HUMAN RELATIONS

Interpersonal, Job-Oriented Skills

Andrew J. DuBrin

Fourth Custom Edition for Lane Community College

Selected by Tim Blood

Taken from:

Human Relations: Interpersonal, Job-Oriented Skills
Ninth Edition, by Andrew J. DuBrin

Human Relations: Career and Personal Success
Seventh Edition, by Andrew J. DuBrin

PEARSON CUSTOM PUBLISHING
501 Boylston Street, Suite 900, Boston, MA 02116
A Pearson Education Company

CONTENTS

HUMAN RELATIONS AT WORK—CG 203

Course Description:

This course presents the interpersonal "people skills" that are important in the modern workplace. Topics include communicating effectively, assertive behavior, teamwork, conflict resolution, and work ethics. Students will gain awareness of their individual work styles and how to work effectively with people with different styles in a diverse workplace. Specific techniques for coping with job stress and managing anger will also be emphasized. Class activities and assignments will stress practical application of skills. Course content is also applicable in other settings (such as family, social, and school).

Course web site: http://Teach.lanecc.edu/~bloodt/hrw.htm

Objectives:

Upon successfully completing this course, students will be able to:

1. Identify their individual work style (i.e., where they like to focus their attention, the way they like to take in information and the way they like to make decisions), and the strengths and weak-nesses of that style. Describe the strengths of other work styles and how to work cooperatively with workers with different styles. (Chapter 1)

2. Describe and utilize appropriate communication skills including non verbal communication and active listening. Describe barriers to communication and how to overcome them (Ch 2) Recognize, describe, and demonstrate Assertive behavior and describe how it differs from Passive and Aggressive behavior. Demonstrate how to send a "whole message" (Appendix 1)

3. Describe the characteristics of an effective work team, the typical stages of team development, and how to be a capable team member. (Ch 3)

4. Understand the issues involved in working with people from different cultural backgrounds and how to work effectively in a diverse workplace. (Ch 4)

5. Describe and demonstrate the rules of "principled negotiation" and conflict resolution. Understand what sexual harassment is, how to prevent it, and how to deal with it if it occurs. (Ch 5)

6. Describe and demonstrate customer satisfaction skills for "internal" and "external" customers. (Ch 6)

7. Identify character traits associated with being an ethical person and use a systematic method for making ethical decisions and behaving ethically. (Ch 7)

8. Describe and give examples of how to effectively manage workplace stress and anger. (Ch 8, Appendix 2)

CHAPTER 1

Understanding Individual Differences

After reading and studying this chapter and doing the exercises you should be able to

1. Take into account the individual differences among people in dealing with them on the job.
2. Develop insight into how your personality, mental ability, emotional intelligence, and values differ from others.
3. Respond to personality differences among people.
4. Respond to mental ability differences among people.
5. Respond to differences in values among people.

How old is too old to be flying hundreds of passengers has long been a difficult question. Right now, the United States kicks commercial airline pilots out of the cockpit before they hit their 60th birthday. But that may change. As pensions erode, there is a growing push to raise that age to 65, and there's an increased likelihood that travelers will start seeing older captains in the cockpit. Some other nations are already moving in this direction, and in Congress, lawmakers have introduced legislation that would bump up the age. Even the Air Line Pilots Association, which in the past has successfully blocked attempts to raise the age, now says it is studying whether a change makes sense.

Gray-haired pilots have the advantage of extensive and wide-ranging experience at the controls, enabling smart, well-informed decision making—which is just what you want, if, say, a plane runs into trouble. Consider that in 1989, United Airlines Captain David Cronin flew a Boeing 747 back to Honolulu after a large section of the fuselage blew out, sucking nine passengers to their death. Two of four engines quit and wing flaps were damaged, but Cronin's flying skills saved 327 passengers. Then, within a month, he was deemed too old to fly.

Yet older pilots may also run a greater risk of sudden incapacitation, slower reactions, or declining mental facilities. While medical studies provide no clear-cut answers, many show that skills do deteriorate with aging.

Discussion Question

1. What should the Federal Aviation Administration do about potential differences in flying ability based on age?

Source: Scott McCartney, "How Old Is too Old to Fly an Airliner?" February 22, 2005, pp. D1, D4. *The Wall Street Journal.* Reprinted with permission.

It might be true that in general people 60 and younger have the top vision and quick reaction time necessary to perform satisfactorily as a commercial airline pilot. However, there is still a wide variation in these abilities with different age groups. Some younger people have poor vision, poor reaction time, and poor judgment to boot. In general, **individual differences** exert a profound effect on job performance and behavior. Such differences refer to variations in how people respond to the same situation based on personal characteristics. One of hundreds of possible examples is that some people can concentrate longer and harder on their work, thereby producing more and higher quality work, than others.

This chapter describes several of the major sources of individual differences on the job. It also gives you the chance to measure your standing on several key dimensions of behavior and helps you develop skill in responding to individual differences. Knowing how to respond to such differences is the cornerstone of effective interpersonal relations.

individual differences Variations in how people respond to the same situation based on personal characteristics.

PERSONALITY

◄ Learning Objective 1

◄ Learning Objective 2

"We're not going to promote you to department head," said the vice president to the analyst. "Although you are a great troubleshooter, you've alienated too many people in the company. You're too blunt and insensitive." As just implied, most successes and failures in people-contact jobs are attributed largely to interpersonal skills. And personality traits are important contributors to interpersonal, or human relations, skills.

Personality refers to those persistent and enduring behavior patterns and tend to be expressed in a wide variety of situations. A person who is brash and insensitive in one situation is likely to behave similarly in many other situations. Your personality is what makes you unique. Your walk, your talk, your appearance, your speech, and your inner values and conflicts all contribute to your personality. Have you ever noticed that when you know a person well you can identify that person by his or her footsteps even though you do not see the individual? This is true because many people have a distinctive gait.

personality Persistent and enduring behavior patterns that tend to be expressed in a wide variety of situations.

I will illustrate the importance of personality to interpersonal relations in organizations by describing eight key personality traits and psychological types related to cognitive styles. In addition, you will be given guidelines for dealing effectively with different personality types.

EIGHT MAJOR PERSONALITY FACTORS AND TRAITS

Many psychologists believe that the basic structure of human personality is represented by five broad factors, known as the Five Factor Model (or Big Five): neuroticism, extraversion (the scientific spelling of *extroversion*), openness, agreeableness, and conscientiousness. Three more key personality factors—self-monitoring of behavior, risk taking and thrill seeking, and optimism—are so important for human relations to be considered here.

All eight factors have a substantial impact on interpersonal relations and job performance. The interpretations and meanings of these factors provide useful information because they help you pinpoint important areas for personal development. Although these factors are partially inherited, most people can improve them providing they exert much conscious effort over a period of time. For example, it

4

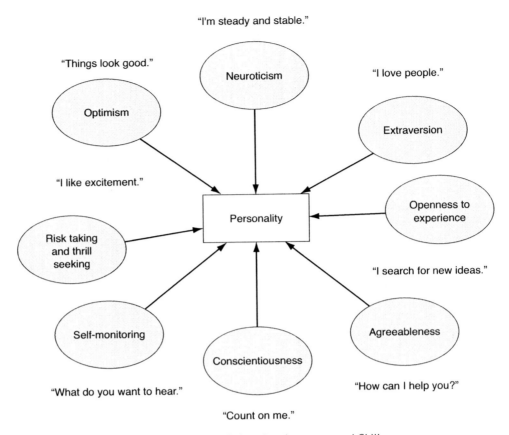

FIGURE 2-1 Eight Personality Factors Related to Interpersonal Skills

usually takes a minimum of three months of effort before a person is perceived to be more agreeable. The eight factors, shown in Figure 2-1, are described in the following list.

1. *Neuroticism* reflects emotional instability and identifies people prone to psychological distress and coping with problems in unproductive ways. Traits associated with this personality factor include being anxious, insecure, angry, embarrassed, emotional, and worried. A person of low neuroticism—or high emotional stability—is calm and confident, and usually in control.

2. *Extraversion* reflects the quantity or intensity of social interactions, the need for social stimulation, self-confidence, and competition. Traits associated with extraversion include being sociable, gregarious, assertive, talkative, and active. An outgoing person is often described as extraverted, whereas introverted persons are described as reserved, timid, and quiet.

3. *Openness* reflects the proactive seeking of experience for its own sake. Traits associated with openness include being creative, cultured, intellectually curious, broadminded, and artistically sensitive. People low on this personality factor are practical, with narrow interests.

4. *Agreeableness* reflects the quality of one's interpersonal orientation. Traits associated with the agreeableness factor include being courteous, flexible, trusting, good-natured, cooperative, forgiving, softhearted, and tolerant. The other end of the continuum includes disagreeable, cold, and antagonistic people.

5. *Conscientiousness* reflects organization, self-restraint, persistence, and motivation toward attaining goals. Traits associated with conscientiousness include being hardworking, dependable, well organized, and thorough. The person low in conscientiousness is lazy, disorganized, and unreliable.

6. *Self-monitoring* of behavior refers to the process of observing and controlling how we are perceived by others. High self-monitors are pragmatic and even chameleonlike actors in social groups. They often say what others want to hear. Low self-monitors avoid situations that require them to adapt to outer images. In this way their outer behavior adheres to their inner values. Low self-monitoring can often lead to inflexibility.

7. *Risk taking and thrill seeking* refers to the propensity to take risks and pursue thrills. Persons with high standing on this personality trait are sensation-seekers who pursue novel, intense, and complex sensations. They are willing to take risks for the sake of such experiences. The search for giant payoffs and daily thrills motivates people with an intense need for risk taking and thrill seeking.[11] Take Self-Assessment Quiz 2-1 to measure your propensity for risk taking and thrill seeking.

 ## SELF-ASSESSMENT QUIZ 2-1

THE RISK-TAKING SCALE

Directions: Answer true or false to the following questions to obtain an approximate idea of your tendency to take risks, or your desire to do so:

	True	False
1. I eat sushi or other raw fish.	☐	☐
2. I think that amusement park roller coasters should be abolished.	☐	☐
3. I don't like trying foods from other cultures.	☐	☐
4. I would choose bonds over growth stocks.	☐	☐
5. I like to challenge people in positions of power.	☐	☐
6. I don't always wear a seat belt while driving.	☐	☐
7. I sometimes talk on my cell phone while driving at highway speeds.	☐	☐
8. I would love to be an entrepreneur (or I love being one).	☐	☐
9. I would like helping out in a crisis such as a product recall.	☐	☐
10. I would like to go cave exploring (or already have done so).	☐	☐
11. I would be willing to have at least one-third of my compensation based on a bonus for good performance.	☐	☐
12. I would be willing to visit a maximum security prison on a job assignment.	☐	☐

Scoring and Interpretation: Give yourself one point each time your answer agrees with the key. If you score 10–12, you are probably a high risk taker; 6–9, you are a moderate risk taker; 3–5, you are cautious; 0–2, you are a very low risk taker.

1. T	5. T	9. T
2. F	6. T	10. T
3. F	7. T	11. T
4. F	8. T	12. T

Source: The idea of a test about risk-taking comfort, as well as several of the statements on the quiz, comes from psychologist Frank Farley.

8. *Optimism* refers to a tendency to experience positive emotional states, and to typically believe that positive outcomes will be forthcoming from most activities. The other end of the scale is *pessimism*—a tendency to experience negative emotional states, and to typically believe that negative outcomes will be forthcoming from most activities. Optimism versus pessimism is also referred to in more technical terms as positive affectivity versus negative affectivity, and is considered a major personality trait. A person's tendency toward having positive affectivity (optimism) versus negative affectivity (pessimism) also influences job satisfaction. Being optimistic, as you would suspect, tends to enhance job satisfaction.[2]

Evidence for the relevance of the Five Factor Model (traits one through five of the previous list) of personality in understanding human behavior comes from a cross-cultural study involving 7,134 individuals. The five-factor structure of the American personality was also found to hold true for German, Portuguese, Hebrew, Chinese, Korean, and Japanese samples when the personality test questions were translated into each of these languages. Based on this extensive study, it was concluded that personality structure is universal, much like the structure of the brain or the body.[3] Another look at the evidence found that extraversion, agreeableness, and conscientiousness are major personality factors in most cultures. Neuroticism and openness are more dependent on the culture and are particularly relevant in the United States.[4]

THE EIGHT FACTORS AND TRAITS AND JOB PERFORMANCE

Depending on the job, any one of the preceding personality factors can be important for success. One explanation for personality being tied to performance is that a particular personality trait gives us a bias or positive spin to certain actions.[5] A person high in conscientiousness, for example, believes that if people are diligent they will accomplish more work and receive just rewards. Conscientiousness relates to job performance for many different occupations, and has proven to be the personality trait most consistently related to success. However, there are a few instances in which being highly conscientious can interfere with job success. If the job requires considerable spontaneity and imagination, a highly conscientious person might perform poorly because he or she dislikes breaking the rules or straying from conventional thinking.[6] For example, a conscientious advertising worker might hesitate to develop a television advertisement that depicted a woman jumping out of a building onto a UPS delivery truck.

Another important research finding is that extraversion is associated with success for managers and sales representatives. The explanation is that managers and salespeople are required to interact extensively with other people.[7] For people who want to advance in their careers, being a high self-monitor is important. An analysis was made of the self-monitoring personality by combining 136 studies involving 23,101 people. A major finding was that high self-monitors tend to receive better performance ratings than low self-monitors. High self-monitors were also more likely to emerge as leaders and work their way into top management positions.[8] Another advantage to being a high self-monitor is that the individual is more likely to help out other workers, even when not required.[9] An example would be helping a worker outside your department with a currency exchange problem even though this was not your responsibility. The willingness to go beyond one's job description is referred to as **organizational citizenship behavior.** Good organizational citizens are highly valued by employers.

A combination of personality factors will sometimes be more closely associated with job success than one factor alone. A study about personality and job performance ratings was conducted with diverse occupations including clerical workers and wholesale appliance sales representatives. A key finding was that conscientious workers who also scored high on agreeableness performed better than conscien-

organizational citizenship behavior
The willingness to go beyond one's job description.

tious workers who were less agreeable.[10] (Being agreeable toward your manager helps elevate performance evaluations!) A study with experienced pharmaceutical sales representatives found that the combination of extraversion and conscientiousness was associated with higher sales. However, being conscientious was the personality factor most closely associated with growth in sales over several years for the experienced sales representatives.[11]

The extent to which a person has a high standing on agreeableness influences whether or not the supervisor perceives him or her as requiring high maintenance (needing a lot of attention). A study with 338 clerical workers in a manufacturing setting found that among employees who had a high standing on conscientiousness, being disagreeable prompted supervisors to rate them as engaging in high-maintenance behavior.[12]

Optimism and pessimism also can be linked to job performance. Optimism can be quite helpful when attempting such tasks as selling a product or service or motivating a group of people. Yet psychologist Julie Normen has gathered considerable evidence that pessimism can sometimes enhance job performance. Pessimists usually assume that something will go wrong, and will carefully prepare to prevent botches and bad luck. A pessimist, for example, will carefully back up computer files or plan for emergencies that might shut down operations.[13]

COGNITIVE STYLES AND PERSONALITY TYPES

People go about solving problems in various ways. You may have observed, for example, that some people are more analytical and systematic while others are more intuitive. The most widely used method of classifying problem-solving styles is the Myers-Briggs Type Indicator (MBTI).[14] Many readers of this book will have already taken the MBTI. Modes of problem solving are referred to as **cognitive styles**. According to this method of understanding problem-solving styles, your personality traits influence strongly how you approach problems, such as being introverted pointing you toward dealing with ideas. Knowledge of these cognitive styles can help you relate better to people because you can better appreciate how they make decisions.

According to the famous psychoanalyst Carl Jung, how people gather and evaluate information determines their cognitive style. Jung's analysis became the basis for the MBTI. Jung reasoned that there are four dimensions of psychological functioning:

1. **Introverted versus Extraverted.** Introverts are oriented toward the inner world of ideas and feelings, whereas extraverts are oriented toward the outer world of people and objects.

2. **Thinking versus Feeling.** Thinkers prefer to make decisions logically based on facts and figures, whereas feelers base decisions on subjective information.

3. **Sensing versus Intuiting.** Sensing individuals prefer to concentrate on details, whereas intuitive individuals prefer to focus on broad issues (the "big picture").

4. **Judging versus Perceiving.** Judging types seek to resolve issues, whereas perceiving types are relatively flexible and search for additional information.

Combining the four types with each other results in 16 personality types, as shown in Figure 2-2. Research evidence for the MBTI is generally positive with respect to the 16 types, and the fact that people with different cognitive styles prefer different occupations.[15] For example, the ENTP cognitive type is labeled the "conceptualizer." He or she is passionate about new opportunities and dislikes routine, and is more likely to be an entrepreneur than a corporate manager. The ISTJ cognitive type is labeled the "traditionalist," and will often become an accountant or financial analyst. The INJT type is labeled the "visionary." Although a small proportion of the population, these individuals are often chief executives of business firms. One of the most common types among people in general, as well as among managers, is the ESTJ, labeled the "organizer."

cognitive style
Mental processes used to perceive and make judgments from situations.

ENTP (Conceptualizer)	ISTJ (Traditionalist)	INTJ (Visionary)	ESTJ (Organizer)
Quick, ingenious, will argue either side of issue for fun, may neglect routine assign-ments. (Good for creative work where deadlines are not crucial.)	Serious, quiet, practical, logical, dependable. (Good for work requiring careful attention to detail such as accountant or auditor.)	Skeptical, critical, independent, determined, original. (Good for major leadership role such as CEO.)	Practical, realistic, has a natural mind for business or mechanics, likes to organize and run activities. (Good for manufacturing supervisor.)

FIGURE 2-2 Four Cognitive Styles of the Myers-Briggs Typology

Note: I = Introvert, *E* = Extrovert, *T* = Thinking, *F* = Feeling, *S* = Sensing, *N* = Intuitive, *J* = Judging, and *P* = Perceiving.

Source: The personality descriptions are based on information from *Meyers-Briggs Type Indicator* by Katharine C. Briggs and Isabel Briggs Myers. Copyright 1983 by Consulting Psychologists Press, Inc. All rights reserved.

Many people who use the Myers-Briggs are unaware that it is an approximate measure, and not a definitive scale such as a measure of physical weight. The most reliable dimension appears to be thinking versus feeling, which is similar to reflect-ing about details versus jumping to a quick decision based on feel and experience, or being reflective versus impulsive.

If you take the Myers-Briggs Type Indicator, often available in career centers, you will discover your type. You can also study these four types and make a tentative judgment as to whether one of them fits your problem-solving style. Recognizing your problem-solving style can help you identify work that you are likely to perform well, as detailed in Figure 2-2.

GUIDELINES FOR DEALING WITH DIFFERENT PERSONALITY TYPES

Learning Objective 3 ▶

A key purpose in presenting information about a sampling of various personality types is to provide guidelines for individualizing your approach to people. As a basic exam-ple, if you wanted to score points with an introvert, you would approach that person in a restrained, laid-back fashion. In contrast, a more gregarious, lighthearted approach might be more effective with an extravert. The purpose of individualizing your ap-proach is to build a better working relationship or to establish rapport with the other person. To match your approach to dealing with a given personality type, you must first arrive at an approximate diagnosis of the individual's personality. The following sug-gestions are therefore restricted to readily observable aspects of personality.

1. When relating to a person who appears to be neurotic based on symptoms of worry and tension, be laid back and reassuring. Attempt not to project your own anxiety and fears. Be a good listener. If possible, minimize the em-phasis on deadlines and the dire consequences of a project's failing. Show concern and interest in the person's welfare.

2. When relating to an extraverted individual, emphasize friendliness, warmth, and a stream of chatter. Talk about people more than ideas, things, or data. Express an interest in a continuing working relationship.

3. When relating to an introverted individual, move slowly in forming a working relationship. Do not confuse quietness with a lack of interest. Tolerate moments of silence. Emphasize ideas, things, and data more heavily than people.

4. When relating to a person who is open to experience, emphasize information sharing, idea generation, and creative approaches to problems. Appeal to his or her intellect by discussing topics of substance rather than ordinary chatter and gossip.

5. When relating to a person who is closed to experience, stick closely to the facts of the situation at hand. Recognize that the person prefers to think small and deal with the here and now.

6. When relating to an agreeable person, just relax and be yourself. Reciprocate with kindness to sustain a potentially excellent working relationship.

7. When relating to a disagreeable person, be patient and tolerant. At the same time, set limits on how much mistreatment you will take. Disagreeable people sometimes secretly want others to put brakes on their antisocial behavior.

8. When relating to a conscientious person, give him or her freedom and do not nag. The person will probably honor commitments without prompting. Conscientious people are often taken for granted, so remember to acknowledge the person's dependability.

9. When relating to a person of low conscientiousness, keep close tabs on him or her, especially if you need the person's output to do your job. Do not assume that because the person has an honest face and a pleasing smile he or she will deliver as promised. Frequently follow up on your requests, and impose deadlines if you have the authority. Express deep appreciation when the person does follow through.

10. When dealing with a person whom you suspect is a high self-monitor, be cautious in thinking that the person is really in support of your position. The person could just be following his or her natural tendency to appear to please others, but not really feel that way.

11. When relating to a person with a high propensity for risk taking and thrill seeking, emphasize the risky and daring aspects of activities familiar to you. Talk about a new product introduction in a highly competitive market, stock options, investment in high-technology startup firms, skydiving, and race car driving.

12. When relating to a person with a low propensity for risk taking and thrill seeking, emphasize the safe and secure aspects of activities familiar to you. Talk about the success of an established product in a stable market (like pencils and paperclips), investment in U.S. Treasury bonds, life insurance, camping, and gardening.

13. When dealing with a sensing-type person, emphasize facts, figures, and conventional thinking without sacrificing your own values. To convince the sensing type, emphasize logic more than emotional appeal. Focus on details more than the big picture.

14. When dealing with an intuiting-type individual, emphasize feelings, judgments, playing with ideas, imagination, and creativity. Focus more on the big picture than details.

To start putting these guidelines into practice, do the role-plays in Skill-Building Exercise 2-1. Remember that a role-player is an extemporaneous actor. Put yourself in the shoes of the character you play and visualize how he or she would act. Because you are given only the general idea of a script, use your imagination to fill in the details.

10

PERSONALITY ROLE-PLAYS

The Extravert: One student assumes the role of a successful outside sales representative who has just signed a $3 million order for the company. The sales rep comes back to the office elated. The other student assumes the role of a member of the office support staff. He or she decides this is a splendid opportunity to build a good relationship with the triumphant sales rep. Run the role-play for about seven minutes. The people not involved in the role-play will observe and then provide feedback when the role-play is completed. (These directions regarding time, observation, and feedback also apply to the two other role-plays in this exercise and throughout the book.)

Openness: One student plays the role of an experienced worker in the department who is told to spend some time orienting a new co-op student or intern. It appears that this new person is open to experience. Another student plays the role of the co-op student who is open to experience and eager to be successful in this new position.

Sensing and Intuiting Types: One student plays the role of a sensing-type individual who is responsible for reviewing the company expense accounts. The other student plays the role of a manager in whose department many expense account abuses (such as lack of documentation and high expenses) have been uncovered. This manager is an intuitive type. The person in charge of the accounts is visiting the manager in the latter's office to discuss this problem.

MENTAL ABILITY

intelligence The capacity to acquire and apply knowledge, including solving problems.

Mental ability, or intelligence, is one of the major sources of individual differences that affects job performance and behavior. **Intelligence** is the capacity to acquire and apply knowledge, including solving problems. Intelligent workers can best solve abstract problems. In an exceedingly simple job, such as packing shoes into boxes, having below-average intelligence can be an advantage because the employee is not likely to become bored.

Understanding the nature of intelligence contributes to effective interpersonal relations in the workplace. Your evaluation of a person's intelligence can influence how you relate to that person. For example, if you think a person is intelligent you will tend to seek his or her input on a difficult problem. If you realize that different types of intelligence exist, you are more likely to appreciate people's strengths. You are thus less likely to judge others as being either good or poor problem solvers.

g (general) factor A factor in intelligence that contributes to the ability to perform well in many tasks.

Four important aspects of mental ability include: (1) the components of traditional intelligence, (2) practical intelligence, (3) multiple intelligences, and (4) emotional intelligence. (This fourth type of intelligence can also be regarded as personality, not mental ability.) Knowledge of the four aspects will enrich your understanding of other workers and yourself.

COMPONENTS OF TRADITIONAL INTELLIGENCE

s (special) factors Specific components of intelligence that contribute to problem-solving ability.

Intelligence consists of more than one component. A component of intelligence is much like a separate mental aptitude. Evidence suggests that intelligence consists of a **g (general) factor** and **s (special) factors** that contribute to problem-solving ability. Scores of tests of almost any type (such as math, aptitude for spatial relations, or reading skill) are somewhat influenced by the *g* factor. The *g* factor helps explain why some people perform well in so many different mental tasks. Substantial evidence has accumulated over the years that workers with high intelligence tend to perform better. The relationship between *g* and job performance is likely to be strongest for those aspects of jobs involving thinking and knowledge, such as problem solving and technical expertise.[16]

Over the years various investigators have arrived at different special factors contributing to overall mental aptitude. The following seven factors have been identified consistently:

1. **Verbal comprehension.** The ability to understand the meaning of words and their relationship to each other and to comprehend written and spoken information.

2. **Word fluency.** The ability to use words quickly and easily, without an emphasis on verbal comprehension.

3. **Numerical acuity.** The ability to handle numbers, engage in mathematical analysis, and to do arithmetic calculations.

4. **Spatial perception.** The ability to visualize forms in space and manipulate objects mentally, particularly in three dimensions.

5. **Memory.** Having a good rote memory for symbols, words, and lists of numbers, along with other associations.

6. **Perceptual speed.** The ability to perceive visual details, to pick out similarities and differences, and to perform tasks requiring visual perception.

7. **Inductive reasoning.** The ability to discover a rule or principle and apply it in solving a problem and to make judgments and decisions that are logically sound.

Being strong in any of the preceding mental aptitudes often leads to an enjoyment of work associated with that aptitude. The reverse can also be true: enjoying a type of mental activity might lead to the development of an aptitude for the activity. Self-Assessment Quiz 2-2 gives you the opportunity to measure your preferences for numerical information.

PRACTICAL INTELLIGENCE

Many people, including psychologists, are concerned that the traditional way of understanding intelligence inadequately describes mental ability. An unfortunate implication of intelligence testing is that intelligence as traditionally calculated is largely the ability to perform tasks related to scholastic work. Thus, a person who scored very high on an intelligence test could follow a complicated instruction manual, but might not be street smart.

To overcome the limited idea that intelligence mostly involves the ability to solve abstract problems, the **triarchic theory of intelligence** has been proposed. The theory holds that intelligence is composed of three different subtypes: analytical, creative, and practical. The *analytical* subtype is the traditional intelligence needed for solving difficult problems. Analytical intelligence is required to perform well in most school subjects. The *creative* subtype is the type of intelligence required for imagination and combining things in novel ways. The *practical* subtype is the type of intelligence required for adapting your environment to suit your needs.[17] The idea of practical intelligence helps explain why a person who has a difficult time getting through school can still be a successful businessperson, politician, or athlete. Practical intelligence incorporates the ideas of common sense, wisdom, and street smarts.

A person with high practical intelligence would also have good **intuition,** an experience-based way of knowing or reasoning in which the weighing and balancing

The best measure of a person's intelligence is the type of life he or she leads.
—David Wechsler, developer of one of the most widely used IQ tests

triarchic theory of intelligence An explanation of mental ability holding that intelligence is composed of three different subtypes: analytical, creative, and practical.

intuition An experience-based way of knowing or reasoning in which the weighing and balancing of evidence are done automatically.

SELF-ASSESSMENT QUIZ 2-2

ATTITUDES TOWARD NUMERICAL INFORMATION

Directions:: Describe how well you agree with each of the following statements, using the following scale: disagree strongly (DS); disagree (D); neutral (N); agree (A); agree strongly (AS). Circle the number in the appropriate column.

	DS	D	N	A	AS
1. I enjoy work that requires the use of numbers.	1	2	3	4	5
2. I think quantitative information is difficult to understand.	5	4	3	2	1
3. I find it satisfying to solve day-to-day problems involving numbers.	1	2	3	4	5
4. Numerical information is very useful in everyday life.	1	2	3	4	5
5. I prefer not to pay attention to information involving numbers.	5	4	3	2	1
6. I think more information should be available in numerical form.	1	2	3	4	5
7. I don't like to think about issues involving numbers.	5	4	3	2	1
8. Numbers are not necessary for most situations.	5	4	3	2	1
9. Thinking is more enjoyable when it does not involve quantitative information.	5	4	3	2	1
10. I like to make calculations involving numerical information.	1	2	3	4	5
11. Quantitative information is vital for accurate decisions.	1	2	3	4	5
12. I enjoy thinking about issues that involve numerical information.	1	2	3	4	5
13. Understanding numbers is as important in daily life as reading or writing.	1	2	3	4	5
14. I easily lose interest in graphs, percentages, and other quantitative information.	5	4	3	2	1
15. I find numerical information to be relevant to most situations.	1	2	3	4	5
16. I think it is important to learn and use numerical information to make well-informed decisions.	1	2	3	4	5
17. Numbers are redundant for most situations.	5	4	3	2	1
18. It is a waste of time to learn information containing a lot of numbers.	5	4	3	2	1
19. I like to go over numbers in my mind.	1	2	3	4	5
20. It helps me think if I put down information as numbers.	1	2	3	4	5

Total Score _____

Scoring and Interpretation: Add the numbers you circled to obtain your total score.

85–100 You have strong positive attitudes toward numerical information and working with quantitative data.

55–84 You have moderately favorable attitudes toward numerical information and working with quantitative data.

20–54 You have very negative attitudes toward numerical information and working with quantitative data. Your dislike for quantitative solutions to problems is so strong that you are quick to distrust statistical analysis.

Source: Table from Madhubalan Viswanathan, "Measurement of Individual Differences in Preference for Numerical Information," *Journal of Applied Psychology,* October 1993, p. 745. Reprinted with permission.

of evidence are done automatically. Examples of good intuition include a merchandiser who develops a hunch that a particular style will be hot next season, a basketball coach who sees the possibilities in a gangly youngster, and a supervisor who has a hunch that a neighbor would be a great fit for her department. Intuition is also required for creative intelligence.

One major reservation some have about practical intelligence is the implication that people who are highly intelligent in the traditional sense are not practical thinkers. In truth, most executives and other high-level workers score quite well on tests of mental ability. These tests usually measure analytical intelligence.

Back to the Opening Case

You will recall the concern about how long to let senior pilots keep flying commercial airplanes. The fact that these experienced flyers currently are allowed to work as pilots up to age 60 shows the importance of practical intelligence. You need good judgment when you have 350 passengers on board. The Federal Aviation Administration maintains that retirement at age 60 has proved to be a safe standard, so why change if you might risk safety? However, as people maintain productive capacity into later years, the FAA might change its position.

MULTIPLE INTELLIGENCES

Another approach to understanding the diverse nature of mental ability is the theory of **multiple intelligences.** According to Howard Gardner, people know and understand the world in distinctly different ways and learn in different ways. Individuals possess the following eight intelligences, or faculties, in varying degrees:

multiple intelligences A theory of intelligence contending that people know and understand the world in distinctly different ways and learn in different ways.

1. **Linguistic.** Enables people to communicate through language, including reading, writing, and speaking.
2. **Logical-mathematical.** Enables individuals to see relationships between objects and solve problems, as in calculus and statistics.
3. **Musical.** Gives people the capacity to create and understand meanings made out of sounds and to enjoy different types of music.
4. **Spatial.** Enables people to perceive and manipulate images in the brain and to recreate them from memory, as is required in making graphic designs.
5. **Bodily-kinesthetic.** Enables people to use their body and perceptual and motor systems in skilled ways such as dancing, playing sports, and expressing emotion through facial expressions.
6. **Intrapersonal.** Enables people to distinguish among their own feelings and acquire accurate self-knowledge.
7. **Interpersonal.** Makes it possible for individuals to recognize and make distinctions among the feelings, motives, and intentions of others as in managing or parenting.
8. **Naturalist.** Enables individuals to differentiate among, classify, and utilize various features of the physical external environment.

Your profile of intelligences influences how you best learn and to which types of jobs you are best suited. Gardner believes that it is possible to develop these separate intelligences through concentrated effort. However, any of these intelligences might fade if not put to use.[18] The components of multiple intelligences might also be perceived as different talents or abilities. Having high general problem-solving ability (*g*) would contribute to high standing on each of the eight intelligences.

EMOTIONAL INTELLIGENCE

Later research has updated and expanded the idea of practical intelligence, suggesting that how effectively people use their emotions has a major impact on their success. **Emotional intelligence** refers to qualities such as understanding one's own feelings, having empathy for others, and regulating one's emotion to enhance living. A person with high emotional intelligence would be able to engage in such behaviors as sizing up people, pleasing others, and influencing them. Four key factors included in a recent analysis of emotional intelligence are as follows:[19]

1. **Self-awareness.** The ability to understand your moods, emotions, and needs as well as their impact on others. Self-awareness also includes using intuition to make decisions you can live with happily. (A person with good self-awareness knows whether he or she is pushing other people too far.)

2. **Self-management.** The ability to control one's emotions and act with honesty and integrity in a consistent and acceptable manner. The right degree of self-management helps prevent a person from throwing temper tantrums when activities do not go as planned. Effective workers do not let their occasional bad moods ruin their day. If they cannot overcome the bad mood, they let coworkers know of their problem and how long it might last. (A person with low self-management would suddenly decide to drop a project because the work was frustrating.)

3. **Social awareness.** Includes having empathy for others and having intuition about work problems. A team leader with social awareness, or empathy, would be able to assess whether a team member has enough enthusiasm for a project to assign him to that project. Another facet of social skill is the ability to interpret nonverbal communication, such as frowns and types of smiles.[20] (A supervisor with social awareness, or empathy, would take into account the most likely reaction of group members before making a decision affecting them.)

4. **Relationship management.** Includes the interpersonal skills of being able to communicate clearly and convincingly, disarm conflicts, and build strong personal bonds. Effective workers use relationship management skills to spread their enthusiasm and solve disagreements, often with kindness and humor. (A worker with relationship management skill would use a method of persuasion that is likely to work well with a particular group or individual.)

Emotional intelligence thus incorporates many of the skills and attitudes necessary to achieve effective interpersonal relations in organizations. Most of the topics in this book, such as resolving conflict, helping others develop, and possessing positive political skills, would be included in emotional intelligence. As mentioned earlier, emotional intelligence might also be regarded as a major aspect of personality rather than true intelligence. For example, if you can read the feelings of other people, aren't you just being smart? Self-Assessment Quiz 2-3 gives you an opportunity to measure your emotional intelligence, but you will need persistence to get the information.

GUIDELINES FOR RELATING TO PEOPLE OF DIFFERENT LEVELS AND TYPES OF INTELLIGENCE

Learning Objective 4 ▶

Certainly you cannot expect to administer mental ability and emotional intelligence tests to all your work associates, gather their scores, and then relate to associates differently based on their scores. Yet it is possible to intuitively develop a sense for the mental quickness of people and the types of mental tasks they perform best. For example, managers must make judgments about mental ability in selecting people for

SELF-ASSESSMENT QUIZ 2-3

WHAT IS YOUR EMOTIONAL INTELLIGENCE?

Psychologists have developed various measures of emotional intelligence. The EIQ test found by visiting *http://www.myskillsprofile.com* deals with 16 emotional competencies. The feedback report provides a chart of your emotional competencies together with a detailed description of your profile. An advantage of this quiz is that it is based on the work of two of the original researchers in emotional intelligence, not the later popularizers of the concept.

jobs and assigning them to tasks. Following are several guidelines worth considering for enhancing your working relationships with others.

1. If you perceive another worker (your manager included) to be mentally quick, present your ideas in technical depth. Incorporate difficult words into your conversation and reports. Ask the person challenging questions.

2. If you perceive another worker to be mentally slow, present your ideas with a minimum of technical depth. Use a basic vocabulary, without going so far as to be patronizing. Ask for frequent feedback about having been clear.

3. If you perceive a work associate to relish crunching numbers, use quantitative information when attempting to persuade that person. Instead of using phrases such as "most people," say "about 65 percent of people."

4. If you perceive a work associate to have high creative intelligence, solicit his or her input on problems requiring a creative solution. Use statements such as "Here's a problem that requires a sharp, creative mind, so I've come to you."

5. If you perceive a work associate to have low emotional intelligence, explain your feelings and attitudes clearly. The person may not get the point of hints and indirect expressions.

To start putting these guidelines into practice, do the role-play in Skill-Building Exercise 2-2.

VALUES AS A SOURCE OF INDIVIDUAL DIFFERENCES

Another group of factors influencing how a person behaves on the job is that person's values and beliefs. A **value** refers to the importance a person attaches to something. Values are also tied to the enduring belief that one's mode of conduct is better than another mode of conduct. If you believe that good interpersonal relations are the most important part of your life, your humanistic values are strong. Similarly, you may think that people who are not highly concerned about interpersonal relations have poor values.

Values are closely tied in with **ethics,** or the moral choices a person makes. A person's values influence which kinds of behaviors he or she believes are ethical. Ethics convert values into action. An executive who strongly values profits might not find it unethical to raise prices higher than needed to cover additional costs. Another executive who strongly values family life might suggest that the company invest money in an on-site childcare center. Ethics is such an important part of interpersonal relations in organizations that the topic receives separate mention in Chapter 13.

value The importance a person attaches to something.

ethics The moral choices a person makes. Also, what is good and bad, right and wrong, just and unjust, and what people should do.

SKILL-BUILDING EXERCISE 2-2

ADAPTING TO PEOPLE OF
DIFFERENT MENTAL ABILITY

The Mentally Sharp Coworker: One student plays the role of a worker who needs to learn a new software package in a hurry. You intend to approach a particular coworker who is known for having a sharp mind. You wonder whether this highly intelligent person will be interested in your problem. The other person plays the role of the computer whiz who ordinarily does not like to solve problems for people that they should be able to solve themselves. The first worker meets with the second to discuss loading the software.

The Mentally Average Team Member: One student plays the role of a supervisor who needs to explain to a team member how to calculate discounts for customers. To the supervisor's knowledge, the team member does not know how to calculate discounts, although it will be an important part of the team member's new job. The supervisor and the team member get together for a session on calculating discounts.

Differences in values among people often stem from age, or generational, differences. Workers over age 50, in general, may have different values than people who are much younger. These age differences in values have often been seen as a clash between Baby Boomers and members of Generation X and Generation Y. According to the stereotype, Boomers see Generation Xers and Yers as disrespectful of rules, not willing to pay their dues, and being disloyal to employers. Generation Xers and Yers see Boomers as worshipping hierarchy (layers of authority), being overcautious, and wanting to preserve the status quo.

Table 2-1 summarizes these stereotypes with the understanding that massive group stereotypes like this are only partially accurate because there are literally millions of exceptions. For example, many Baby Boomers are fascinated with technology, and many Generation Yers like hierarchy.

HOW VALUES ARE LEARNED

People acquire values in the process of growing up, and many values are learned by the age of four. One important way we acquire values is through observing others, or modeling. Models can be teachers, friends, brothers, sisters, and even public figures. If we identify with a particular person, the probability is high that we will develop some of his or her major values.

> *Derek, a restaurant owner, was known for his ability to offer employment to troubled teenagers and then help them get back on their feet. Asked why he put so much effort into helping youths in trouble, he explained, "I was greatly influenced as a boy by my Uncle Clarence. I was going through troubled times—stealing from a variety store and getting drunk on beer.*
>
> *"Uncle Clarence took me under his wing and spent hours listening to my problems. He would take me fishing and ask if there was anything he could do to help me. Finally, I straightened out. I decided that I would be like Uncle Clarence if someday I had a chance to help young people."*

Another major way values are learned is through the communication of attitudes. The attitudes that we hear expressed directly or indirectly help shape our values. Assume that using credit to purchase goods and services was considered an evil

TABLE 2-1 Value Stereotypes for Several Generations of Workers

Baby Boomers (1946–1964)	*Generation X (1965–1977)*	*Generation Y (1978–1984)*
Use technology as necessary tool	Techno-savvy	Techno-savvy
Appreciate hierarchy	Teamwork very important	Teamwork very important
Tolerate teams but value independent work	Dislike hierarchy	Dislike hierarchy
Strong career orientation	Strive for work–life balance but will work long hours for now	Strive for work–life balance but will work long hours for now
More loyalty to organization	Loyalty to own career and profession	Believe in informality
		Want to strike it rich quickly
Favor diplomacy	Candid in conversation	Ultracandid in conversation
Favor old economy	Appreciate old and new economy	Prefer the new economy
Expect a bonus based on performance	Would appreciate a signing bonus	Expected a signing bonus before the dot-com crash
Believe that issues should be formally discussed	Believe that feedback can be administered informally	Believe that feedback can be given informally, even on the fly

Sources: Several of the ideas in this table are from Robert McGarvey, "The Coming of Gen X Bosses," *Entrepreneur,* November 1999, pp. 60–64; Joanne M. Glenn, "Teaching the Net Generation," *Business Education Forum,* February 2000, pp. 6–14; Anita Bruzzese, "There Needn't Be a Generation Gap," Gannett News Service, April 22, 2002.

practice among your family and friends. You might therefore hold negative values about installment purchases. Unstated but implied attitudes may also shape your values. If key people in your life showed no enthusiasm when you talked about work accomplishments, you might not place such a high value on achieving outstanding results. If, however, your family and friends centered their lives on their careers, you might develop similar values. (Or you might rebel against such a value because it interfered with a more relaxed lifestyle.) Many key values are also learned through religion and thus become the basis for society's morals. For example, most religions emphasize treating other people fairly and kindly. To "knife somebody in the back" is considered immoral both on and off the job.

CLARIFYING YOUR VALUES

The values that you develop early in life are directly related to the kind of person you are and to the quality of the relationships you form.[21] Recognition of this fact has led to exercises designed to help people clarify and understand some of their own values. Self-Assessment Quiz 2-4 gives you an opportunity to clarify your values.

THE MESH BETWEEN INDIVIDUAL AND JOB VALUES

Under the best of circumstances, the values of employees mesh with those required by the job. When this state of congruence exists, job performance is likely to be higher. Suppose that Jacquelyn strongly values giving people with limited formal education an opportunity to work and avoid being placed on welfare. So she takes a job as a manager of a dollar store that employs many people who would ordinarily

SELF-ASSESSMENT QUIZ 2-4

CLARIFYING YOUR VALUES

Directions: Rank from 1 to 20 the importance of the following values to you as a person. The most important value on the list receives a rank of 1; the least important a rank of 20. Use the space next to "Other" if the list has left out an important value in your life.

_____ Having my own place to live
_____ Having one or more children
_____ Having an interesting job and career
_____ Owning a car
_____ Having a good relationship with coworkers
_____ Having good health
_____ Sending and receiving e-mail messages, and using the Web
_____ Being able to stay in frequent contact with friends by cell phone
_____ Watching my favorite television shows
_____ Participating in sports or other pastimes
_____ Following a sports team, athlete, music group, or other entertainer
_____ Being a religious person
_____ Helping people less fortunate than myself
_____ Loving and being loved by another person
_____ Having physical intimacy with another person
_____ Making an above-average income
_____ Being in good physical condition
_____ Being a knowledgeable, informed person
_____ Completing my formal education
_____ Other

1. Discuss and compare your ranking of these values with the person next to you.
2. Perhaps your class, assisted by your instructor, can arrive at a class average on each of these values. How does your ranking compare to the class ranking?
3. Look back at your own ranking. Does it surprise you?
4. Are there any surprises in the class ranking? Which values did you think would be highest and lowest?

person–role conflict
The situation that occurs when the demands made by the organization clash with the basic values of the individual.

have limited opportunity for employment. Jacquelyn is satisfied because her employer and she share a similar value.

When the demands made by the organization or a superior clash with the basic values of the individual, that person suffers from **person–role conflict.** The individual wants to obey orders, but does not want to perform an act that seems inconsistent with his or her values. A situation such as this might occur when an employee is asked to produce a product that he or she feels is unsafe or of no value to society.

A manager of a commercial weight-reduction center resigned after two years of service. The owners pleaded with her to stay, based on her excellent performance. The man-

ager replied, "Sorry, I think my job is immoral. We sign up all these people with great expectations of losing weight permanently. Most of them do achieve short-term weight reduction. My conflict is that over 90 percent of our clientele regain the weight they lost once they go back to eating standard food. I think we are deceiving them by not telling them up front that they will most likely gain back the weight they lose."

GUIDELINES FOR USING VALUES TO ENHANCE INTERPERSONAL RELATIONS

◄ Learning Objective 5

Values are intangible and abstract, and thus not easy to manipulate to help improve your interpersonal relations on the job. Despite their vagueness, values are an important driver of interpersonal effectiveness. Ponder the following guidelines:

1. Establish the values you will use in your relationships with others on the job, and then use those values as firm guidelines in working with others. For example, following the Golden Rule, you might establish the value of treating other people as you want to be treated. You would then not lie to others to gain personal advantage, and you would not backstab your rivals.

2. Establish the values that will guide you as an employee. When you believe that your values are being compromised, express your concern to your manager in a tactful and constructive manner. You might say to your manager, "Sorry, I choose not to tell our customers that our competitor's product is inferior just to make a sale. I choose not to say this because our competitor makes a fine product. But what I will say is that our service is exceptional."

3. Remember that many values are a question of opinion, not a statement of being right versus wrong. If you believe that your values are right, and anybody who disagrees is wrong, you will have frequent conflict. For example, you may believe that the most important value top managers should have is to bring shareholders a high return on their investment. Another worker believes that profits are important, but providing jobs for as many people as possible is an equally important value. Both of you have a good point, but neither is right or wrong. So it is better to discuss these differences rather than hold grudges because of them.

To help you put these guidelines into practice, do Skill-Building Exercise 2-3. Remember, however, that being skilled at using your values requires day-by-day monitoring.

SKILL-BUILDING EXERCISE 2-3

THE VALUE-CONFLICT ROLE-PLAY

One student plays the role of a company president who makes an announcement to the group that the company must soon lay off 10 percent of the workforce in order to remain profitable. The president also points out that the company has a policy against laying off good performers. He or she then asks four of the company managers to purposely give below-average performance ratings to 10 percent of employees. In this way, laying them off will fit company policy.

Four other students play the role of the company managers who receive this directive. If such manipulation of performance evaluations clashes with your values, engage in a dialogue with your manager expressing your conflict. Remember, however, that you may not want to jeopardize your job.

Conduct this group role-play for about seven minutes, with other class members observing and being prepared to offer feedback.

SUMMARY

Individual differences are among the most important factors influencing the behavior of people in the workplace. Knowing how to respond to such differences is the cornerstone of effective interpersonal relations.

Personality is one of the major sources of individual differences. The eight major personality factors described in this chapter are neuroticism, extraversion, openness, agreeableness, conscientiousness, self-monitoring of behavior, risk taking and thrill seeking, and optimism. Depending on the job, any one of these personality factors can be important for success, and they also affect interpersonal relations.

Personality also influences a person's cognitive style, or the mental processes used to perceive and make judgments from information. According to the Myers-Briggs Type Indicator (MBTI), four dimensions of psychological functioning are as follows: introverted versus extraverted; thinking versus feeling; sensing versus intuiting; and judging versus perceiving. Combining the four types with each other results in 16 personality types, such as a person being a conceptualizer, traditionalist, visionary, or organizer. For example, the organizer (ESTJ) scores high on extraversion, sensing, thinking, and judging.

Mental ability, or intelligence, is one of the major sources of individual differences that affects job performance and behavior. Understanding the nature of intelligence contributes to effective interpersonal relations in organizations. For example, understanding that different types of intelligence exist will help a person appreciate the strengths of people.

Intelligence consists of many components. The traditional perspective is that intelligence includes a general factor (g) along with special factors (s) that contribute to problem-solving ability. A related perspective is that intelligence consists of seven components: verbal comprehension, word fluency, numerical acuity, spatial perception, memory, perceptual speed, and inductive reasoning.

To overcome the idea that intelligence involves mostly the ability to solve abstract problems, the triarchic theory of intelligence has been proposed. According to this theory, intelligence has three subtypes: analytical, creative, and practical (street smarts included). Another approach to understanding mental ability contends that people have multiple intelligences, or faculties, including linguistic, logical-mathematical, musical, spatial, bodily-kinesthetic, intrapersonal, interpersonal, and naturalist.

Emotional intelligence refers to factors other than traditional mental ability that influence a person's success. The four components of emotional intelligence are (1) self-awareness, (2) self-management, (3) social awareness, and (4) relationship management.

Values and beliefs are another set of factors that influence behavior on the job, including interpersonal relations. Values are closely tied in with ethics. People acquire values in the process of growing up and modeling others. The values a person develops early in life are directly related to the kind of adult he or she becomes and to the quality of relationships formed. Values-clarification exercises help people identify their values. Person–role conflict occurs when the demands made by an organization or a superior clash with the basic values of an individual.

QUESTIONS FOR DISCUSSION AND REVIEW

1. Why is responding to individual differences considered to be the cornerstone of effective interpersonal relations?
2. How can knowledge of major personality factors help a person form better interpersonal relations on the job?

3. In what way might the personality trait of optimism versus pessimism be relevant for job performance?

4. Suppose a high self-monitoring person is attending a company-sponsored social event and that person dislikes such events. How is he or she likely to behave?

5. Identify two business occupations for which a high propensity for risk taking and thrill seeking would be an asset.

6. What kind of problems would a *sensing* type individual prefer to tackle?

7. Which of the seven components of traditional intelligence represents your best mental aptitude? What is your evidence?

8. How could you use the concept of multiple intelligences to raise the self-esteem of people who did not consider themselves to be very smart?

9. Why is emotional intelligence so important for success in business?

10. How can you use information about a person's values to help you relate more effectively to him or her?

GO TO THE WEB

http://www.iVillage.com
(See the quizzes relating to memory loss because they provide clues to keeping your mental ability in top form.)

http://www.queendom.com
(This site provides many tests and quizzes related to cognitive factors and personality.)

AN INTERPERSONAL RELATIONS CASE PROBLEM

MULTIPLE INTELLIGENCES IN THE OFFICE

Liz Russo is the general manager of the Student Loan Division of a major bank. She prides herself on being a modern manager who searches continuously for new ways to manage the student loan business and to manage people. Recently she attended a talk by Harvard University psychologist Howard Gardner given to the management group at the bank. Russo and the other managers listened intently as Gardner explained his theories of intelligence.

The psychologist emphasized that managers must discard the notion that there is only one kind of intelligence. Most of the managers nodded in agreement. Gardner explained that he wants people in charge of managing human resources to recognize that there are at least eight different kinds of intelligence. People with linguistic intelligence are really good at communicating with words. If you have logical-mathematical intelligence, you can deal with abstract relationships like formulating new ideas for products. People with musical intelligence can do wonders with sounds. Those who have spatial intelligence can work well with images and designs.

People who have bodily-kinesthetic intelligence can move their bodies easily, like dancers and athletes. Individuals gifted with intrapersonal intelligence can understand their own feelings well. People with interpersonal intelligence can read other people well. And finally, people with naturalist intelligence can understand and make good use of the environment.

During a lunch following the talk, Russo said to one of the other managers, "What liberating thoughts. The way I interpret Dr. Gardner's theories, people who are talented athletes or dancers are just as intelligent as computer whizzes. It's just that they have a different kind of intelligence."

(Continued)

"Why stop there?" responded the other manager. "One of my kids is a great banjo player, but we're wondering if he'll ever make it through high school. His mom and I used to think he was mentally challenged. Now we know his intelligence is the musical type, not the logical type."

Gardner's ideas kept spinning through Russo's mind. She bought a copy of one of his books for each of her managers and asked them all to study the book carefully. Later she scheduled a half-day meeting in a hotel to discuss how to apply the idea of eight human intelligences to the Student Loan Division. Russo said to her management team, "You all seem to agree with the idea that there are eight human intelligences. Now I want us to figure out how to apply Dr. Gardner's theories to make us a more productive business."

Molly Gerbrach, the head of information systems, said with a smirk on her face, "I have a suggestion. If I

hire a programmer who proves to be poor at programming, I'll just ask him or her to be the department's official musician!"

"I appreciate the humor, Molly," said Russo, "but now let's get down to business. Let's figure out how to implement these great ideas about different human intelligences."

Case Questions

1. Is Liz Russo being realistic about applying the concept of eight human intelligences to the office setting?

2. Suggest at least two ways in which the theory of eight human intelligences could be applied to improving productivity in the Student Loan Division.

AN INTERPERSONAL RELATIONS CASE PROBLEM

"WE'VE GOT TO MAKE OUR NUMBERS"

Bruce Malone works as an account manager for an office-supply company with branches in most cities of the United States. The company has two lines of business, retail and commercial. Among the many products the company sells are computers and related equipment, office furniture, copy paper, and other basic office supplies.

The retail trade is served by customers walking directly into the store or ordering online. Many of the customers are small business owners or corporate employees who work at home part of their work week. The commercial trade also does some walk-in purchasing and online ordering. However, each large customer is also assigned an account manager who calls on them periodically to discuss their needs for larger purchases such as office furniture and multiple copiers and desktop computers.

Malone is meeting his sales targets for the year despite a flat economy in the city where the office supplier is located. Shortly before Thanksgiving, Malone was analyzing his sales to estimate his performance for the year. According to his projections, his total sales would be 1 percent beyond his quota, giving him a satisfactory year. Making his quota would qualify him for a year-end bonus.

The Friday after Thanksgiving, Malone received an e-mail message from his boss Lucille Whitman requesting that the two meet Monday morning before Bruce began working with his customers. At the start of the meeting, Whitman told Malone that she had something very important to discuss with him. "Bruce, we are getting a lot of heat from corporate headquarters," Whitman began. "If we don't make our numbers [attaining the sales goals] the stock price could dip big time, and the home office executives will be in trouble. Even their bonuses will be at risk"

"I've done what I can," responded Malone. "I'm going to make my quota for the year plus a little extra margin. So I guess I'm covered. There isn't much I can do about the company as a whole."

"Let me be a little more specific," replied Whitman. "The company is in trouble, so we all have to pitch in and show better numbers for the year. What we need our account managers to do is to pump up the sales figures a little. Maybe you could count as December sales a few of the purchases your customers have planned for early January. Or maybe you could ship extra-large orders at a discount, and tell your customers they can pay as late as February or March.

"You're smart, Bruce. Beef up your sales figures for the year a little because we have got to make our numbers."

"Lucille, maybe I could work extra hard to pull in a few more sales in the next four weeks. But I would feel rotten faking my sales figures for December. I'm a professional."

With an angry tone, Whitman responded, "I don't care what you call yourself; we have got to make our numbers. Get back to me soon with your plan for increasing your numbers for December."

Case Questions

1. What is the nature of the conflict Bruce Malone is facing?
2. What type of values is Lucille Whitman demonstrating?
3. What do you recommend Bruce should have done to work his way out of the problem he was facing?
4. Is Bruce too naïve for a career in business?

INTERPERSONAL SKILLS ROLE-PLAY

The "Making the Numbers" Conundrum

Here is an opportunity to practice dealing with the type of conflict facing Bruce Malone. One person plays Bruce who has a follow-up conversation with Lucille Whitman about improving his December sales figures by less than straightforward means. Another student plays the role of Lucille Whitman who is focused on the corporate demands of "making the numbers." Bruce wants to communicate clearly how uncomfortable he feels about fudging the facts, while Lucille feels enormous pressure to meet the demands of the executive group. Ideally, the two role-players will reach a solution acceptable to both sides.

CHAPTER 2

Interpersonal Communication

Learning Objectives

After reading and studying this chapter and doing the exercises you should be able to

1. Explain the basic steps in the communication process.
2. Explain the relationship-building aspect of interpersonal communication.
3. Understand nonverbal communication and improve your nonverbal communication skills.
4. Understand barriers to communication, including gender differences, and know how to overcome them.
5. Enhance your listening skills.

Three months after she joined an infomercial company in January 2002, 23-year-old Kristy Pinand moved up to producer from production assistant. The promotion was like, so cool. But Ms. Pinand's routine of such "teen speak" bothered her boss. "She sounded very young," potentially hurting her ability to win clients' respect, recalls Collette Liantonio, president of Concepts TV Productions in Boonton, New Jersey. She urged the youthful-looking staffer to watch her words.[1]

Discussion Question

1. Why shouldn't Kristy Pinand continue with her teen speak? Shouldn't a person be natural on the job?

The manager's reaction to the young producer illustrates once again (you have heard this many times) the importance of effective communication skills for career success. **Communication** is the sending, receiving, and understanding of messages. It is also the basic process by which managers, customer-contact workers, and professionals accomplish their work. For example, a customer service representative cannot resolve a thorny customer problem without carefully receiving and sending information. Communication is also important because communication skills are a success factor for workers in a wide variety of jobs.

The information in this chapter is aimed at reducing communication problems among people and helping you enhance your communication effectiveness. The chapter approaches these ends in two ways. First, it explains the nature of a few key facets of interpersonal communication. Second, it presents guidelines for improving your effectiveness, along with skill-building exercises.

communication The sending, receiving, and understanding of messages.

STEPS IN THE COMMUNICATION PROCESS

One way to understand how people communicate is to examine the steps involved ◀ Learning Objective 1 in transmitting and receiving a message, as shown in Figure 3-1. For effective communication to take place, six components must be present: a sender, a message, a channel, a receiver, feedback, and the environment. In addition, a seventh component, noise, affects the entire communication process. To help understand the communication process, assume that a production manager in a bicycle factory wants to inform a team leader that quality in her department slipped last month.

1. **Sender (or source).** The sender in a communication event is usually a person (in this case the production manager) attempting to send a spoken, written, sign language, or nonverbal message to another person or persons. The perceived authority and credibility of the sender are important factors in influencing how much attention the message will receive.

2. **Message.** The heart of the communication event is the **message**, a purpose or idea to be conveyed. Many factors influence how a message is received. Among them are clarity, the alertness of the receiver, the complexity and length of the message, and how the information is organized. The production manager's message will most likely get across if he says directly, "I need to talk to you about last month's below-average quality figures."

message A purpose or idea to be conveyed.

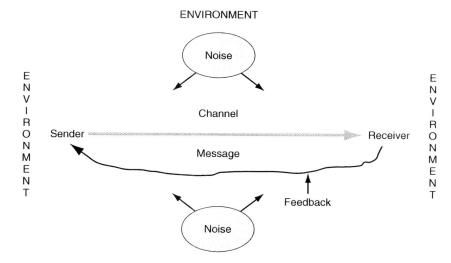

FIGURE 3-1 A Basic Model of the Communication Process

3. **Channel (medium).** Several communication channels, or media, are usually available for sending messages in organizations. Typically, messages are written (usually electronically), spoken, or a combination of the two. Some kind of nonverbal signal such as a smile or hand gesture accompanies most spoken messages. In the production manager's case, he has chosen to drop by the team leader's office and deliver his message in a serious tone.

4. **Receiver.** A communication event can be complete only when another party receives the message and understands it properly. In the example here, the team leader is the receiver. Perceptual distortions of various types act as filters that can prevent a message from being received as intended by the sender. If the team leader is worried that her job is at stake, she might get defensive when she hears the production manager's message.

feedback In communication, messages sent back from the receiver to the sender.

5. **Feedback.** Messages sent back from the receiver to the sender are referred to as **feedback.** Without feedback it is difficult to know whether a message has been received and understood. The feedback step also includes the reactions of the receiver. If the receiver takes action as intended by the sender, the message has been received satisfactorily. The production manager will know his message got across if the team leader says, "Okay, when would you like to review last month's quality reports?" Effective interpersonal communication therefore involves an exchange of messages between two people. The two communicators take turns being receivers and senders.

6. **Environment.** A full understanding of communication requires knowledge of the environment in which messages are transmitted and received. The organizational culture (attitudes and atmosphere) is a key environmental factor that influences communication. It is easier to transmit controversial messages when trust and respect are high than when they are low.

noise Anything that disrupts communication, including the attitudes and emotions of the receiver.

7. **Noise.** Distractions such as noise have a pervasive influence on the components of the communication process. In this context, **noise** is anything that disrupts communication, including the attitudes and emotions of the receiver. Noise includes such factors as stress, fear, negative attitudes, and low motivation.

RELATIONSHIP BUILDING AND INTERPERSONAL COMMUNICATION

Learning Objective 2 ▶ Another way of understanding the process of interpersonal communication is to examine how communication is a vehicle for building relationships. According to Ritch Sorenson, Grace DeBord, and Ida Ramirez, we establish relationships along two primary dimensions: dominate–subordinate, and cold–warm. In the process of communicating we attempt to dominate or subordinate. When we dominate, we attempt to control communication. When we subordinate we attempt to yield control, or think first of the wishes and needs of the other person. Dominators expect the receiver of messages to be submit to them; subordinate people send a signal that they expect the other person to dominate.[2]

We indicate whether we want to dominate or subordinate by the way we speak, write, or by the nonverbal signals we send. The dominator might speak loudly or enthusiastically, write forceful messages filled with exclamation points, or gesture with exaggerated, rapid hand movements. He or she might write a harsh e-mail message such as, "It's about time you started taking your job seriously, and put in some real effort."

In the subordinate mode, we might speak quietly and hesitantly, in a meek tone, and being apologetic. A subordinate person might ask, "I know you have better things on your mind than to worry about me, but I was wondering when I can expect my reimbursement for travel expenses?" In a work setting we ordinarily expect people with more formal authority to have the dominant role in conversations. However, in more democratic, informal companies, workers with more authority are less likely to feel the need to dominate conversations.

The *cold–warm dimension* also shapes communication because we invite the same behavior that we send. Cold, impersonal, negative messages evoke similar messages from others. In contrast, warm verbal and nonverbal messages evoke similar behavior from others. Getting back to the inquiry about the travel-expense check, here is a colder versus warmer response by the manager:

Colder: Travel vouchers really aren't my responsibility. You'll just have to wait like everybody else.

Warmer: I understand your problem. Not getting reimbursed on time is a bummer. I'll follow up on the status of your expense check sometime today or tomorrow.

The combination of dominant and cold communication sends the signal that the sender of the message wants to control and to limit, or even withdraw from a personal relationship. A team leader might say that she cannot attend a Saturday morning meeting because she has to go out of town for her brother's wedding. A dominant and cold manager might say, "I don't want to hear about your personal life. Everyone in this department has to attend our Saturday meeting."

Subordinate actions combined with warm communication signal a desire to maintain or build the relationship while yielding to the other person. A manager communicating in a warm and subordinate manner in relation to the wedding request might say, "We'll miss you on Saturday morning because you are a key player in our department. However, I recognize that major events in personal life sometimes take priority over a business meeting."

Figure 3-2 summarizes how the dual dimensions of dominate–subordinate and cold–warm influence the relationship-building aspects of communication. Rather

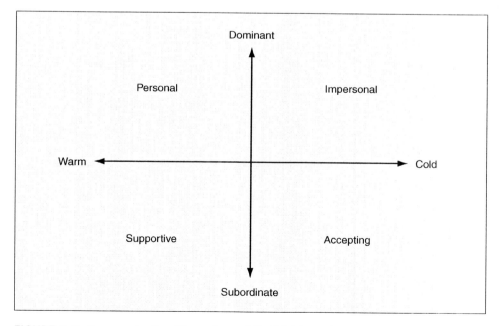

FIGURE 3–2 Communication Dimensions of Establishing a Relationship

Source: Sorenson, Ritch; Debord, Grace; Ramirez, Ida, *Business and Management Communication: A Guide Book*, 4th Edition, © 2001. Adapted by permission of Pearson Education, Inc. Upper Saddle River, NJ.

than regarding these four quadrants of relationships as good or bad, think of your purposes. In some situations you might want to dominate and be cold, yet in most situations you might want to submit a little and be warm in order to build a relationship. For example, being dominant and cold might be necessary for a security officer who is trying to control an unruly crowd at a sporting event.

Observe that the person in the quadrant *dominant–cold* has an impersonal relationship with the receiver, and the person in the *warm–subordinate* quadrant has a supportive relationship with the receiver. Being *dominant and warm* leads to a personal relationship, whereas being *submissive and cold* leads to an accepting relationship. The combinations of *dominant–cold* and *warm–subordinate* are more likely to produce the results indicated.

NONVERBAL COMMUNICATION IN ORGANIZATIONS

Learning Objective 3 ▶

nonverbal communication The transmission of messages through means other than words.

Our discussion so far has emphasized the use of words, or verbal communication. A substantial amount of communication between people, however, takes place at the nonverbal level. **Nonverbal communication** refers to the transmission of messages through means other than words. These messages accompany verbal messages or sometimes stand alone. The general purpose of nonverbal communication is to communicate the feeling behind a message. For instance, you can say no with either a clenched fist or a smile to communicate the intensity of your negative or positive feelings.

The following paragraphs summarize the major modes of transmission of nonverbal communication and provide guidelines for improving nonverbal communication. Chapter 6, about cross-cultural relations, describes cultural differences in nonverbal communication.

MODES OF TRANSMISSION OF NONVERBAL COMMUNICATION

Nonverbal communication can be transmitted in many modes. You may be surprised that certain factors, such as dress and appearance, are considered part of nonverbal communication.

Environment
The setting or environment in which you send a message can influence how that message is received. Assume that your manager invites you out to lunch at an upscale restaurant to discuss a problem. You will think it is a more important topic under these circumstances than you would if the manager had lunch with you in the company cafeteria.

Other important environmental silent messages include room color, temperature, lighting, and furniture arrangement. A person who sits behind a large, uncluttered desk, for example, appears more powerful than a person who sits behind a small, messy desk.

Interpersonal Distance
The placement of one's body in relation to someone else is widely used to transmit messages (see Figure 3-3). In general, getting physically close to another person conveys a positive attitude toward that person. Putting your arm around someone is generally interpreted as a friendly act. (Some people, however, recoil when touched by someone other than a close friend. Touching others on the job can also be interpreted as sexual harassment.) Watch out for cultural differences in preferences for

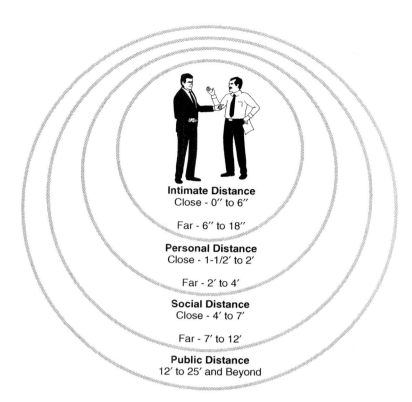

Intimate Distance
Close - 0″ to 6″

Far - 6″ to 18″

Personal Distance
Close - 1-1/2′ to 2′

Far - 2′ to 4′

Social Distance
Close - 4′ to 7′

Far - 7′ to 12′

Public Distance
12′ to 25′ and Beyond

FIGURE 3-3 Four Circles of Intimacy

interpersonal distance, such as French people standing much closer to each other while conversing than do Americans.

Closely related to interpersonal distance is where and how you sit in relation to another person during a meeting. Sitting across the table from a person during a negotiation session creates a defensive, competitive atmosphere, often leading to each party taking a firm stand on his or her point of view. The table becomes a tangible and psychological barrier between both parties. Recognition of this observation leads many managers and salespeople to sit down with another person with either no table or a coffee table between the two. Even when seated on separate chairs instead of a sofa, removal of a large table or desk separating the two parties leads to a friendlier, more open negotiation or sales discussion.[3]

Posture

Posture communicates a variety of messages. Standing erect usually conveys the message that the person is self-confident and experiencing positive emotion. Slumping makes a person appear to be lacking in self-confidence or down in the dumps. Another interpersonal message conveyed by posture involves the direction of leaning. Leaning toward the sender suggests that you are favorably disposed toward his or her message; leaning backward communicates the opposite. Openness of the arms or legs serves as an indicator of liking or caring. In general, people establish closed postures (arms folded and legs crossed) when speaking to people they dislike.

Can you think of an aspect of your posture that conveys a specific message?

Hand Gestures

Frequent hand movements show positive attitudes toward another person. In contrast, dislike or disinterest usually produces few gestures. An important exception is that some people wave their hands furiously while arguing. Gestures are also said to provide clues to a person's levels of dominance and submission. The gestures of dominant people are typically directed outward toward the other person. Examples include a steady, unwavering gaze and touching one's partner. Submissive gestures are usually protective, such as touching oneself or shrugging one's shoulders.

Facial Expressions

Using your head, face, and eyes in combination provides the clearest indications of interpersonal attitudes. Looking at the ceiling (without tilting your head), combined with a serious expression, almost always communicates the message "I doubt what you're saying is true." Maintaining eye contact with another person improves communication. To maintain eye contact, it is usually necessary to move your face and eyes with the other person. Moving your face and eyes away from the other person is often interpreted as defensiveness or a lack of self-confidence.

Facial expressions are also important because many people rely on them as indicators of whether or not a person is telling the truth. In general, fabrication is suggested by facial tics and nervous mannerisms that reveal how uncomfortable the sender is with telling something false. Looking away from a person is often interpreted as covering up a lie. Computer scientists at the Salk Institute in La Jolla, California, have documented the difference between a truthful smile and a lying smile. An authentic smile is most frequently characterized by crinkly eyes and a generally relaxed expression. A lying smile reveals itself in subtle ways, particularly eye wrinkles that resemble crow's feet more than laugh lines.[4]

Voice Quality

Often more significance is attached to the *way* something is said than to *what* is said. A forceful voice, which includes a consistent tone without vocalized pauses, connotes power and control. Closely related to voice tone are volume, pitch, and rate of speaking. Anger, boredom, and joy often can be interpreted from voice quality. Anger is noted when the person speaks loudly, with a high pitch and at a fast rate. Boredom is indicated by a monotone. Joy is indicated by loud volume. Avoiding an annoying voice quality can make a positive impact on others. The research of voice coach Jeffrey Jacobi provides some useful suggestions. He surveyed a nationwide sample of 1,000 men and women and asked, "Which irritating or unpleasant voice annoys you the most?" The most irritating was a whining, complaining, or nagging tone.

Jacobi notes that we are judged by the way we sound. He also notes that careers can be damaged by voice problems such as those indicated in the survey. "We think about how we look and dress," says Jacobi, "and that gets most of the attention. But people judge our intelligence much more by how we sound than how we dress."[5] Do Self-Assessment Quiz 3-1 to apply Jacobi's findings to your development.

Personal Appearance

Your external image plays an important role in communicating messages to others. A favorable personal appearance enhances a person's ability to persuade others, whether you are dealing with an individual receiver or an audience.[6] Job seekers show recognition of the personal appearance aspect of nonverbal communication when they carefully groom for a job interview. People pay more respect and grant more privileges to those they perceive as being well dressed and neatly groomed. The meaning of being well dressed depends heavily on the situation. In an information technology firm, neatly pressed jeans, a stylish T-shirt, and clean sport shoes might qualify as being well dressed. The same attire worn in a financial service firm would qualify as being poorly dressed.

A recent tendency is a return to more formal business attire, to suggest that a person is ambitious and successful. The best advice for using appearance to communicate nonverbal messages is to size up the environment to figure out what type of appearance and dress connotes the image you want to project.

SELF-ASSESSMENT QUIZ 3-1

VOICE-QUALITY CHECKUP

The voice-quality study cited in the text ranked voice quality in decreasing order of annoyance, as follows:

- Whining, complaining, or nagging tone—44.0 percent
- High-pitched, squeaky voice—15.9 percent
- Mumbling—11.1 percent
- Very fast talking—4.9 percent
- Weak and wimpy voice—3.6 percent
- Flat, monotonous tone—3.5 percent
- Thick accent—2.4 percent

Directions: Ask yourself and two other people familiar with your voice whether you have one or more of the preceding voice-quality problems. If your self-analysis and feedback from others does indicate a serious problem, get started on self-improvement. Record your voice on tape and attempt to modify the biggest problem. Another avenue of improvement is to consult with a speech coach or therapist.

GUIDELINES FOR IMPROVING NONVERBAL COMMUNICATION

Nonverbal communication, like verbal communication, can be improved. Here are six suggestions to consider.

1. **Obtain feedback on your body language by asking others to comment upon the gestures and facial expressions you use in conversations.** Be videotaped conferring with another individual. After studying your body language, attempt to eliminate those mannerisms and gestures that you think detract from your effectiveness. Common examples include nervous gestures such as moving knees from side to side, cracking knuckles, rubbing the eyes or nose, head scratching, and jingling coins.

2. **Learn to relax when communicating with others.** Take a deep breath and consciously allow your body muscles to loosen. Tension-reducing techniques should be helpful here. A relaxed person makes it easier for other people to relax. You are likely to elicit more useful information from other people when you are relaxed.

3. **Use facial, hand, and body gestures to supplement your speech, but don't overdo it.** A good starting point is to use hand gestures to express enthusiasm. You can increase the potency of enthusiastic comments by shaking the other person's hand, nodding approval, or smiling.

4. **Avoid using the same nonverbal gesture indiscriminately.** If you want to use nodding to convey approval, do not nod with approval when you dislike what somebody else is saying. Also, do not pat everybody on the back. Nonverbal gestures that are used indiscriminately lose their communication effectiveness.

SKILL-BUILDING EXERCISE 3-1

THE MIRRORING TECHNIQUE

To practice mirroring, during the next 10 days each class member schedules one mirroring session with an unsuspecting subject. An ideal opportunity would be an upcoming meeting on the job. Another possibility would be to ask a friend if you could practice your interviewing techniques with him or her—but do not mention the mirroring technique. A third possibility would be to sit down with a friend and conduct a social conversation.

While holding an interview or discussion with the other party, use the mirroring technique. Imitate the person's breathing pattern, rate of speech, hand movements, eye movements, leg movements, or any other noticeable aspect of behavior.

After the mirroring sessions have been conducted, hold a class discussion about the results. Questions include:

1. Did the other person notice the mirroring and comment on the behavior of the person doing the mirroring?

2. Was the rapport enhanced (or hindered) by the mirroring?

3. How many of the students intend to repeat the mirroring technique in the future?

5. **Use role-playing to practice various forms of nonverbal communication.** A good starting point would be to practice selling your ideas about an important project or concept to another person. During your interchange, supplement your spoken messages with appropriate nonverbal cues such as posture, voice intonation, gestures, and so forth. Later, obtain the other person's perception of the effectiveness of your nonverbal communication.

6. **Use mirroring to establish rapport.** Nonverbal communication can be improved through **mirroring,** or subtly imitating someone. The most successful mirroring technique is to imitate the breathing pattern of another person. If you adjust your own breathing rate to match someone else's, you will soon establish rapport with that individual. Another effective mirroring technique is to adopt the voice speed of the person with whom you are communicating. If the other person speaks more slowly than you typically do, slow down to mirror him or her.

You can also use mirroring by imitating a manager to win favor. Many subordinates have a relentless tendency to copy the boss's mannerisms, gestures, way of speaking, and dress. As a consequence, without realizing why, your manager may think more favorably of you.

Caution: Do not use mirroring to the extent that you appear to be mocking another person, thereby adversely affecting rapport. Do Skill-Building Exercise 3-1 to get started developing your mirroring skills.

mirroring Subtly imitating someone.

GUIDELINES FOR OVERCOMING COMMUNICATION PROBLEMS AND BARRIERS

Learning Objective 4 ▶ Communication problems in organizations are ever present. Some interference usually takes place between ideation and action, as suggested earlier by the noise factor in Figure 3-1. The type of message influences the amount of interference. Routine

1. Understand the receiver.
2. Minimize defensive communication.
3. Use multiple channels.
4. Use verbal and nonverbal feedback.
5. Display a positive attitude.
6. Use persuasive communication.
7. Engage in active listening.
8. Prepare for stressful conversations.
9. Engage in metacommunication.
10. Recognize gender differences in communication.

FIGURE 3-4 Overcoming Communication Problems and Barriers

or neutral messages are the easiest to communicate. Interference is most likely to occur when a message is complex, emotionally arousing, or clashes with a receiver's mental set.

An emotionally arousing message deals with topics such as money or a relationship between two people. A message that clashes with a receiver's mental set requires the person to change his or her typical pattern of receiving messages. Try this experiment. The next time you visit a restaurant, order dessert first and the main meal second. The server probably will not receive your dessert order because it deviates from the normal sequence.

Here we will describe strategies and tactics for overcoming some of the more frequently observed communication problems in the workplace, as outlined in Figure 3-4.

UNDERSTAND THE RECEIVER

Understanding the person you are trying to reach is a fundamental principle of overcoming communication barriers. The more you know about your receiver, the better able you are to deliver your message effectively. Three important aspects of understanding the receiver are (1) developing empathy, (2) recognizing his or her motivational state, and (3) understanding the other person's frame of reference.

Developing **empathy** requires placing yourself in the receiver's shoes. To accomplish this you have to imagine yourself in the other person's role and assume the viewpoints and emotions of that individual. For example, if a supervisor were trying to communicate the importance of customer service to sales associates, the supervisor might ask himself or herself, "If I were a part-time employee being paid close to the minimum wage, how receptive would I be to messages about high-quality customer service?" To empathize you have to understand another person. *Sympathy* means that you understand and agree.

The receiver's **motivational state** could include any active needs and interests operating at the time. People tend to listen attentively to messages that show promise of satisfying an active need or interest. Management usually listens attentively to a suggestion framed in terms of cost savings or increased profits. A coworker is likely to be attentive to your message if you explain how your idea can lead to a better year-end financial bonus for the group.

People perceive words and concepts differently because their vantage points and perspectives differ. Such differences in **frame of reference** create barriers to communication. A frame of reference can also be considered a lens through which we view the world. A manager attempted to chastise a team member by saying, "If

empathy In communication, imagining oneself in the receiver's role, and assuming the viewpoints and emotions of that individual.

motivational state Any active needs and interests operating at a given time.

frame of reference The fact that people perceive words and concepts differently because their vantage points and perspectives differ.

you keep up your present level of performance, you'll be a repair technician all your life." The technician replied, "That's good news," because he was proud of being the first person in his family to hold a skilled job. Understanding another person's frame of reference requires empathy.

MINIMIZE DEFENSIVE COMMUNICATION

defensive communication The tendency to receive messages in such a way that our self-esteem is protected.

An important general communication barrier is **defensive communication**—the tendency to receive messages in such a way that our self-esteem is protected. Defensive communication is also responsible for people sending messages to make them look good. For example, when being criticized for low production, a financial sales consultant might blame the advertising agency used by his or her firm.

Overcoming the barrier of defensive communication requires two steps. First, people have to recognize the existence of defensive communication. Second, they have to try not to be defensive when questioned or criticized. Such behavior is not easy because of the unconscious or semiconscious process of **denial**—the suppression of information we find uncomfortable. For example, the sales consultant just cited would find it uncomfortable to think of himself or herself as being responsible for below-average performance.

denial The suppression of information we find uncomfortable.

USE MULTIPLE CHANNELS

Repetition enhances communication, particularly when different channels are used to convey the same message. Effective communicators at many job levels follow spoken agreements with written documentation. Since most communication is subject to at least some distortion, the chances of a message being received as intended increase when two or more channels are used. Many firms have a policy of using a multiple-channel approach to communicate the results of a performance evaluation. The worker receives an oral explanation from the manager of the results of the review. The worker is also required to read the form and indicate by signature that he or she has read and understands the meaning of the review. Another useful way of using multiple channels is to follow up a telephone call or in-person conversation with an e-mail message summarizing key facts or agreements.

USE VERBAL AND NONVERBAL FEEDBACK

Ask for feedback to determine whether your message has been received as intended. A frequent managerial practice is to conclude a meeting with a question such as, "Okay, what have we agreed upon?" Unless feedback of this nature is obtained, you will not know whether your message has been received until the receiver carries out your request. If the request is carried out improperly, or if no action is taken, you will know that the message was received poorly.

Obtaining feedback is important because it results in two-way communication in which people take turns being sender and receiver, thereby having a dialogue. Dialogues take time because they require people to speak more slowly and listen more carefully. The results of having employees engage in dialogue are said to include a deeper sense of community (a feeling of belongingness) and greater trust among employees.[7] Relate this finding to your own experiences. Do you trust people more when you both exchange ideas and listen to each other?

Feedback is also important because it provides reinforcement to the sender, and few people will continue to communicate without any reinforcement. The sender is reinforced when the receiver indicates understanding of the message. When the original receiver indicates that he or she understands the message, that person becomes the sender. A nod of approval would be an appropriate type of nonverbal reinforcement for the sender to receive.

DISPLAY A POSITIVE ATTITUDE

Being perceived as having a positive attitude helps melt communication barriers. This is true because most people prefer to communicate with a positive person. According to Sharon Lund O'Neil, you must establish credibility and trustworthiness if you expect others to listen, let alone get them to react positively to your communication.[8] Being positive helps make you appear more credible and trustworthy, whereas being consistently negative makes you less credible and trustworthy. As one coworker said about a chronic complainer in his office, "Why take Margot seriously? She finds something wrong with everybody and everything."

USE PERSUASIVE COMMUNICATION

A powerful tactic for overcoming communication barriers is to communicate so persuasively that obstacles disappear. Persuasiveness refers to the sender convincing the receiver to accept his or her message. Persuasion thus involves selling to others. Hundreds of articles, books, audiotapes, and videos have been developed to help people become more persuasive. Following are some representative suggestions for becoming a more persuasive communicator, both in speaking and in writing.[9]

1. **Know exactly what you want.** Your chances of selling an idea increase to the extent that you have clarified the idea in your own mind. The clearer and more committed you are at the outset of a selling or negotiating session, the stronger you are as a persuader.

2. **Never suggest an action without telling its end benefit.** In asking for a raise, you might say, "If I get this raise, I'll be able to afford to stay with this job as long as the company likes."

3. **Get a yes response early on.** It is helpful to give the persuading session a positive tone by establishing a "yes pattern" at the outset. Assume that an employee wanted to convince the boss to allow the employee to perform some work at home during normal working hours. The employee might begin the idea-selling questions with "Is it important for the company to obtain maximum productivity from all its employees?"

4. **Use power words.** An expert tactic for being persuasive is to sprinkle your speech with power (meaning powerful) words. Power words stir emotion and bring forth images of exciting events. Examples of power words include decimating the competition, bonding with customers, surpassing previous profits, capturing customer loyalty, and attaining the unattainable. Using power words is part of having a broad vocabulary.

5. **Minimize raising your pitch at the end of sentences.** Part of being persuasive is to not sound unsure and apologetic. In English and several other languages, a convenient way to ask a question or to express doubt is to raise the pitch of your voice at the end of a sentence or phrase. As a test, use the sentence "You like my ideas." First say *ideas* using approximately the same pitch and tone as with every other word. Then say the same sentence by pronouncing *ideas* with a higher pitch and louder tone. By saying *ideas* loudly, you sound much less certain and are less persuasive.

6. **Talk to your audience, not the screen.** Computer graphic presentations have become standard practice even in small-group meetings. Many presenters rely so heavily on computer-generated slides and transparencies that they basically read the slides and transparencies to the audience. Jean Mausehund and R. Neil Dortch remind us that in an oral presentation, the predominant means of connection between sender and receiver should be eye contact. When your audience is frequently distracted by movement on the screen,

For more information on Ragland's product, see http://www. executivevocabulary. com. (The Web site includes an impressive video clip.)

computer sounds, garish colors, or your looking at the screen, eye contact suffers. As a result the message is weakened, and you are less persuasive.[10]

7. **Back up conclusions with data.** You will be more persuasive if you support your spoken and written presentations with solid data. You can collect the data yourself or quote from a printed or electronic source. Relying too much on research has a potential disadvantage, however. Being too dependent on data could suggest that you have little faith in your intuition. For example, you might convey a weak impression if, when asked your opinion, you respond, "I can't answer until I collect some data."

8. **Minimize "wimp" phrases.** Persuasive communicators minimize statements that make them appear weak and indecisive. Such phrases convey the impression that they are not in control of their actions. Wimp phrases include: "It's one of those days," "I'm not sure about that," "Don't quote me on that," and "I'll try my best to get it done." (It is better to commit yourself forcibly by saying, "I'll get it done.")

9. **Avoid or minimize common language errors.** You will enhance your persuasiveness if you minimize common language errors because you will appear more articulate and informed. Here are several common language errors:

   a. "Just between you and I" is wrong. "Just between you and me" is correct.

   b. *Irregardless* is not a word; *regardless* is correct.

   c. Avoid double negatives when you want to express the negative, despite the increasing popularity of double negatives. Common examples of double negatives are "I got no nothing from my best customer this week" and "We don't have no money in the budget for travel." If expressed with the right inflection, a double negative can be correct. For example, to say "We don't have no money" with an emphasis on *no money* means that the budget is not completely depleted. Yet in general, double negatives make the sender appear so ill-informed that they fail to persuade.

   d. "We are customer-oriented" is correct. "We are customer-orientated" is wrong. Here is an example of an error so widely committed that it would be fair to wonder if dictionaries will soon include *orientated.*

10. **Avoid overuse of jargon and clichés.** To feel "in" and hip many workers rely heavily on jargon and clichés, such as referring to their "fave" (for *favorite*) product, or that "At the end of the day" something counts, or that software is "scalable" (meaning it can get bigger). Add to the list "a seamless company," to mean the various departments cooperate with one another. The caution is that if a person uses jargon and hip phrases too frequently the person appears to be too contrived, and lacking in imagination.[11]

If you can learn to implement most of the preceding 10 suggestions, you are on your way toward becoming a persuasive communicator. In addition, you will need solid facts behind you, and you will need to make skillful use of nonverbal communication.

Back to the Opening Case

Kristy Pinand decided that her boss was offering her constructive advice if she wanted to be perceived as a professional. Pinand, who still gets mistaken for a teenager, now rehearses her remarks aloud before she calls a client. "How you talk should not be how you're judged, but of course it is," she observes. As a result of accepting her manager's constructive advice, Pinand now projects a more professional image.

ENGAGE IN ACTIVE LISTENING

Persuasion deals primarily with sending messages. Improving one's receiving of messages is another part of developing better communication skills. Unless you receive messages as they are intended, you cannot perform your job properly or be a good companion. A major challenge in developing good listening skills is that we process information much more quickly than most people speak. The average speaking rate is about 130 words per minute. In contrast, the average rate of processing information is about 300 words per minute.[12] So, you have to slow down mentally to listen well. ◀ **Learning Objective 5**

Listening can be even more essential than talking when engaged in face-to-face communication. Listening is a particularly important skill for anybody whose job involves troubleshooting, since one needs to gather information in order to solve problems. Another reason that improving the listening skills of employees is important is that insufficient listening is extraordinarily costly. Listening mistakes lead to reprocessing letters, rescheduling appointments, reshipping orders, and recalling defective products. Effective listening also improves interpersonal relations because the people listened to feel understood and respected.

A major component of effective listening is to be an **active listener.** The active listener listens intensely, with the goal of empathizing with the speaker. As a result of listening actively, the listener can feed back to the speaker what he or she thinks the speaker meant. Feedback of this type relies on both verbal and nonverbal communication. Active listening also involves **summarization.** When you summarize, you pull together, condense, and thereby clarify the main points communicated by the other person. Here are three examples of summarization statements:

"What I heard you say during our meeting is that . . ."

"As I understand it, your position is that . . ."

"Your major objection then is that . . ."

Another component to active listening is to indicate by your body language that you are listening intently. When a coworker comes to you with a question or concern, focus on that person and exclude all else. If you tap your fingers on the desk or glance around the room, you send the message that the other person and his or her concerns do not warrant your full attention. Listening intently through nonverbal communication also facilitates active listening because it demonstrates respect for the receiver.

Specific suggestions for improving active listening skills are summarized in Figure 3-5. These suggestions relate to good listening in general, as well as active listening. As with any other suggestions for developing a new skill, considerable practice (with some supervision) is needed to bring about actual changes in behavior. One of the problems a poor listener would encounter is the difficulty of breaking old habits in order to acquire new ones. Self-Assessment Quiz 3-2 gives you an opportunity to think about bad listening habits you may have acquired. To practice your listening skills, do Skill-Building Exercise 3-2.

PREPARE FOR STRESSFUL CONVERSATIONS

Communication barriers will frequently surface when two or more people are engaged in conversation fraught with emotion, such as giving highly negative performance feedback, rejecting a person for membership in your team, or firing an employee. Giving praise is another exchange that can make both or either parties uncomfortable. The sender might feel that he or she is patronizing the receiver, and the receiver might feel unworthy of the praise. One technique for reducing the stress in potentially stressful conversations is to prepare for them in advance.

A starting point in preparing for a stressful conversation is self-awareness about how you react to certain uncomfortable exchanges. For example, how do you feel

active listener A person who listens intensely, with the goal of empathizing with the speaker.

summarization The process of summarizing, pulling together, condensing, and thereby clarifying the main points communicated by another person.

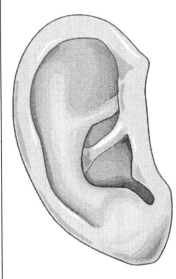

- ☺ *While your target is talking, look at him or her intently.* At the same time, maintain steady eye contact.
- ☺ *Be patient about your turn to speak.* A common barrier to effective listening is to mentally prepare an answer while another person is speaking.
- ☺ *Nod your head in agreement from time to time.*
- ☺ *Mutter "mmh" or "uh-huh" periodically but not incessantly.*
- ☺ *Ask open-ended questions to encourage the other person to talk.* For example, you encourage more conversation by saying "What do you think of . . . ?" rather than asking "Do you agree that . . . ?"
- ☺ *Reflect your target's content or meaning.* Rephrase and summarize concisely what the other person is saying.
- ☺ *Reflect the other person's feelings.* Reflection-of-feeling responses typically begin with "You feel that . . . "
- ☺ *Keep your ratio of talking to listening down to about one to five.* In other words, spend 20 percent of your time talking, and 80 percent listening to be perceived as a great listener.
- ☺ *Ask yourself whether anything the other person is saying could benefit you.* Maintaining this perspective will enable you to benefit from most listening episodes and will motivate you to listen intently.

FIGURE 3-5 Suggestions for Active Listening

when the receiver of the negative feedback reacts with hostility? Do you clam up, or do you become counterhostile? If you anticipate a hostile reception to an upcoming conversation, rehearse the scenario with a neutral friend. Deliver the controversial content that you will be delivering during the real event. Practice the body language you will use when you deliver a phrase such as, "As team leader, I must tell you that you have contributed almost nothing of value to our current project. Another part of the rehearsal is to practice delivering clear content—be explicit about what you mean." "Almost nothing of value to our current project" is much more explicit than "Your contribution has much room for improvement."

Also, practice *temperate phrasing,* or being tactful while delivering negative feedback. Communications specialist Holly Weeks suggests the following: Instead of snapping at someone, "Stop interrupting me"—try this: "Can you hold on a minute? I want to finish before I lose my train of thought." Temperate phrasing will take some of the sting out of a stressful conversation.[13]

ENGAGE IN METACOMMUNICATION

metacommunication
To communicate about your communication to help overcome barriers or resolve a problem.

Sometimes the best way to overcome a communication barrier with another person is to describe the nature of the relationship between you two at the moment. **Metacommunication** is to communicate about your communication to help overcome barriers or resolve a problem. If you as a team leader were facing heavy deadline pressures, you may say to a team member, "I might appear brusque today and tomorrow. Please don't take it personally. It's just that I have to make heavy demands on you because the team is facing a gruesome deadline." A more common situation is when the person with whom you are attempting to communicate appears angry or indifferent. Instead of wasting the communication event, it would be better to say, "You do not seem receptive to listening to me now. Are we having a problem? Should I try again later?"

SELF-ASSESSMENT QUIZ 3-2

LISTENING TRAPS

Communication specialists at Purdue University have identified certain behavior patterns that interfere with effective hearing and listening. After thinking carefully about each trap, check how well the trap applies to you: *not a problem,* or *need improvement.* To respond to the statements accurately, visualize how you acted when you recently were in a situation calling for listening.

	Not a problem	*Need improvement*
• **Mind reader.** You will receive limited information if you constantly think "What is this person really thinking or feeling?"	☐	☐
• **Rehearser.** Your mental rehearsals for "Here's what I'll say next" tune out the sender.	☐	☐
• **Filterer.** You engage in selective listening by hearing only what you want to hear. (Could be difficult to judge because the process is often unconscious.)	☐	☐
• **Dreamer.** You drift off during a face-to-face conversation, which often leads you to an embarrassing "What did you say?" or "Could you repeat that?"	☐	☐
• **Identifier.** If you refer everything you hear to your experience, you probably did not really listen to what was said.	☐	☐
• **Comparer.** When you get sidetracked sizing up the sender, you are sure to miss the message.	☐	☐
• **Derailer.** You change the subject too quickly, giving the impression that you are not interested in anything the sender has to say.	☐	☐
• **Sparrer.** You hear what is said, but quickly belittle or discount it, putting you in the same class as the derailer.	☐	☐
• **Placater.** You agree with everything you hear just to be nice or to avoid conflict. By behaving this way you miss out on the opportunity for authentic dialogue.	☐	☐

Interpretation: If you checked *need improvement* for five or more of the above statements, you are correct—your listening needs improvement! If you checked only two or fewer of the above traps, you are probably an effective listener and a supportive person.

Source: Listening Traps Quiz from *Messages: The Communication Skills Handbook* (Oakland, CA: New Harbinger Publications, 1983).

RECOGNIZE GENDER DIFFERENCES IN COMMUNICATION STYLE

A trend in organizations for many years has been to move toward gender equality. Despite this trend, substantial interest has arisen in identifying differences in communication styles between men and women. People who are aware of these differences face fewer communication barriers between themselves and members of the opposite sex. As we discuss these differences, recognize that they are group stereotypes. Individual differences in communication style usually are more important

SKILL-BUILDING EXERCISE 3-2

LISTENING TO A COWORKER

Before conducting the following role-plays, review the suggestions for effective listening presented in the text and Figure 3-5. Restating what you hear (summarization) is particularly important when listening to a person who is talking about an emotional topic.

The Elated Coworker: One student plays the role of a coworker who has just been offered a six-month assignment to the Rome, Italy, unit of the company. She will be receiving a 30 percent pay increase during the assignment plus a supplementary living allowance. She is eager to describe full details of her good fortune to a coworker. Another student plays the role of the coworker to whom the first worker wants to describe her good fortune. The second worker decides to listen intently to the first worker. Other class members will rate the second student on his or her listening ability.

The Discouraged Coworker: One student plays the role of a coworker who has just been placed on probation for poor job performance. His boss thinks that his performance is below standard and that his attendance and punctuality are poor. He is afraid that if he tells his girlfriend, she will leave him. He is eager to tell his tale of woe to a coworker. Another student plays the role of a coworker he corners to discuss his problems. The second worker decides to listen intently to his problems but is pressed for time. Other class members will rate the second student on his or her listening ability.

than group (men versus women) differences. Here we will discuss the major findings of gender differences in communication patterns.[14]

1. **Women prefer to use conversation for rapport building.** For most women, the intent of conversation is to build rapport and connections with people. Women are therefore more likely to emphasize similarities, to listen intently, and to be supportive.

2. **Men prefer to use talk primarily as a means to preserve independence and status by displaying knowledge and skill.** When most men talk they want to receive positive evaluation from others and maintain their hierarchical status within the group. Men are therefore more oriented to giving a *report* while women are more interested in establishing *rapport*.

3. **Women want empathy, not solutions.** When women share feelings of being stressed out, they seek empathy and understanding. If they feel they have been listened to carefully, they begin to relax. When listening to the woman, the man may feel blamed for her problems or that he has failed the woman in some way. To feel useful, the man might offer solutions to the woman's problems.

4. **Men prefer to work out their problems by themselves, whereas women prefer to talk out solutions with another person.** Women look upon having and sharing problems as an opportunity to build and deepen relationships. Men are more likely to look upon problems as challenges they must meet on their own. The communication consequence of these differences is that men may become uncommunicative when they have a problem.

5. **Women are more likely to compliment the work of a coworker, whereas men are more likely to be critical.** A communication problem may occur

when a woman compliments the work of a male coworker and expects reciprocal praise.

6. **Men tend to be more directive in their conversation, whereas women emphasize politeness.** Women are therefore more likely to frequently use the phrases "I'm sorry" and "Thank you," even when there is no need to express apology or gratitude. For example, a supermarket manager notices that the store has suddenly become busy. She would therefore say to a store associate unpacking boxes, "I'm sorry Pedro, but we've become busy all of a sudden. Could you please open up a new lane up front? Thank you." A manager who is a stereotyped male might say, "Pedro, we need you to open a line up front, pronto. Put down the boxes and get up there."

7. **Women tend to be more conciliatory when facing differences, whereas men become more intimidating.** Again, women are more interested in building relationships, whereas men are more concerned about coming out ahead.

8. **Men are more interested than women in calling attention to their accomplishments or hogging recognition.** In one instance a sales representative who had already made her sales quota for the month turned over an excellent prospect to a coworker. She reasoned, "It's somebody else's turn. I've received more than my fair share of bonuses for the month."

9. **Men tend to dominate discussions during meetings.** One study of college faculty meetings found that women's longest turns at speaking were, on the average, of shorter duration than men's shortest turns. A possible explanation here is that women are still less assertive than men in the workplace.

How can the information just presented help overcome communication problems on the job? As a starting point, remember that these gender differences often exist. Understanding these differences will help you interpret the communication behavior of people. For example, if a male coworker is not as effusive with praise as you would like, remember that he is simply engaging in gender-typical behavior. Do not take it personally.

A woman can remind herself to speak up more in meetings because her natural tendency might be toward diffidence. She might say to herself, "I must watch out to avoid gender-typical behavior in this situation." A man might remind himself to be more complimentary and supportive toward coworkers. The problem is that although such behavior is important, his natural tendency might be to skip the praise.

A woman should not take it personally when a male coworker or subordinate is tight-lipped when faced with a problem. She should recognize that he needs more encouragement to talk about his problems than would a woman. If the man persists in not wanting to talk about the problem, the woman might say, "It looks like you want to work out this problem on your own. Go ahead. I'm available if you want to talk about the problem."

Men and women should recognize that when women talk over problems, they might not be seeking hard-hitting advice. Instead, they might simply be searching for a sympathetic ear so they can deal with the emotional aspect of the problem.

A general suggestion for overcoming gender-related communication barriers is for men to improve communication by becoming more empathic (showing more empathy) listeners. Women can improve communication by becoming more direct.

Ruth Sherman, a speech and communications consultant, advises you to be more aware of how you talk at work. If you feel that you are not be listened to in meetings or have trouble persuading managers of your ability or accomplishments, get feedback from others. As a colleague you trust, to watch you during a meeting and provide analysis.[15]

SUMMARY

Communication is the basic process by which managers, customer-contact workers, and professionals accomplish their work, yet many communication problems exist in organizations. Communication among people is a complex process that can be divided into six components: sender or source, message, channel (or medium), receiver, feedback, and environment. Noise, or interference, can disrupt communication within any component.

Nonverbal communication plays an important part in sending and receiving messages and is especially important for imparting the emotional aspects of a message. The modes of nonverbal communication include the environment in which the message is sent, interpersonal distance, posture, gestures, facial expressions, voice quality, and personal appearance.

Nonverbal communication can be improved through such means as obtaining feedback, learning to relax, using gestures more discriminately, role-playing, and mirroring. The latter refers to subtly imitating someone.

Methods of overcoming communication barriers include the following: (1) understand the receiver, (2) minimize defensive communication, (3) use multiple channels, (4) use verbal and nonverbal feedback, (5) display a positive attitude, (6) use persuasive communication, (7) engage in active listening, (8) prepare for stressful conversation, (9) engage in metacommunication (communicating about your communication), and (10) recognize gender differences in communication styles.

QUESTIONS FOR DISCUSSION AND REVIEW

1. What are the reasons so many workers need improvement in communication skills?

2. How can knowing the steps in the communication process help a person become a more effective communicator?

3. How can people use their automobiles to send nonverbal messages?

4. What type of voice quality do you think would be effective in most work situations?

5. How could watching television provide some useful ideas for improving your job-oriented communication skills?

6. Should a person use power words when he or she is not in a powerful job? Explain.

7. Why is summarization such a powerful communication technique?

8. Identify three scenarios in the workplace that are likely to result in stressful conversations.

9. Suppose your manager does not listen to your suggestions for job improvements. How would you metacommunicate to deal with this problem?

10. What are the implications of gender differences in communication for conducting meetings?

GO TO THE WEB

http://www.optimalthinking.com/quiz-communication-skills.asp
(Rate your level of communication.)

http://www.queendom.com
(Look for the Communication Skills Test.)

AN INTERPERSONAL RELATIONS CASE PROBLEM

THE SCRUTINIZED TEAM MEMBER CANDIDATE

HRmanager.com is a human resource management firm that provides human resource services such as payroll, benefits administration, affirmative action programs, and technical training to other firms. By signing up with HRmanager, other firms can outsource part or all of their human resource functions. During its seven years of operation, HRmanager has grown from 3 to 50 employees, and last year it had total revenues of $21 million.

Teams perform most of the work, led by a rotating team leader. Each team member takes an 18-month turn at being a team leader. CEO and founder Jerry Clune regards the four-person new ventures team as vital for the future of the company. In addition to developing ideas for new services, the team members are responsible for obtaining clients for any new service they propose that Clune approves. The new ventures team thus develops and sells new services. After the service is launched and working well, the sales group is responsible for developing more clients.

As with other teams at HRmanager, the team members have a voice as to who is hired to join their team. In conjunction with Clune, the new ventures team decided it should expand to five members. The team posted the job opening for a new member on an Internet recruiting service, ran classified ads in the local newspaper, and also asked present employees for referrals. One of the finalists for the position was Gina Cleveland, a 27-year-old business graduate. In addition to interviewing with Clune and the two company vice presidents, Cleveland spent one-half day with the new ventures team, breakfast and lunch included. About two-and-one-half hours of the time was spent in a team interview in which Gina sat in a conference room with the four team members.

The team members agreed that Cleveland appeared to be a strong candidate on paper. Her education and experience were satisfactory, her résumé was impressive, and she presented herself well during a telephone-screening interview. After Cleveland completed her time with the new ventures team, Lauren Nielsen, the team leader, suggested that the group hold a debriefing session. The purpose of the session would be to share ideas about Cleveland's suitability for joining the team.

Nielsen commented, "It seems like we think that Gina is a strong candidate based on her credentials and what she said. But I'm a big believer in nonverbal communication. Studying Gina's body language can give us a lot of valuable information. Let's each share our obser-

vations about what Gina's body language tells us she is *really* like. I'll go first.

Lauren: I liked the way Gina looked so cool and polished when she joined us for breakfast. She's got all the superficial movements right to project self-confidence. But did anybody else notice how she looked concerned when she had to make a choice from the menu? She finally did choose a ham-and-cheese omelet, but she raised her voice at the end of the sentence when she ordered it. I got the hint that Gina is not very confident.

I also noticed Gina biting her lips a little when we asked her how creative she thought she was. I know that Gina said she was creative, and gave us an example of a creative project she completed. Yet nibbling at her lips like that suggests she's not filled with firepower.

Michael: I didn't make any direct observations about Gina's self-confidence or lack of, but I did notice something that could be related. I think Gina is on a power trip, and this could indicate high or low self-confidence. Did anybody notice how Gina put her hands on her hips when she was standing up? That's a pure and clear signal of somebody who wants to be in control. Her haircut is almost the same length and style like most women who've made it to the top in Fortune 500 companies. I think she cloned her hairstyle from Carly Fiorina, the former HP honcho who is called a "celebrity CEO."

Another hint I get of Gina's power trip is the way she eyed the check in the restaurant at lunch. I could see it in her eyes that she really wanted to pay for the entire team. That could mean a desire to control, and show us that she is very important. Do we want someone on the team with such a strong desire to control?

Brenda: I observed a different picture of Gina based on her nonverbal communication. She dressed just right for the occasion: not too conservatively and not too business casual. This tells me she can fit into our environment. Did you notice how well groomed her shoes were? This tells you she is well organized and good at details. Her briefcase was a soft, inviting leather. If she were really into power and control she would carry a hard vinyl or aluminum briefcase. I see Gina as a confident and assertive person who could blend right into our team.

(Continued)

Larry: I hope that because I'm last, I'm not too influenced by the observations that you three have shared so far. My take is that Gina looks great on paper, but that she may have a problem being a good team player. She's too laid back and distant. Did you notice her handshake? She gave me the impression of wanting to have the least possible physical contact with me. Her handshake was so insincere. I could feel her hand and arm withdrawing from me as she shook my hand.

I also couldn't help noticing that Gina did not lean toward us during the round-table discussion. Do you remember how she would pull her chair back ever so slightly when we got into a heavy discussion? I interpreted that as a sign that Gina does not want to be part of a close-knit group.

Lauren: As you have probably noticed, I've been typing as fast as I can with my laptop, taking notes on what you have said. We have some mixed observations here, and I want to summarize and integrate them before we make a decision. I'll send you an e-mail with an attached file of my summary observations by tomorrow morning. Make any changes you see fit and get back to me. After we have finished evaluating Gina carefully, we will be able to make our recommendations to Jerry (Clune).

Case Questions

1. To what extent are new ventures team members making appropriate use of nonverbal communication to size up Gina Cleveland?

2. Which team member do you think made the most realistic interpretation of nonverbal behavior? Why?

3. Should Lauren, the team leader, have told Gina in advance that the team would be scrutinizing her nonverbal behavior? Justify your answer.

AN INTERPERSONAL RELATIONS CASE PROBLEM

THE DENTAL FLOSS COMMUNICATION CHALLENGE

Claudia Telfair has worked as a dental hygienist for five years in the same large dental practice in suburban Columbus, Ohio. She treats patients about 25 hours per week. In her words, "If I work too much more than 25 hours per week I'm liable to get tendonitis and carpal tunnel syndrome. All that precision scraping takes a toll on my right hand, and to some extent on my left hand. Hovering over patients can also give me back pains, if I do it for too long each week.

"I feel that my work is so important that I am willing to put up with a little physical pain to help my patients have healthy teeth and gums."

"You would then say that the biggest frustration in your work is its physical demands?" asked the case researcher.

"I never said that. You said that," replied Telfair. "The part of my job with the biggest impact on the health of patients is getting across my message about healthy habits to prevent tooth decay and gum disease. I lecture my patients. I demonstrate how they should be brushing and flossing, and how they should use soft wood plaque removers [such as Stim-u-Dents]. I give out samples.

"I do everything I can think of to convince my patients to take good care of their teeth and gums between cleaning appointments."

"What is so frustrating about what you have just described?"

"The frustration is that my patients don't seem to listen. They smile, they nod in agreement, and they pack the samples. Yet four months later when the patients return, it appears that most of them are engaging in the same old sloppy dental habits. They continue with superficial brushing with an old toothbrush instead of using a battery-powered or electric one. It looks like they forgot my message about using wooden plaque removers. Yet flossing is the least used preventive treatment of them all."

"When you ask patients why they neglect flossing between their cleaning appointments, what do they say?" asked the case researcher.

"I hear more excuses than you get from violators in traffic court," said Telfair. Some of the typical excuses are that the patients forget, that they are too busy, and that flossing is too painful. A patient told me the other day that he dislikes flossing because the ritual is so ugly and weird."

"What do you tell the patients when you observe that they are not following your advice?"

"I usually just tell them that are doing a poor job of taking care of their teeth and gums. Also, I will usually give them more samples of floss and plaque remover so they will be reminded to do better. Sometimes I give them another brochure about a battery-powered toothbrush.

"I guess you could say that I'm doing a much better job treating tooth and gum problems than preventing them."

Case Questions

1. What communication problems is Claudia Telfair facing in her role as a dental hygienist?

2. What communication errors might Telfair be making?

3. Offer Telfair a couple of suggestions to help her accomplish her goal of being more effective at preventing dental and gum problems, based on your knowledge of interpersonal communication.

INTERPERSONAL SKILLS ROLE-PLAY

The Dental Hygienist and Dental Patient Role-Play

One student sits on a chair pretending to be a dental patient who does a sloppy job of dental care, such as brushing regularly and flossing. Another student plays the role of dental hygienist Claudia. (She can use a pencil or pen to simulate a metal gum scraper.) With the patient in the chair, engage in a dialogue about the importance of using dental floss. Claudia wants this patient to practice much better dental hygiene, whereas the patient is somewhat skeptical about her advice. Perhaps two or three different pairs can conduct the role-play in front of the class. Other class members will observe the effectiveness of the communication episode in terms of Claudia getting her message across.

CHAPTER 3

Developing Teamwork Skills

Learning Objectives

After reading and studying this chapter and doing the exercises you should be able to

1. Identify several types of teams in organizations.
2. Understand the advantages and disadvantages of teams.
3. Identify various team member roles.
4. Be ready to apply interpersonal-related tactics for effective team play.
5. Be ready to apply task-related tactics for effective team play.

altimore's Chesapeake Habitat for Humanity (CHH) is a nonprofit organization that renovates vacant houses and sells them at noninterest mortgage rates to low-income home buyers. This year, the nonprofit's 11 employees will oversee 2,000 local volunteers renovating 11 homes.

But CHH is renovating much more than houses; it's also updating its business model. In June, CHH launched its own for-profit venture called TeamBuilds, where corporate teams pay $7,500 for an all-day team-building session with an organization development consultant while working together to rebuild an old house. Amid nail guns and drywall, teams will work out their problems and increase their competitiveness.[1]

Discussion Question

1. Why would companies spend so much time and money developing teamwork skills? Doesn't everybody know how to be a team player?

The enthusiasm of companies to send groups of workers to TeamBuilds illustrates the importance of teamwork in organizations. Many firms rely more on teamwork than on individuals acting alone to accomplish work. To be successful in the modern organization, it is therefore necessary to be an effective team player. You have to work smoothly with other members of the team to accomplish your goals. Teamwork is more important as people work their way up through the organization. Executives, such as CEOs, preach teamwork but tend to dominate meetings and make more decisions by themselves.[2]

The challenges a team member faces come to light when the true nature of a team is recognized. A **team** is a special type of group. Team members have complementary skills and are committed to a common purpose, a set of performance goals, and an approach to the task. In other words, the members of a team work together smoothly, and all pull in the same direction. A workplace team should be more like an effective athletic team than a group of individuals out for individual glory.[3]

This chapter gives you the information, insights, and preliminary practice necessary to develop effective teamwork skills. Self-Assessment Quiz 4-1 will help you assess your current mental readiness to be a contributing team member.

Team A small number of people with complementary skills who are committed to a common purpose, set of performance goals, and approach for which they hold themselves mutually accountable.

 ## SELF-ASSESSMENT QUIZ 4-1

TEAM PLAYER ATTITUDES

Directions: Describe how well you agree with each of the following statements, using the following scale: disagree strongly (DS); disagree (D); neutral (N); agree (A); agree strongly (AS). Circle the number in the appropriate column.

	DS	D	N	A	AS
1. I am at my best when working alone.	5	4	3	2	1
2. I have belonged to clubs and teams ever since I was a child.	1	2	3	4	5
3. It takes far too long to get work accomplished with a group.	5	4	3	2	1
4. I like the friendship of working in a group.	1	2	3	4	5
5. I would prefer to run a one-person business than to be a member of a large firm.	5	4	3	2	1
6. It's difficult to trust others in the group on key assignments.	5	4	3	2	1
7. Encouraging others comes to me naturally.	1	2	3	4	5
8. I like the give-and-take of ideas that is possible in a group.	1	2	3	4	5
9. It is fun for me to share responsibility with other group members.	1	2	3	4	5
10. Much more can be accomplished by a team than by the same number of people working alone.	1	2	3	4	5

Total Score _____

Scoring and Interpretation: Add the numbers you circled to obtain your total score.

41–50 You have strong positive attitudes toward being a team member and working cooperatively with other members.

30–40 You have moderately favorable attitudes toward being a team member and working cooperatively with other members.

10–29 You much prefer working by yourself to being a team member. To work effectively in a company that emphasizes teamwork, you may need to develop more positive attitudes toward working jointly with others.

TYPES OF TEAMS

Learning Objective 1 ▶ All teams in the workplace have the common element of people working together cooperatively and members possessing a mix of skills. Nevertheless, many specific types of work teams can be identified. Successful people will usually have the opportunity to be a member of several different types of teams.

Four representative work teams are self-managing work teams, cross-functional teams, virtual teams and crews. Projects, task forces, and committees are similar in design to cross-functional teams, so they do not receive separate mention here. No matter what label the team carries, its broad purpose is to contribute to a *collaborative workplace* in which people help each other achieve constructive goals. The idea is for workers to collaborate (a high level of cooperation) rather than compete with or prevent others from getting their work done.

As teams have become more common in the workplace, effort has been directed toward specifying the skills and knowledge a person needs to function effectively on a team, particularly a self-managing work team. Self-Assessment Quiz 4-2 presents a representative listing of team skills as perceived by employers.

SELF-MANAGING WORK TEAMS

The best-known work team is a group of workers who take much of the responsibility for managing their own work. The same type of team is referred to as a self-managing work team, a self-directing work team, a production work team, or a team. A **self-managing work team** is a small group of employees responsible for managing and performing technical tasks to deliver a product or service to an external or internal customer.[4] The vast majority of large- and medium-size firms make some use of self-managing work teams. Work teams are used in a wide variety of activities including producing motorcycles, telephone directories, or a major component for a large computer.

Members of a self-managing work team typically work together on an ongoing, day-by-day basis, thus differentiating it from a task force or a committee. The work team is often given total responsibility for or "ownership" of an entire product or service, such as producing a telephone directory. At other times, the team is given responsibility for a major chunk of a job, such as building an airplane engine (but not the entire airplane).

A major hurdle in forming self-managing teams is to help employees overcome the attitude reflected in the statement "I'm not paid to think." Work teams rely less on supervisors and more on the workers assuming more responsibilities for managing their own activities. For example, work team members may be required to discipline other team members who have attendance, performance, or behavioral problems.[5]

As with all teams, mutual trust among members contributes to team effectiveness. A study conducted with business students, however, showed that if the members trust each other too much they may not monitor (check up on) each other's work enough. As a result, group performance will suffer. This problem of too much trust surfaces primarily when the team members have individual assignments that do not bring them into frequent contact with each other.[6] An example of an individual, or autonomous, project would be preparing a statistical report that would later be given to the group.

self-managing work team A small group of employees responsible for managing and performing technical tasks to deliver a product or service to an external or internal customer.

cross-functional team A work group composed of workers from different specialties, and about the same organizational level, who come together to accomplish a task.

CROSS-FUNCTIONAL TEAMS

It is common practice for teams to be composed of workers from different specialties. A **cross-functional team** is a work group composed of workers from different specialties, who come together to accomplish a task. The purpose of the cross-functional team is to get workers from different specialties to blend their talents toward accomplishing a task that requires such a mix.

SELF-ASSESSMENT QUIZ 4-2

TEAM SKILLS

A variety of skills are required to be an effective member of various types of teams. Several different business firms use the skill inventory here to help guide team members toward the competencies they need to become high-performing team members.

Directions: Review each team skill listed and rate your skill level for each one using the following classification:

    S = strong (capable and comfortable with effectively implementing the skill)

    M = moderate (demonstrated skill in the past)

    B = basic (minimum ability in this area)

    N = not applicable (not relevant to the type of work I do)

Communication skills	*Skill level (S, M, B, or N)*
Speak effectively	_____
Foster open communications	_____
Listen to others	_____
Deliver presentations	_____
Prepare written communication	_____

Self-management skills	
Act with integrity	_____
Demonstrate adaptability	_____
Engage in personal development	_____
Strive for results	_____
Display a commitment to work	_____

Thought process skills	
Innovate solutions to problems	_____
Use sound judgment	_____
Analyze issues	_____
Think "outside the box"	_____

Organizational skills	
Know the business	_____
Use technical/functional expertise	_____
Use financial/quantitative data	_____

Strategic (broad business perspective) skills	
Recognize "big picture" impact	_____
Promote corporate citizenship	_____
Focus on customer needs	_____
Commit to quality	_____
Manage profitability	_____

Interpretation: There is no scoring key for this questionnaire. Its purpose is to raise your awareness of the types of skills that are required to be a successful team member in business.

A typical application of a cross-functional team would be to develop a new product such as a video cell phone. Among the specialties needed on such a team would be computer science, engineering, manufacturing, industrial design, marketing, and finance. (The finance person would help guide the team toward producing a video cell phone that could be sold at a profit.) When members from different specialties work together, they can take into account each other's perspectives when making their contribution. For example, if the manufacturing representative knows that a video cell phone must sell for about one-half the price of a plasma screen TV, then he or she will have to build the device inexpensively. A major advantage of cross-functional teams for product development is that they enhance communication across groups, thereby saving time. In addition to product development, cross-functional teams are used for such purposes as improving quality, reducing costs, and running a company (in the form of a top management team).

To perform well on a cross-functional team a person would have to think in terms of the good of the larger organization, rather than in terms of his or her own specialty. For example, a manufacturing technician might say, "If I proposed using expensive components for the video phone, would the product cost too much for its intended market?"

VIRTUAL TEAMS

virtual team A small group of people who conduct almost all of their collaborative work by electronic communication rather than face-to-face meetings.

Some teams conduct most of their work by sending electronic messages to each other rather than conducting face-to-face meetings. A **virtual team** is a small group of people who conduct almost all of their collaborative work by electronic communication rather than face-to-face meetings. E-mail, including **IM** (instant messaging), is the usual medium for sharing information and conducting meetings. *Groupware* is another widely used approach to conducting an electronic meeting. Using groupware, several people can edit a document at the same time, or in sequence. Desktop videoconferencing is another technological advance that facilitates the virtual team. Electronic brainstorming, as described in Chapter 5, is well suited for a virtual team.

Most high-tech companies make some use of virtual teams and electronic meetings. Strategic alliances in which geographically dispersed companies work with each other are a natural for virtual teams. It is less expensive for the field technician in Iceland to hold an electronic meeting with her counterparts in South Africa, Mexico, and California than it is to bring them all together in one physical location. Virtual teams are sometimes the answer to the challenge of hiring workers with essential skills who do not want to relocate. With team members geographically dispersed, precise communications are all the more important for virtual teams. The virtual team members usually need a formal document outlining the objectives, job responsibilities, and team goals. Another communication problem takes place when the virtual team is composed of both in-house workers and those in remote locations. The office-bound members become jealous of the seemingly cushy setup enjoyed by the telecommuters. One solution to this problem is for every member of the team to be given a chance to prove he or she can work off-site.[7]

Despite the efficiency of virtual teams, there are times when face-to-face interaction is necessary to deal with complex and emotional issues. Negotiating a new contract between management and a labor union, for example, is not well suited to an electronic meeting.

CREWS

crew A group of specialists each of whom have specific roles, perform brief events that are closely synchronized with each other, and repeat these events under different environmental conditions.

We are all familiar with common usage of the term *crew* in relation to such groups as those who operate airplanes, boats, and firefighting equipment. The technical meaning of the term means virtually the same thing. A **crew** is a group of specialists each of who have specific roles, perform brief events that are closely synchronized with each other, and repeat these events under different environmental conditions. A crew is identified by the technology it handles, such as an aircraft crew, or a deep-sea salvage operation. The crewmembers rarely rotate specialties, such as the flight attendant taking over for the chief pilot. (Special training and licensing would be required.) The following are several criteria of a group qualifying as a crew:[8]

- Clear roles and responsibilities
- Workflow well established before anyone joins the team
- Careful coordination required with other members in order to perform the task
- Group needs to be in a specific environment to complete its task
- Different people can join the group without interfering with its operation or mission

Because of the specialized roles they play, and the essential tasks they perform, much is expected of crews. The future of crews is promising. For example, computer-virus-fighting crews would be a welcome addition to business and society. Mutual trust is especially important in a crew because good cooperation could save one's life, such as in a firefighting crew.

THE ADVANTAGES AND DISADVANTAGES OF TEAMS AND TEAMWORK

Groups have always been the building blocks of organizations. Yet groups and teams have recently grown in importance as the basic unit for organizing work. In an attempt to cope with numerous changes in the outside world, many organizations have granted teams increased independence and flexibility. Furthermore, teams are often required to work more closely with customers and suppliers. ◀ **Learning Objective 2**

The increased acceptance of teams suggests that group work offers many advantages. Nevertheless, it is useful to specify several of these advantages and also examine the potential problems of groups. Being aware of these potential pitfalls can often help a person avoid them. These same advantages and disadvantages also apply to group decision making, to be described in Chapter 5.

ADVANTAGES OF GROUP WORK AND TEAMWORK

Group work and group decision making offer several advantages over individual effort. If several knowledgeable people are brought into the decision-making process, a number of worthwhile possibilities may be uncovered. It is also possible to gain **synergy,** whereby the group's total output exceeds the sum of each individual's contribution. For example, it would be a rare person working alone who could build a racing car.

Group decision making is also helpful in gaining acceptance and commitment. The argument is that people who contribute to making a decision will feel some ownership about implementing the decision. Team members often evaluate each other's thinking, so the team is likely to avoid major errors. An advertising specialist was developing an advertising campaign to attract seniors to live in a retirement community. The proposed ads had photographs of senior citizens engaged in playing shuffleboard, visiting the pharmacy, and sleeping in a hammock. Another team member on the project pointed out that many seniors perceive themselves to be energetic and youthful. Ads emphasizing advanced age might therefore backfire. A successful advertising campaign was then developed that featured seniors in more youthful activities such as jogging and dancing.

Working in teams and groups also enhances the job satisfaction of members. Being a member of a work group makes it possible to satisfy more needs than working

synergy A situation in which the group's total output exceeds the sum of each individual's contribution.

alone. Among these needs are affiliation, security, self-esteem, and self-fulfillment. (Chapter 9 provides more details about psychological needs.)

DISADVANTAGES OF GROUP WORK AND TEAMWORK

Group activity has some potential disadvantages for both individuals and the organization. Teams and other groups often waste time because they talk too much and act too little. Committees appear to suffer from more inaction than teams. Abigail Johnson, president of Fidelity Investments, the financial services giant, says that committees are not effective decision makers. "They have tended to be slow and overly risk averse. Even worse, I believe, they can drain an organization of talent, because the group can only be as good as the average."[9] A major problem is that members face pressures to conform to group standards of performance and conduct, as just implied. Some teams might shun a person who is much more productive than his or her coworkers. Shirking of individual responsibility is another problem frequently noted in groups. Unless work is assigned carefully to each team member, an under-motivated person can often squeeze by without contributing his or her fair share to a group effort.

social loafing The psychological term for shirking individual responsibility in a group setting.

Social loafing is the psychological term for shirking individual responsibility in a group setting. The social loafer risks being ostracized (shunned) by the group but may be willing to pay the price rather than work hard. Loafing of this type is sometimes found in groups such as committees and project teams. Have you ever encountered a social loafer on a group project at school?

At their worst, teams and other groups foster conflict on the job. People within the work group often bicker about such matters as doing a fair share of the undesirable tasks within the department. Cohesive work groups can also become xenophobic (fearful of outsiders). As a consequence, they may grow to dislike other groups and enter into conflict with them. A customer service group might put considerable effort into showing up a sales group because the latter makes promises to customers that the customer service group cannot keep. For example, a sales representative might promise that a customer can get a loaner if his or her equipment needs repair, although customer service has no such policy.

groupthink A deterioration of mental efficiency, reality testing, and moral judgment in the interest of group solidarity.

A well-publicized disadvantage of group decision making is **groupthink,** a deterioration of mental efficiency, reality testing, and moral judgment in the interest of group solidarity. Simply put, groupthink is an extreme form of consensus. The group atmosphere values getting along more than getting things done. The group thinks as a unit, believes it is impervious to outside criticism, and begins to have illusions about its own invincibility. As a consequence, the group loses its powers of critical analysis.[10] Groupthink appears to have contributed to several of the major financial scandals of the previous decade. Members of top management got together to vote themselves huge bonuses just before filing bankruptcy for their company. Several of the executives, including a few from Enron Corporation, were later sent to prison for their outrageous decisions.

Two conditions are important for overcoming the potential disadvantages of teams and groups. First, the members must strive to act like a team,[11] following some of the suggestions given in the upcoming pages. Second, the task given to the group should require collective effort instead of being a task that could better be performed by individuals. For example, an international business specialist would probably learn to conjugate verbs in a foreign language better by working alone than on a team. What is your opinion on this issue? Figure 4-1 presents more information about key factors associated with effective work teams and groups. The more of these factors that are present, the more likely it is that a given team or group will be productive.

- The team has clear-cut goals linked to organizational goals so that group members feel connected to the entire organization. Group members are empowered so they learn to think for themselves rather than expecting a supervisor to solve all the difficult problems. At the same time, the group believes it has the authority to solve a variety of problems without first obtaining approval from management.

- Group members are assigned work they perceive to be challenging, exciting, and rewarding. As a consequence, the work is self-rewarding.

- Members depend on one another to accomplish tasks, and work toward a common goal.

- Members learn to think "outside the box" (are creative).

- Members receive extensive training in technical knowledge, problem-solving skills, and interpersonal skills.

- Members inspect their own work for quality.

- Members receive part of their pay related to team or group incentives rather than strictly based on individual performance.

- Group size is generally about 6 people, rather than 10 or more.

- Team members have good intelligence and personality factors, such as conscientiousness and pride that contribute to good performance.

- There is honest and open communication among group members and with other groups in the organization.

- Members have the philosophy of working as a team—25 brains, not just 50 hands.

- Members are familiar with their jobs, coworkers, and the work environment. This experience adds to their expertise. The beneficial effects of experience may diminish after awhile because the team needs fresh ideas and approaches.

- The team has emotional intelligence in the sense that it builds relationships both inside and outside the team. Included in emotional intelligence are norms that establish mutual trust among members, a feeling of group identity, and group efficacy.

FIGURE 4-1 Key Characteristics of Effective Teams and Work Groups

Sources: Ben Nagler, "Recasting Employees into Teams," *Workforce,* January 1998, p. 104; Gerben S. Van Der Vegt et al., "Patterns of Interdependence in Work Teams: A Two-Level Investigation of the Relations with Job and Team Satisfaction," *Personnel Psychology,* Spring 2001, pp. 51–69; Shawn L. Berman, Vanessa Urch Druskat, and Steven B. Wolff, "Building the Emotional Intelligence of Groups," *Harvard Business Review,* March 2001, pp. 80–90; Claus W. Langred, "Too Much of a Good Thing? Negative Effects of High Trust and Individual Autonomy in Self-Managing Work Teams," *Academy of Management Journal,* June 2004, pp. 385–389.

TEAM MEMBER ROLES

A major challenge in learning to become an effective team member is to choose the ◀ **Learning Objective 3** right roles to occupy. A role is a tendency to behave, contribute, and relate to others in a particular way. If you carry out positive roles, you will be perceived as a contributor to team effort. If you neglect carrying out these roles, you will be perceived as a poor contributor. Self-Assessment Quiz 4-3 will help you evaluate your present inclinations toward occupying effective roles as a team member. In this section we describe a number of the most frequently observed positive roles played by team members. [12] We will also mention a group of negative roles. The description will be followed by an activity in which the roles can be practiced.

SELF-ASSESSMENT QUIZ 4-3

TEAM PLAYER ROLES

Directions: For each of the following statements about team activity, check *mostly agree* or *mostly disagree*. If you have not experienced such a situation, imagine how you would act or think if placed in that situation. In responding to the statements, assume that you are taking the questionnaire with the intent of learning something about yourself.

	Mostly agree	*Mostly disagree*
1. It is rare that I ever miss a team meeting.	_____	_____
2. I regularly compliment team members when they do something exceptional.	_____	_____
3. Whenever I can, I avoid being the notetaker at a team meeting.	_____	_____
4. From time to time, other team members come to me for advice on technical matters.	_____	_____
5. I like to hide some information from other team members so I can be in control.	_____	_____
6. I welcome new team members coming to me for advice and learning the ropes.	_____	_____
7. My priorities come first, which leaves me with very little time to help other team members.	_____	_____
8. During a team meeting, it is not unusual for several other people at a time to look toward me for my opinion.	_____	
9. If I think the team is moving in an unethical direction, I will say so explicitly.	_____	_____
10. Rarely will I criticize the progress of the team even if I think such criticism is deserved.	_____	_____
11. It is typical for me to summarize the progress in a team meeting, even if not asked.	_____	_____
12. To conserve time, I attempt to minimize contact with my teammates outside our meetings.	_____	_____
13. I intensely dislike going along with a consensus decision if the decision runs contrary to my thoughts on the issue.	_____	_____
14. I rarely remind teammates of our mission statement as we go about our work.	_____	_____
15. Once I have made up my mind on an issue facing the team, I am unlikely to be persuaded in another direction.	_____	_____
16. I am willing to accept negative feedback from team members.	_____	_____
17. Just to get a new member of the team involved, I will ask his or her opinion.	_____	_____
18. Even if the team has decided on a course of action, I am not hesitant to bring in new information that supports another position.	_____	_____
19. Quite often I talk negatively about one team member to another.	_____	_____

	Mostly agree	Mostly disagree
20. My teammates are almost a family to me because I am truly concerned about their welfare.	_____	_____
21. When it seems appropriate, I joke and kid with teammates.	_____	_____
22. My contribution to team tasks is as important to me as my individual work.	_____	_____
23. From time to time I have pointed out to the team how we can all improve in reaching our goals.	_____	_____
24. I will fight to the last when the team does not support my viewpoint and wants to move toward consensus.	_____	_____
25. I will confront the team if I believe that the members are thinking too much alike.	_____	_____
Total Score	_____	

Scoring and Interpretation: Give yourself one point (+1) for each statement you gave in agreement with the keyed answer. The keyed answer indicates carrying out a positive, as opposed to a negative, role.

Question number	Positive role answer	Question number	Positive role answer
1.	Mostly agree	14.	Mostly disagree
2.	Mostly agree	15.	Mostly disagree
3.	Mostly disagree	16.	Mostly agree
4.	Mostly agree	17.	Mostly agree
5.	Mostly disagree	18.	Mostly agree
6.	Mostly agree	19.	Mostly disagree
7.	Mostly disagree	20.	Mostly agree
8.	Mostly agree	21.	Mostly agree
9.	Mostly agree	22.	Mostly agree
10.	Mostly disagree	23.	Mostly agree
11.	Mostly agree	24.	Mostly disagree
12.	Mostly disagree	25.	Mostly agree
13.	Mostly disagree		

20–25 You carry out a well-above-average number of positive team roles. Behavior of this type contributes substantially to being an effective team player. Study the information in this chapter to build upon your already laudable sensitivity to occupying various positive roles within the team.

10–19 You carry out an average number of positive team roles. Study carefully the roles described in this chapter to search for ways to carry out a greater number of positive roles.

0–9 You carry out a substantially above average number of negative team roles. If becoming an effective team player is important to you, you will have to diligently search for ways to play positive team roles. Study the information in this chapter carefully.

According to the role theory developed by R. Meredith Belbin and his group of researchers, there are nine frequent roles occupied by team members. All of these roles are influenced to some extent by an individual's personality.

1. **Plant.** The plant is creative, imaginative, and unorthodox. Such a person solves difficult problems. A potential weakness of this role is that the person tends to ignore fine details and becomes too immersed in the problem to communicate effectively.

2. **Resource investigator.** The resource investigator is extroverted, enthusiastic, and communicates freely with other team members. He or she will explore opportunities and develop valuable contacts. A potential weakness of this role is that the person can be overly optimistic and may lose interest after the initial enthusiasm wanes.

3. **Coordinator.** The coordinator is mature, confident, and a natural team leader. He or she clarifies goals, promotes decision making, and delegates effectively. A downside to occupying this role is that the person might be seen as manipulative and controlling. Some coordinators delegate too much by asking others to do some of the work they (the coordinators) should be doing.

4. **Shaper.** The shaper is challenging, dynamic, and thrives under pressure. He or she will use determination and courage to overcome obstacles. A potential weakness of the shaper is that he or she can be easily provoked and may ignore the feelings of others.

5. **Monitor-evaluator.** The monitor-evaluator is even tempered, engages in strategic (big picture and long-term) thinking, and makes accurate judgments. He or she sees all the options and judges accurately. A potential weakness of this role occupant is that he or she might lack drive and the ability to inspire others.

6. **Team worker.** The team worker is cooperative, focuses on relationships, and is sensitive and diplomatic. He or she is a good listener who builds relationships, dislikes confrontation, and averts friction. A potential weakness is that the team worker can be indecisive in a crunch situation or crisis.

7. **Implementer.** The implementer is disciplined, reliable, conservative, and efficient. He or she will act quickly on ideas, and convert them into practical actions. A potential weakness is that the implementer can be inflexible and slow to see new opportunities.

8. **Completer-Finisher.** The completer-finisher is conscientious and eager to get the job done. He or she has a good eye for detail, and is effective at searching out errors. He or she can be counted on for finishing a project and delivering on time. A potential weakness is that the completer-finisher can be a worrier and reluctant to delegate.

9. **Specialist.** The specialist is a single-minded self-starter. He or she is dedicated and provides knowledge and skill in rare supply. A potential weakness of the specialist is that he or she can be stuck in a niche with little interest in other knowledge and may dwell on technicalities.

The weaknesses in the first nine roles point to problems the team leader or manager can expect to emerge, and therefore an allowance should be made. Belbin refers to these potential problems as *allowable weaknesses* because an allowance should be made for them. To illustrate, if a team worker has a tendency to be indecisive in a crisis, the team should not have high expectations of the team worker when faced with a crisis. Team workers will be the most satisfied if the crisis is predicted and decisions involving them are made before the pressure mounts.[13]

Another perspective on team roles is that team members will sometimes engage in *self-oriented roles*. Members will sometimes focus on their own needs rather than those of the group. The individual might be overly aggressive because of a personal need such as wanting a bigger budget for his or her project. The individual might hunger for recognition or power. Similarly the person might attempt to dominate the meeting, block others from contributing, or serve as a distraction. One of the ploys used by distracters recently is to engage in cell phone conversations during a meeting, blaming it on "those people who keep calling me."

The many roles just presented overlap somewhat. For example, the implementer might engage in specialist activities. Do not be concerned about the overlap. Instead, pick and choose from the many roles as the situation dictates—whether or not overlap exists. Skill-Building Exercise 4-1 gives you an opportunity to observe these roles in action. The behavior associated with the roles just described is more important than remembering the labels. For example, remembering to be creative and imaginative is more important than remembering the specific label *plant*.

SKILL-BUILDING EXERCISE 4-1

TEAM MEMBER ROLES

A team of approximately six people is formed to conduct a 20-minute meeting on a significant topic of their choosing. The possible scenarios follow:

Scenario A: Management Team.   A group of managers are pondering whether to lay off one-third of the workforce in order to increase profits. The company has had a tradition of caring for employees and regarding them as the company's most precious asset. However, the CEO has said privately that times have changed in our competitive world, and the company must do whatever possible to enhance profits. The group wants to think through the advisability of laying off one-third of the workforce, as well as explore other alternatives.

Scenario B: Group of Sports Fans.   A group of fans have volunteered to find a new team name to replace "Redskins" for the local basketball team. One person among the group of volunteers believes that the name "Redskins" should be retained because it is a compliment, rather than an insult to Native Americans. The other members of the group believe that a name change is in order, but they lack any good ideas for replacing a mascot team name that has endured for over 50 years.

Scenario C: Community Group.   A community group is attempting to launch an initiative to help battered adults and children. Opinions differ strongly as to what initiative would be truly helpful to battered adults and children. Among the alternatives are establishing a shelter for battered people, giving workshops on preventing violence, and providing self-defense training. Each group member with an idea strongly believes that he or she has come up with a workable possibility for helping with the problem of battered people.

While the team members are conducting their heated discussion, other class members make notes on which team members carry out which roles. Students should watch for the different roles as developed by Belbin and his associates, as well as the self-oriented roles. For example, students in the first row might look for examples of the plant. Use the role worksheet that follows to help make your observations. Summarize the comment that is indicative of the role. An example would

(Continued)

be noting in the shaper category: "Linda said naming the team the 'Washington Rainbows' seems like too much of an attempt to be politically correct."

Plant _____
Resource Investigator _____
Coordinator _____
Shaper _____
Monitor-Evaluator _____
Team Worker _____
Implementer _____
Completer-Finisher _____
Specialist _____
Self-Oriented Roles _____

GUIDELINES FOR THE INTERPERSONAL ASPECTS OF TEAM PLAY

Learning Objective 4 ▶ The purpose of this and the following section is to help you enhance your effectiveness as a team player by describing the skills, actions, and attitudes required to be an effective team player. You can regard these behaviors (the collective term for skills, actions, and attitudes) as goals for personal improvement. Identify the actions and attitudes for which you need the most improvement, and proceed accordingly with self-development. Apply the model for skill development presented in Chapter 1.

One convenient method for classifying team activities in pursuit of goals is to categorize them as people-related or task-related. Remember, however, that the categorization of people- versus task-related activities is not entirely accurate. For example, if you are challenging your teammates with a difficult goal, are you focusing more on the people (offering them a motivational challenge) or the task (achieving the goal)? We begin first with people-related actions and attitudes, followed in the next section by task-related actions and attitudes.

Back to the Opening Case

Companies spend enormous amounts of time and money in developing the teamwork skills of employees who work on teams, including a variety of outdoor activities. Although almost everybody has had some experience with teams in school or athletics, most people are not natural team players—they need to develop skills. Workers who rebuild old houses to help homeless or low-income people often find the experience educational and morally uplifting. Teamwork is dramatized because working alone, for example, it is almost impossible to install a new roof.

TRUSTING TEAM MEMBERS

The cornerstone attitude of an outstanding team player is to trust team members, including the leader. Working on a team is akin to a small-business partnership. If you do not believe that the other team members have your best interests at heart, it will be difficult for you to share opinions and ideas. You will fear that others will make negative statements behind your back.

Trusting team members also includes believing that their ideas are technically sound and rational until proven otherwise. Another manifestation of trust is taking risks with others. You can take a risk by trying out one of their unproved ideas. You can also take a risk by submitting an unproved idea and not worrying about being ridiculed.

DISPLAYING A HIGH LEVEL OF COOPERATION AND COLLABORATION

Cooperation and collaboration are synonymous with teamwork. If you display a willingness to help others by working cooperatively with them, you will be regarded as a team player. If you do not cooperate with other team members, the team structure breaks down. Collaboration at a team level refers to working jointly with others to solve mutual problems. Although working with another person on a given problem may take longer than working through a problem alone, the long-term payoff is important. You have established a climate favorable to working on joint problems where collective action is necessary.

Achieving a cooperative team spirit is often a question of making the first move. Instead of grumbling about poor teamwork, take the initiative and launch a cooperative spirit in your group. Target the most individualistic, least cooperative member of the group. Ask the person for his or her input on an idea you are formulating. Thank the person, then state that you would be privileged to return the favor.

Another way of attaining good cooperation is to minimize confrontations. If you disagree with the opinion of another team member, patiently explain the reasons for your differences and look for a workable way to integrate both your ideas. A teammate might suggest, for example, that the team stay until midnight to get a project completed today. You have plans for the evening and are angered by the suggestion. Instead of lashing out at your teammate, you might say, "I agree we need to put in extra time and effort to get the job done. But why can't we spread out this extra effort over a few days? In this way those of us who cannot work until midnight this evening can still contribute."

Skill-Building Exercise 4-2 is a widely used technique for demonstrating the importance of cooperation and collaboration.

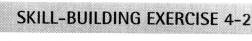

SKILL-BUILDING EXERCISE 4-2

THE SCAVENGER HUNT

The purpose of this teamwork exercise is to demonstrate the importance of cooperation and collaboration in accomplishing a task under pressure. The class is divided into teams of about five students. How much time you can devote to the task depends upon your particular class schedule. The instructor will supply each team with a list of items to find within a prescribed period of time—usually about 35 minutes. Given the time constraints, the group will usually have to conduct the hunt on campus. Following is a representative list of items to find in an on-campus scavenger hunt:

- A fountain pen
- A tie
- A brick
- A cap from a beer bottle
- A pocket knife
- A flash drive

When the groups return within 30 minutes, you hold a public discussion about what you learned about teamwork and what insights you acquired.

RECOGNIZING THE INTERESTS AND ACHIEVEMENTS OF OTHERS

A fundamental tactic for establishing yourself as a solid team player is to actively recognize the interests and achievements of others. Let others know you care about their interests. After you make a suggestion during a team meeting, ask: "Would my suggestion create any problems for anybody else?" or "How do my ideas fit into what you have planned?"

Recognizing the achievements of others is more straightforward than recognizing interests. Be prepared to compliment any tangible achievement. Give realistic compliments by making the compliment commensurate with the achievement. To do otherwise is to compromise your sincerity. For example, do not call someone a genius just because he or she showed you how to compute an exchange rate from one currency to another. Instead, you might say, "Thank you. I am very impressed by your knowledge of exchange rates."

A technique has been developed to enable the entire team to recognize the interests and achievements of others. Playing the anonymous praise game, each team member lists what he or she admires about a specific coworker. The team leader collects the responses and sends each team member the comments made about him or her. Using this technique, team members see a compilation of praise based on how coworkers perceive them. The anonymous praise game helps overcome the hesitancy some people have to praise another person face-to-face.[14]

GIVING HELPFUL CRITICISM

The outstanding team player offers constructive criticism when needed, but does so diplomatically. To do otherwise is to let down the team. A high-performance team demands sincere and tactful criticism among members. No matter how diplomatic you are, keep your ratio of criticism to praise small. Keep two time-tested principles in mind. First, attempt to criticize the person's work, not the person. It is better to say "The conclusion is missing from your analysis" than "You left out the conclusion." (The latter statement hurts because it sounds like your teammate did something wrong.)

Another key guideline for criticism is to ask a question rather than to make a declarative statement. By answering a question, the person being criticized is involved in improving his or her work. In the example at hand, it would be effective to ask, "Do you think your report would have a greater impact if it contained a conclusion?" In this way, the person being criticized contributes a judgment about the conclusion. The person has a chance to say, "Yes, I will prepare a conclusion."

SHARING THE GLORY

An effective team player shares praise and other rewards for accomplishment even if he or she is the most deserving. Shared praise is usually merited to some extent because teammates have probably made at least some contribution to the achievement that received praise. For example, if a team member comes up with a powerful suggestion for cutting costs, it is likely that somebody else in the group sparked his or her thinking. Effective examples of sharing glory are easy to find. Think back to watching athletes and other entertainers who win a title or an award. Many of them are gracious enough to share the glory. Shortly after he retired, hockey legend Wayne Gretzky told a television reporter, "I never would have accomplished what I did if I hadn't played with such a great group of guys."

TAKING CARE NOT TO RAIN ON ANOTHER PERSON'S PARADE

As teamwork specialist Pamela Lovell observes, we all have achievements and accomplishments that are sources of pride. Belittling the achievements of others for no legitimate reason brings about tension and anger. Suppress your feelings of petty jealousy.[15] An example would be saying to someone who is proudly describing an accomplishment, "Don't take too much credit. It looks to me like you were at the right place at the right time." If you support teammates by acknowledging their accomplishments, you are more likely to receive their support when needed.

GUIDELINES FOR THE TASK ASPECTS OF TEAM PLAY

The task aspects of team play also make a key contribution to becoming an effective ◄ Learning Objective 5 team player. Here we describe six major task-related tactics. As mentioned earlier, a task aspect usually has interpersonal consequences.

PROVIDING TECHNICAL EXPERTISE (OR KNOWLEDGE OF THE TASK)

Most people are selected for a work team primarily because of their technical expertise. *Technical* refers to the intimate details of any task, not just tasks in engineering, physical science, and information technology. The sales promotion specialist on a product development team has technical expertise about sales promotion, whether or not sales promotion requires knowledge of engineering or computers.

As team consultant Glenn Parker observes, to use your technical expertise to outstanding advantage you must have the willingness to share that expertise.[16] Some experts perceive their esoteric knowledge as a source of power. As a consequence, they are hesitant to let others share their knowledge for fear of relinquishing power. It is also necessary for the technical expert to be able to communicate with team members in other disciplines who lack the same technical background. The technical person who cannot explain the potential value of his or her contribution may fail to receive much attention.

ASSUMING RESPONSIBILITY FOR PROBLEMS

The outstanding team player assumes responsibilities for problems. If a problem is not yet assigned to anybody, he or she says, "I'll do it." One team member might note that true progress on the team's effort is blocked until the team benchmarks (compares itself) with other successful teams. The effective team player might say, "You are right, we need to benchmark. If it's okay with everybody else, I'll get started on the benchmarking project tomorrow. It will be my responsibility." Taking responsibility must be combined with dependability. The person who takes responsibility for a task must produce, time after time.

SEEING THE BIG PICTURE

Effective team players need to think conceptually, or see the big picture. A trap in team effort is that discussion can get bogged down in small details and the team might lose sight of what it is trying to accomplish. The team player (including the team leader) who can help the group focus on its broader purpose plays a vital role. The following case history illustrates what it means to see the big picture.

A sales process improvement team was asked to make it easier for customers to purchase office equipment when they visited the company's retail center. Under the existing process, five different people had to handle the sales transaction. The customer was often kept waiting for up to an hour. During its second meeting, the team vented its hostility toward the warehouse specialists. As the conversation became more heated, several team members discussed documenting all the problems created by the warehouse personnel and then reporting them to the vice president of marketing. As emotions intensified, several team members ridiculed the warehouse workers.

Beth, the store manager and one of the team members, helped the group step back and see the big picture. She challenged the group in these words: "Hold on. Why are we here? Is our purpose to improve the sales process or to attack the very people who keep items for sale in stock?" The team accepted the suggestion and praised Beth for her contribution. The team then refocused its effort on reducing the paperwork required to complete a sales transaction.

BELIEVING IN CONSENSUS

consensus General acceptance by the group of a decision.

A major task-related attitude for outstanding team play is to believe that consensus has merit. **Consensus** is general acceptance of a decision by the group. Every member may not be thrilled about the decision, yet they are unopposed and are willing to support the decision. Believing that consensus is valuable enables you to participate fully in team decisions without thinking that you have sacrificed your beliefs or the right to think independently. To believe in consensus is to believe that the democratic process has relevance for organizations and that ideal solutions are not always possible.

FOCUSING ON DEADLINES

A notable source of individual differences among work group members is how much importance they attach to deadlines. Some work group members may regard deadlines as a moral contract, to be missed only in case of emergency. Others may view deadlines as an arbitrary date imposed by someone external to the group. Other work group members may perceive deadlines as moderately important. Differences in perception about the importance of deadlines influence the group's ability to meet deadlines.[17]

Keeping the group focused on the deadline is a valuable task behavior because meeting deadlines is vital to team success. Discussing the importance of the deadlines is helpful because of the varying attitudes about deadlines likely to be found among group members.

HELPING TEAM MEMBERS DO THEIR JOBS BETTER

Your stature as a team player will increase if you take the initiative to help coworkers make needed work improvements. Helping other team members with their work assignments is a high-level form of cooperation. Make the suggestions in a constructive spirit rather than displaying an air of superiority. Identify a problem that a coworker is having, and then suggest alternatives he or she might be interested in exploring. Avoid saying to team members that they "should" do something, because many people become defensive when told what they should do. The term *should* is usually perceived as a moral judgment given to one person by another, such as being told that you should save money, should learn a second language, or should improve your math skills.

BEING A GOOD ORGANIZATIONAL CITIZEN

A comprehensive way of carrying out the task aspects of team play (as well as relationship aspects) is to help out beyond the requirements of your job description. As discussed in Chapter 2, such extra-role activity is referred to as organizational citizenship behavior—working for the good of the organization even without the promise of a specific reward. As a result of many workers being good organizational citizens, the organization functions more effectively in such ways as improved product quantity and quality.[18] Good citizenship on the job encompasses many specific behaviors, including helping a coworker with a job task and refraining from complaints or petty grievances. A good organizational citizen would carry out such specific acts as picking up litter in the company parking lot. He or she would also bring a reference to the office that could help a coworker solve a job problem. Most of

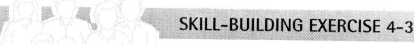

SKILL-BUILDING EXERCISE 4-3

HABITAT FOR HOMELESS PEOPLE

Organize the class into teams of about six people. Each team takes on the assignment of formulating plans for building temporary shelters for homeless people. The task will take about one hour and can be done inside or outside the class. The dwellings you plan to build, for example, might be two-room cottages with electricity and indoor plumbing.

During the time allotted to the task, formulate plans for going ahead with Habitat for Homeless People. Consider dividing up work by assigning certain roles to each team member. Sketch out tentative answers to the following questions:

1. How will you obtain funding for your venture?
2. Which homeless people will you help?
3. Where will your shelters be located?
4. Who will do the actual construction?

After your plan is completed, evaluate the quality of the teamwork that took place within the group. Specify which teamwork skills were evident and which ones did not surface. Search the chapter for techniques you might use to improve teamwork. The skills used to accomplish the habitat task could relate to the team skills presented in Self-Assessment Quiz 4-2, the interpersonal aspects of team play, the task aspects of team play, or some team skill not mentioned in this chapter. Here is a sampling of the many different skills that might be relevant in this exercise:

- Speaks effectively
- Listens to others
- Innovates solutions to problems
- Thinks outside the box

- Displays a high level of cooperation and collaboration
- Provides knowledge of the task
- Sees the big picture
- Focuses on deadlines

the other team player tactics described here are related to organizational citizenship behavior.

Skill-Building Exercise 4-3 will help you integrate the many suggestions presented here for developing teamwork skills.

SUMMARY

To be successful in the modern organization it is necessary to be an effective team player. Team members have complementary skills and are committed to a common purpose. All teams have some elements in common, but four key types of teams are self-managing work teams, cross-functional teams, virtual teams, and crews. (A virtual team does most of its work electronically instead of in face-to-face meetings.)

Groups and teams offer such advantages as gaining synergy, avoiding major errors, and gaining increased acceptance of and commitment to decisions. Working in groups can also enhance job satisfaction. Groups and teams also have disadvantages, such as more talk than action, conformity in thinking and action, social loafing, and the creation of conflict. A serious potential problem is groupthink, whereby bad decisions are made as a by-product of strong consensus. Key characteristics of effective work groups are outlined in Figure 4-1.

An important part of being an effective team player is to choose effective roles. The roles studied here are: plant, resource investigator, coordinator, shaper, monitor-evaluator, team worker, implementer, completer-finisher, and specialist. Self-oriented roles are less effective and detract from group productivity.

Guidelines for effectively contributing to the interpersonal aspects of team play include (1) trusting team members, (2) displaying a high level of cooperation and collaboration, (3) recognizing the interests and achievements of others, (4) giving helpful criticism, (5) sharing the glory, and (6) taking care not to rain on another person's parade.

Guidelines for effectively contributing to the task aspects of team play include (1) providing technical expertise, (2) assuming responsibility for problems, (3) seeing the big picture, (4) believing in consensus, (5) focusing on deadlines, and (6) helping team members do their jobs better.

QUESTIONS FOR DISCUSSION AND REVIEW

1. Part of being a good team player is helping other members. How can members of a workplace team help each other?

2. How do team members know when they have achieved synergy?

3. What should the other team members do when they uncover a social loafer?

4. What is the potential downside of heavily emphasizing the *specialist* role?

5. How can the *monitor-evaluator* role backfire for a person?

6. Assume that you are a team member. What percent of your pay would you be willing to have based on a group reward? Explain your reasoning.

7. How effective do you think the scavenger hunt really is in building cooperation among team members?

8. A number of companies have sent employees to a team-building exercise in which they literally walk over hot coals. The participants receive appropriate training. (*Caution:* Many participants in this exercise do suffer serious burns.) Why would walking over hot coals help build teamwork?

9. The "little picture" in studying this chapter is learning details about teamwork skills. What is the "big picture"?

10. How can a person achieve individual recognition yet still be a team player?

GO TO THE WEB

http://content.monster.com/tools/quizzes/teamplayer/
(Take the quiz Are You a Team Player?)

http://www.skydivingmagazine.com/
(Find the article "How to Be a Team Player" written by a skydiver.)

AN INTERPERSONAL RELATIONS CASE PROBLEM

TEAM BUILDING GONE WILD AT USPS

They bark like a pack of dogs, quack like a flock of ducks and hiss like a nest of vipers. They wrap each other from head to toe in paper toweling and aluminum foil and pipe cleaners. They build sandcastles and gingerbread houses and practice picking up oranges while blindfolded. These are professional auditors and investigators who police the United States Postal Service.

The mission of the USPS Office of Inspector General is to make the mail more efficient and cost-effective by rooting out waste, fraud, abuse and mismanagement. Yet hundreds of IG staffers were taking part in bizarre bonding and team-building exercises and playing goofy games that burn up millions of dollars—and appear to do little or nothing to curb postal inefficiencies, a *New York Daily News* investigation found.

As stamp prices and postal deficits soared over the past few years, the agency's well-paid, highly trained employees got a lesson in scat singing, took an outing to a racetrack—and delved into the history of the Civil War during a $100,000 retreat to the battlefield at Gettysburg. On USPS time, they've composed Christmas Carols, belted out "We Are Family" at sing-alongs, conducted mock trials in which witnesses were paraded before a judge and jury—and played children's games like follow the leader.

Under the supervision of Postal Inspector General Karla Corcoran, civil servants have been paid to emit animal sounds, embark on treasure hunts, dress in cat costumes and seek the counsel of make-believe wizards, magicians and mad scientists at mass gatherings of the workforce.

They've been jetting into the capital from 15 field offices around the nation for "annual recognition conferences" that celebrated the organization and its values. The tab for the last three confabs: $3.6 million, including planning and salary costs. At one such event at the Renaissance Washington D.C. Hotel, a blindfolded and barefoot Corcoran was swaddled in a blue blanket and hoisted into the air above a hotel ballroom on colored ropes and strings manipulated by some 500 of her 725 employees. The point of lifting the boss skyward was to show that by working together as a team, they could accomplish a task that would have been impossible to perform alone.

"Touchy-feely bonding exercises, management retreats at first-class hotels and annual celebratory events all divert resources that could be better invested in audits and investigations," said Debra Ritt, the agency's former No 1 auditor.

"I question whether spending tens of thousands of dollars for an afternoon of treasure hunting sets the gold standard for prudence," said Senate Finance Committee Chairman Chuck Grassley.

In written responses to questions, the agency said its audits and probes of postal operations have identified $2.2 billion in potential, projected and actual savings during the past six years. Its team-and-leadership development programs mirror those offered by corporate giants and consume only minimal resources, officials claim. They help workers learn more about each other, and themselves, so they can discover novel ways to think and work together.

The exercises also teach acceptance of five core workplace values that the agency instills in all staffers: teamwork, leadership, communication, creativity and conceptualization. Wrapping people in paper toweling, for instance displayed teamwork; building sandcastles showed creativity; mimicking animals involved conceptualization. Besides, said agency spokesperson Laura Whitaker, when "fun and humor" are integrated into the workplace, people become more productive and creative and absenteeism and downtime plummet.

Fun and humor, however, is now how ex-employees such as John Rooney, a former special assistant to Corcoran, describe the organization. "We were forced to play silly games, build gingerbread houses and sing songs praising Karla, and I found the whole thing humiliating, demoralizing and nonproductive," Rooney said.

A spokeswoman for Karla Corcoran said that their undoubtedly had a positive effect on the Postal Service's bottom line. Corcoran announced her retirement in August 2003, following a 274-page report by the President's Council in Integrity and Efficiency. She rebutted all the criticism made by the Council, saying that the investigators sat down with all her enemies, and said "Tell me all your dirt."

Case Questions

1. How might Karla Corcoran have accomplished the development of teamwork without triggering so much criticism of her efforts?

2. What defense might you offer for Corcoran's efforts at building teamwork in the U.S. Postal Service?

3. What does this case tell us about the importance Corcoran placed on teamwork?

Sources: Douglas Feiden, "Bizarre Postal Bonding: Goofy Games Cost Public Millions as Stamp Prices Soar," *http://www.nydailynew.com/news/story/*, March 9, 2003; "CAGW Calls for Postal IG's Removal," *http://www.cagw.org/site/*, May 1, 2003; Larry Margasak, "Employees Harshly Criticize Retiring Postal Service Inspector General," Associated Press, August 20, 2003. New York Daily News, L.P. Reprinted with permission.

AN INTERPERSONAL RELATIONS CASE PROBLEM

SHOWBOAT BRENT

Mary Tarkington, CEO of one of the major dot-com retailers, became concerned that too many employees at the company were stressed out and physically unhealthy. Tarkington said, "I have walked through our distribution center at many different times of the day and night, and I see the same troublesome scene. The place is littered with soft-drink cans and fast-food wrappers. Loads of our workers have stomachs bulging out of their pants. You always see a few workers huddled outside the building smoking. The unhealthiness around the company is also reflected in high absenteeism rates, and health insurance costs that are continually rising.

"I want to see a big improvement in the health of our employees. It makes sense from the standpoint of being a socially responsible company, and from the standpoint of becoming more profitable. With this in mind, I am appointing a project team to study how we can best design and implement a company wellness program. Each member of the team will work about five hours per week on the project. I want to receive a full report in 45 days, and I expect to see progress reports along the way."

Five people were appointed to the wellness task force: Ankit, a programmer; Jennifer, a Web site designer; Brent, a systems analyst; Derek, a logistics technician; and Kristine, a human resource specialist. During the first meeting, the group appointed Kristine as the wellness task force head because of her professional specialty. Ankit, Jennifer, and Derek offered Kristine their congratulations, and wished her the best. Brent offered a comment with a slightly different tone: "I can see why the group chose you to head our task force. I voted for you also, but I think we should be starting with a blank tablet. We are making no assumptions that anybody's ideas carry more professional weight than anybody else."

The next time the group met, each member reported some preliminary findings about wellness programs they had researched. Ankit summarized a magazine article on the topic, Jennifer reported on a friend's experience with his company wellness program, Derek presented some data on how wellness programs can boost productivity and morale, and Kristine reported on *workforce.com*, a human resource Web site that carries information about wellness programs. Each spent about six minutes on his or her presentation.

Brent then walked up to the front of the conference room and engaged his laptop computer. He began a 25-minute PowerPoint presentation about what he thought the committee should be doing, along with industry data about wellness programs. At the end of Brent's presentation, Kristine commented with a quizzical look, "Thanks Brent, but I thought we agreed to around a 5-minute presentation this first time around."

Brent replied, "Good point Kristine, yet I'm only doing what I consider best for getting our mission accomplished."

Ten days later, CEO Tarkington visited the task force to discuss its progress. Kristine, as the task force head, began the progress report. She pointed out that the group had gathered substantial information about corporate wellness programs. Kristine also noted that so far, establishing one at the company looked feasible and worthwhile. She commented that the group was beginning to assemble data about the physical requirements for having a wellness program, and the cost of implementation.

With a frown Brent said, "Not so fast, Kristine. Since we last met I have taken another look at the productivity figures about wellness centers. People who run wellness programs apparently supplied these figures, so the information could be tainted. I say that we are rushing too fast to reach a decision. Let's get some objective data before making a recommendation to the company."

Kristine groaned as she looked at Mary Tarkington and the task force members. She whispered to Jennifer to her right, "There goes Brent, showboating again."

Case Questions

1. Which team player roles is Brent attempting to occupy?

2. In what way is Brent occupying self-oriented roles?

3. Which team player roles is Kristine attempting to occupy?

4. What actions, if any, should the other task force members take to make Brent a better team player?

CHAPTER 4

Cross-Cultural Relations and Diversity

Learning Objectives

After reading and studying this chapter and doing the exercises you should be able to

1. Recognize who fits under the diversity umbrella.
2. Describe the major values accounting for cultural differences.
3. Overcome many cross-cultural communication barriers.
4. Specify some of the business implications of being sensitive to cultural differences.
5. Improve your cross-cultural relations.

Joan Weiss is the owner and president of Superior Motors, a dealership that sells a variety of luxury vehicles, both new and previously owned. The average sticker price on new vehicles is over $45,000, and the average price for previously owned vehicles is $26,000. During a year-end strategy meeting with Bill Matteson, the director of marketing, Weiss and Matteson agreed that the dealership needed a way to boost sales.

"It's getting more difficult to cope with the wild discounting in this business, and the fact that many of our potential buyers can invest their discretionary dollars in something other than a $75,000 sports car," said Weiss. "What is your take on this problem, Bill?"

"I'm going to pick on an idea both you and I have talked about before," replied Matteson. "Our sales reps are no longer representative of the clientele we serve. Back when you and your late husband founded the dealership, practically all our customers were white, middle-aged males. Yet our customer mix has changed. Many of our customers are women, African American, Chinese, and Indian. Also, many of our best customers are under age 40.

"So let's join the realities of the market, and recruit a few culturally diverse sales reps. If any existing rep quits, he or she will be replaced by somebody who will help us diversify our sales force. The same goes for employees in our service center."

"Let's start on this plan today," agreed Weiss.

Discussion Question

1. Do you think the initiatives taken by the luxury-car dealership are a publicity stunt to appear more inclusive? Or do you think being culturally diverse actually improves a company's business results?

Top management at business firms continues to recognize the importance of a diverse workforce as well as diverse customers. Minority group members in the United States are growing seven times as fast as the majority population. According to the Bureau of Labor Statistics, women make up about 47 percent of the workforce. Minorities and workers from other countries occupy 26 percent of jobs. Furthermore, white males constitute only 15 percent of new entrants to the workforce.

Not only is the workforce becoming more diverse, but business has also become increasingly international. Small- and medium-size firms, as well as corporate giants, are increasingly dependent on trade with other countries. An estimated 10 to 15 percent of jobs in the United States depend on imports or exports. Furthermore, most manufactured goods contain components from more than one country. Also, more and more work, such as call centers and manufacturing, is subcontracted to companies in other countries.

All this workplace diversity has an important implication for the career-minded individual. To succeed in today's workplace a person must be able to relate effectively to people from different cultural groups from within and outside his or her country. Being able to relate to a culturally diverse customer base is also necessary for success.

This chapter presents concepts and techniques you can use to sharpen your ability to work effectively with people from diverse backgrounds. To get you started thinking about your readiness to work in a culturally diverse environment, take Self-Assessment Quiz 6-1.

THE DIVERSITY UMBRELLA

Learning Objective 1 ▶

In this extreme war for talent, we need to create a culture of inclusion.
—Lynn Weaver, vice president of human resources at Yazaki of North America

Improving cross-cultural relations includes understanding the true meaning of appreciating diversity. To appreciate diversity a person must go beyond tolerating and treating people from different racial and ethnic groups fairly. The true meaning of valuing diversity is to respect and enjoy a wide range of cultural and individual differences. Appreciating these differences is often referred to as *inclusion* to emphasize unity rather than diversity. To be diverse is to be different in some measurable way, even if what is measurable is not visible (such as religion or sexual orientation).

To be highly skilled in interpersonal relations, one must recognize and appreciate individual and demographic (group or category) differences. Some people are more visibly diverse than others because of physical features or disabilities. Yet the diversity umbrella is supposed to include everybody in an organization. To value diversity is therefore to appreciate individual differences among people.

Appreciating cultural diversity in organizations was originally aimed at assisting women and minorities. The diversity umbrella continues to include more people as the workforce encompasses a greater variety of people. For example, in recent years much attention has been paid to the rights of employees included in the group GLBT (gay, lesbian, bisexual, and transsexual). The rights of members of diverse religious groups are also receiving attention. One such group is a Christian employee network that opposes rights for people of nontraditional sexual orientation.[11] The goal of a diverse organization is for persons of all cultural backgrounds to achieve their full potential, not restrained by group identities such as gender, nationality, or race. Another important goal is for these groups to work together harmoniously.

SELF-ASSESSMENT QUIZ 6-1

CROSS-CULTURAL SKILLS AND ATTITUDES

Directions: Listed below are skills and attitudes that various employers and cross-cultural experts think are important for relating effectively to coworkers in a culturally diverse environment. For each of the statements, check *applies to me now* or *not there yet,*

	Applies to me now	Not there yet
1. I have spent some time in another country.	_____	_____
2. At least one of my friends is deaf, blind, or uses a wheelchair.	_____	_____
3. Currency from other countries is as real as the currency from my own country.	_____	_____
4. I can read in a language other than my own.	_____	_____
5. I can speak in a language other than my own.	_____	_____
6. I can write in a language other than my own.	_____	_____
7. I can understand people speaking in a language other than my own.	_____	_____
8. I use my second language regularly.	_____	_____
9. My friends include people of races different from my own.	_____	_____
10. My friends include people of different ages.	_____	_____
11. I feel (or would feel) comfortable having a friend with a sexual orientation different from mine.	_____	_____
12. My attitude is that although another culture may be very different from mine, that culture is equally good.	_____	_____
13. I am willing to eat (or have eaten) food from other countries that are not served in my own country.	_____	_____
14. I would accept (or have already accepted) a work assignment of more than several months in another country.	_____	_____
15. I have a passport.	_____	_____

Interpretation: If you answered *applies to me now* to 10 or more of the preceding questions, you most likely function well in a multicultural work environment. If you answered *not there yet* to 10 or more of the questions, you need to develop more cross-cultural awareness and skills to work effectively in a multicultural work environment. You will notice that being bilingual gives you at least five points on this quiz.

Sources: Several ideas for statements on this quiz are derived from Ruthann Dirks and Janet Buzzard, "What CEOs Expect of Employees Hired for International Work," *Business Education Forum,* April 1997, pp. 3–7; and Gunnar Beeth, "Multicultural Managers Wanted," *Management Review,* May 1997, pp. 17–21.

Figure 6-1 presents a broad sampling of the ways in which workplace associates can differ from one another. Studying this list can help you anticipate the types of differences to understand and appreciate in a diverse workplace. The differences include cultural as well as individual factors. Individual factors are also important because people can be discriminated against for personal characteristics as well as group factors. Many people, for example, believe they are held back from promotion because of their weight-to-height ratio.

- Race
- Sex (or gender)
- Religion
- Age (young, middle-aged, and old)
- Ethnicity (country of origin)
- Education
- Abilities
- Mental disabilities (including attention deficit disorder)
- Physical disabilities (including hearing status, visual status, able-bodied, wheelchair user)
- Values and motivation
- Sexual orientation (heterosexual, homosexual, bisexual, transsexual)
- Marital status (married, single, cohabitating, widow, widower)
- Family status (children, no children, two-parent family, single parent, grandparent)
- Personality traits
- Functional background (area of specialization)
- Technology interest (high-tech, low-tech, technophobe)
- Weight status (average, obese, underweight, anorexic)
- Hair status (full head of hair, bald, wild hair, tame hair, long hair, short hair)
- Tobacco status (smoker versus nonsmoker, chewer versus nonchewer)
- Styles of clothing and appearance (dress up, dress down, professional appearance, casual appearance)

FIGURE 6-1 The Diversity Umbrella

UNDERSTANDING CULTURAL DIFFERENCES

Learning Objective 2 ▶ The groundwork for developing effective cross-cultural relations is to understand cultural differences. The information about different communication patterns between men and women presented in Chapter 3 is relevant here. Some researchers think that men and women represent different cultures! One cultural difference between the two groups is that women tend to speak indirectly and soften criticism. Men, in contrast, tend to be more direct in giving criticism. Here we discuss six aspects of understanding cultural differences: (1) cultural sensitivity, (2) cultural intelligence, (3) respect for all workers (4) cultural fluency (5) dimensions of differences in cultural values, and (6) avoidance of cultural bloopers. To work smoothly with people from other cultures, it is important to become competent in all six areas.

CULTURAL SENSITIVITY

cultural sensitivity
An awareness of and willingness to investigate the reasons why people of another culture act as they do.

In order to relate well to someone from a foreign country, a person must be alert to possible cultural differences. When working in another country a person must be willing to acquire knowledge about local customs and learn how to speak the native language at least passably. When working with people from different cultures, even from his or her own country, the person must be patient, adaptable, flexible, and willing to listen and learn. The characteristics just mentioned are part of **cultural sensitivity,** an awareness of and willingness to investigate the reasons why individuals of another culture act as they do.[2] A person with cultural sensitivity will recognize certain nuances in customs that will help build better relationships from cultural backgrounds other than his or her own.

CULTURAL INTELLIGENCE

An advanced aspect of cultural sensitivity is to be able to fit in comfortably with people of another culture by observing the subtle cues they give about how a person should act in their presence. **Cultural intelligence (CQ)** is an outsider's ability to interpret someone's unfamiliar and ambiguous behavior the same way that person's compatriots would.[3] With high cultural intelligence a person would be able to figure out what behavior would be true of all people and all groups, such as rapid shaking of a clenched fist to communicate anger. Also, the person with high cultural intelligence could figure out what is peculiar to this group, and those aspects of behavior that are neither universal nor peculiar to the group. These ideas are so abstract, that an example will help clarify.

> *An American expatriate manager served on a design team that included two German engineers. As other team members floated their ideas, the engineers condemned them as incomplete or underdeveloped. The manager concluded that the Germans in general are rude and aggressive.*
>
> *With average cultural intelligence the American would have realized he was mistakenly equating the merit of an idea with the merit of the person presenting it. The Germans, however, were able to make a sharp distinction between the two. A manager with more advanced cultural intelligence might have tried to figure out how much of the two Germans' behavior was typically German and how much was explained by the fact that they were engineers.*

Similar to emotional intelligence, cultural intelligence encompasses several different aspects of behavior. The three sources of cultural intelligence relate to the cognitive, emotional/motivational, and the physical, explained as follows:[4]

1. **Cognitive (the Head).** The cognitive part of CQ refers to what a person knows and how he or she can acquire new knowledge. Here you acquire facts about people from another culture such as their passion for football (soccer in North America), their business practices, and their promptness in paying bills. Another aspect of this source of cultural intelligence is figuring out how you can learn more about the other culture.

2. **Emotional/Motivational (the Heart).** The emotional/motivational aspect of CQ refers to energizing one's actions and building personal confidence. You need both confidence and motivation to adapt to another culture. A man on a business trip to Africa might say to himself, "When I greet a work associate in a restaurant, can I really pull off kissing him on both cheeks. What if he thinks I'm weird?" With strong motivation, the same person might say, "I'll give it a try. I kind of greet my grandfather the same way back in the United States."

3. **The Body (Physical).** The body aspect of CQ is the action component. The body is the element for translating intentions into actions and desires. Kissing the same-sex African work associates on both cheeks is the *physical* aspect just mentioned. We often have an idea of what we should do, but implementation is not so easy. You might know, for example, that when entering an Asian person's home you should take off your shoes, yet you might not actually remove them—thereby offending your Asian work (or personal life) associate.

To practice high cultural intelligence, the mind, heart, and body have to work together. You need to figure out how to act with people from another culture; you need motivation and confidence to change; and you have to translate your knowledge and

cultural intelligence (CQ) An outsider's ability to interpret someone's unfamiliar and ambiguous behavior the same way that person's compatriots would.

motivation into action. So when you are on a business trip to London, go ahead and hold your fork in your left hand!

RESPECT FOR ALL WORKERS AND CULTURES

An effective strategy for achieving cross-cultural understanding is to simply respect all others in the workplace, including their cultures. An important component of respect is to believe that although another person's culture is different from yours, it is equally good. Respect comes from valuing differences. Respecting other people's customs can translate into specific attitudes, such as respecting one coworker for wearing a yarmulke on Friday or another for wearing African clothing to celebrate Kwanzaa. Another way of being respectful would be to listen carefully to the opinion of a senior worker who says the company should never have converted to voice mail in place of assistants answering the phone (even though you disagree).

An aspect of respecting all workers that achieves current attention is the importance of respecting the rights of majorities, particularly white males. Many of these men want to be involved in—not excluded from—bringing about cultural diversity in organizations. For example, they might want to mentor minority group members.

Company policies that encourage respect for the rights of others are likely to create a positive influence on tolerance throughout the firm. An example is that many employers have taken steps to recognize and affirm the existence of gay and lesbian workers. Among these steps are publishing formal statements of nondiscrimination, and the inclusion of issues about sexual orientation in diversity training programs. A major policy change has been to grant same-sex couples the same benefits granted to opposite-sex couples.

A study of 537 gay and lesbian employees working for a variety of organizations demonstrated that the more prevalent policies dealing with respect, the more equitably sexual minorities are likely to be treated at work. More equitable treatment, in turn, was associated with gays and lesbians being more satisfied, and less likely to leave the firm.[5]

CULTURAL FLUENCY

cultural fluency The ability to conduct business in a diverse, international environment.

A high-level goal in understanding cultural differences is to achieve **cultural fluency**, the ability to conduct business in a diverse, international environment.[6] Achieving cultural fluency includes a variety of skills, such as relating well to people from different cultures and knowing a second language. Cultural fluency also includes knowledge of the international business environment, such as how the exchange rate can affect profits. Having high cultural intelligence would contribute to cultural fluency because such intelligence makes it easier to work well with people from other cultures.

Skill-Building Exercise 6-1 is a warm-up activity for achieving cultural sensitivity, and perhaps respect for all workers.

DIMENSIONS OF DIFFERENCES IN CULTURAL VALUES

One way to understand how national cultures differ is to examine their values. Table 6-1 presents an introduction to the subject by comparing values in the United States to the collective values of many Western and Eastern countries. You can use this information as a general stereotype of how Americans are likely to differ from people in many other countries.

The focus of our attention is a more detailed look at seven different values and how selected nationalities relate to them, based on the work of several researchers.[7] A summary of these values follows.

individualism A mental set in which people see themselves first as individuals and believe that their own interests take priority.

1. **Individualism versus collectivism.** At one end of the continuum is **individualism,** a mental set in which people see themselves first as individuals and

SKILL-BUILDING EXERCISE 6-1

DEVELOPING CULTURAL SENSITIVITY

Carefully observe products and services such as tennis shoes, notebooks, bicycles, and banking services, and attempt to find out how they are marketed and sold in other countries. For a convenient reference source, interview foreign students and foreigners outside class about these products and services. Your digging for information might uncover such nuggets as the following:

- In India, cricket champions are celebrities comparable to U.S. basketball stars who endorse soft drinks like Coca-Cola and Pepsi.
- In Hungary, peanut butter is considered a luxury food item.
- In some countries in warm climates, meat is freshly killed and hung on hooks for sale—without refrigeration or freezing.

After conducting these product and service interviews, arrive at some kind of interpretation or conclusion. Share your insights with other class members.

Source: "Teaching International Business," *Keying In,* January 1999, p. 1. *National Business Education Association.* Reprinted with permission.

TABLE 6-1 Comparison of U.S. Values with Those in Many Other Countries

In the United States	*In many other countries*
Time is to be controlled	Time is fluid, malleable
Emphasis is on change	Emphasis is on tradition, continuity
Individualism	Group orientation
Personal privacy	Openness, accessibility
Informality	Formality (not as much as in the past)
Individual competition	Cooperation
Equality/egalitarianism	Hierarchy/authority
Short-term emphasis	Long-term emphasis
Work emphasis ("One lives to work.")	Leisure = work emphasis ("One works to live.")
Task emphasis	People emphasis
Direct/explicit communication style	Indirect/implicit communication style
Action bias or emphasis	Planning and preparation emphasis

Source: Adaptation of chart prepared by International Orientation Resources.

believe that their own interests take priority. **Collectivism,** at the other end of the continuum, is a feeling that the group and society receive top priority. Members of a society who value individualism are more concerned with their careers than with the good of the firm. Members of a society who value collectivism, in contrast, are typically more concerned with the organization than with themselves.

Highly individualistic cultures include the United States, Canada, Great Britain, Australia, and the Netherlands. Japan, Taiwan, Mexico, Greece, and Hong Kong are among the countries that strongly value collectivism. The heavy emphasis on teamwork on the job and in sports in the United States is moving it inhabitants more toward collectivism.

collectivism A feeling that the group and society should receive top priority, rather than the individual.

materialism An emphasis on assertiveness and the acquisition of money and material objects.

concern for others An emphasis on personal relationships and a concern for the welfare of others.

formality A cultural characteristic of attaching considerable importance to tradition, ceremony, social rules, and rank.

informality A cultural characteristic of a casual attitude toward tradition, ceremony, social rules, and rank.

urgent time orientation A cultural characteristic of perceiving time as a scarce resource and tending to be impatient.

casual time orientation A cultural characteristic in which people view time as an unlimited and unending resource and therefore tend to be patient.

high-context culture A culture that makes extensive use of body language.

2. **Acceptance of power and authority.** People from some cultures accept the idea that members of an organization have different levels of power and authority. In a culture that believes in concentration of power and authority, the boss makes many decisions simply because he or she is the boss. Group members readily comply because they have a positive orientation toward authority. In a culture with less acceptance of power and authority, employees do not readily recognize a power hierarchy. They accept directions only when they think the boss is right or when they feel threatened. Countries that readily accept power and authority include France, Spain, Japan, Mexico, and Brazil. Countries that have much less acceptance of power and authority are the United States and particularly the Scandinavian countries (e.g., Sweden).

3. **Materialism versus concern for others.** In this context, **materialism** refers to an emphasis on assertiveness and the acquisition of money and material objects. It also means a deemphasis on caring for others. At the other end of the continuum is **concern for others,** an emphasis on personal relations and a concern for the welfare of others. Materialistic countries include Japan, Austria, and Italy. The United States is considered to be moderately materialistic. Scandinavian nations all emphasize caring as a national value. (In the original, the same dimension was referred to as masculinity versus femininity. Such terms are considered to be sexist today.)

4. **Formality versus informality.** A country that values **formality** attaches considerable importance to tradition, ceremony, social rules, and rank. At the other extreme, **informality** refers to a casual attitude toward tradition, ceremony, social rules, and rank. Workers in Latin American countries highly value formality, such as lavish public receptions and processions. Americans, Canadians, and Scandinavians are much more informal.

5. **Urgent time orientation versus casual time orientation.** Individuals and nations attach different importance to time. People with an **urgent time orientation** perceive time as a scarce resource and tend to be impatient. People with a **casual time orientation** view time as an unlimited and unending resource and tend to be patient. Americans are noted for their urgent time orientation. They frequently impose deadlines and are eager to get started doing business. Asians and Middle Easterners, in contrast, are patient negotiators.

6. **Work orientation versus leisure orientation.** A major cultural difference is the number of hours per week and weeks per year people expect to invest in work versus leisure, or other nonwork activities. American corporate professionals typically work about 55 hours per week, take 45-minute lunch breaks, and two weeks of vacation. Japanese workers share similar values with respect to time invested in work. In contrast, many European countries have steadily reduced the work week in recent years, while lengthening vacations. In March 2005, France overturned its 35-hour workweek and restored its 39-hour workweek, illustrating that Europeans have a preference for a modest workweek.

7. **High-context versus low-context cultures.** Cultures differ in how much importance they attach to the surrounding circumstances, or context, of an event. **High-context cultures** make more extensive use of body language. Some cultures, such as the Asian, Hispanic, and African American cultures, are high context. In contrast, northern European cultures are low context and make less use of body language. The Anglo American culture is considered to be medium-low context. People in low-context cultures seldom take time in business dealings to build relationships and establish trust.

How might a person use information about cultural differences to improve his or her interpersonal relations on the job? A starting point would be to recognize that a person's national values might influence his or her behavior. Assume that you wanted to establish a good working relationship with a person from a high-context culture. An effective starting point would be to emphasize body language when communicating with the individual.

Attitudes toward hierarchy and status can make a difference in establishing working relationships. A worker who values deference to age, gender, or title might shy away from offering suggestions to an elder or manager to avoid appearing disrespectful. This worker would need considerable encouragement to collaborate in decision making.[8] *Time-consciousness* may create a conflict if you are committed to making deadlines and a team member has a laid-back attitude toward time. You might explain that although you respect his attitudes toward time, the company insists on getting the project completed on time.

Self-Assessment Quiz 6-2 will help you think about how values might be influencing your interpersonal relations in the workplace.

CULTURAL BLOOPERS

An effective way of being culturally sensitive is to minimize actions that are likely to offend people from another culture based on their values. Cultural bloopers are most likely to take place when you are visiting another country. The same bloopers, however, can also be committed with people from a different culture within your

SELF-ASSESSMENT QUIZ 6-2

CHARTING YOUR CULTURAL VALUE PROFILE

Directions: For each of the seven value dimensions, circle the number that most accurately fits your standing on the dimension. For example, if you perceive yourself to be "highly formal," circle 1 on the fourth dimension (item 4).

1. Individualism — Collectivism
   1   2   3   4   5   6   7

2. High acceptance of power and authority — Low acceptance of power and authority
   1   2   3   4   5   6   7

3. Materialism — Concern for others
   1   2   3   4   5   6   7

4. Formality — Informality
   1   2   3   4   5   6   7

5. Urgent time orientation — Casual time orientation
   1   2   3   4   5   6   7

6. Work orientation — Leisure orientation
   1   2   3   4   5   6   7

7. High-context culture — Low-context culture
   1   2   3   4   5   6   7

Scoring and Interpretation: After circling one number for each dimension, use a felt-tipped pen to connect the circles, thereby giving yourself a profile of cultural values. Do not be concerned if your marker cuts through the names of the dimensions. Compare your profile to others in the class. Should time allow, develop a class profile by computing the class average for each of the seven points and then connecting the points.

own country. To avoid these bloopers, you must carefully observe persons from another culture. Studying another culture through reading is also helpful.

E-commerce and other forms of Internet communication have created new opportunities for creating cultural bloopers. The Web site developers and workers responsible for adding content must have good cross-cultural literacy, including an awareness of how the information might be misinterpreted.

- Numerical date formats can be readily misinterpreted. To an American, 4/9/08 would be interpreted as April 9, 2008 (or 1908!). However, many Europeans would interpret the same numerical expression as September 4, 2008.
- Colors on Web sites must be chosen carefully. For example, in some cultures purple is the color of royalty, whereas in Brazil purple is associated with death.
- Be careful of metaphors that may not make sense to a person for whom your language is a second language. Examples include "We've encountered an ethical meltdown" and "Our biggest competitor is over the hill."

English has become the language of business and science throughout the world, yet communicating in a customer's native tongue has its advantages. International business specialist Rick Borelli says that being able to communicate your message directly in your customer's mother tongue provides a competitive advantage.[9] Furthermore, according to the research firm IDC, consumers are four times more likely to purchase a product online if the Web site is in their preferred language.[10] The translator, of course, must have good knowledge of the subtleties of the language to avoid a blooper. An English-to-French translator used the verb *baiser* instead of *baisser* to describe a program of lowering prices. *Baisser* is the French verb "to lower," whereas *baiser* is the verb "to kiss." Worse, in slang *baiser* is a verb that refers to having intimate physical relationships!

Keep two key facts in mind when attempting to avoid cultural mistakes. One is that members of any cultural group show individual differences. What one member of the group might regard as an insensitive act, another might welcome. Recognize also that one or two cultural mistakes will not peg you permanently as a boor. Skill-Building Exercise 6-2 will help you minimize certain cultural bloopers.

SKILL–BUILDING EXERCISE 6–2

CULTURAL MISTAKES TO AVOID
WITH SELECTED CULTURAL GROUPS

EUROPE

Great Britain
- Asking personal questions. The British protect their privacy.
- Thinking that a businessperson from England is unenthusiastic when he or she says, "Not bad at all." English people understate their positive emotion.
- Gossiping about royalty.

France
- Expecting to complete work during the French two-hour lunch.
- Attempting to conduct significant business during August—*les vacances* (vacation time).
- Greeting a French person for the first time and not using a title such as "sir," or "madam," or "miss" (*monsieur, madame,* or *mademoiselle*).

Italy
- Eating too much pasta, as it is not the main course.
- Handing out business cards freely. Italians use them infrequently.

Spain	• Expecting punctuality. Your appointments will usually arrive 20 to 30 minutes late.
	• Making the American sign for "okay" with your thumb and forefinger. In Spain (and many other countries) this is vulgar.
Scandinavia (Denmark, Sweden, Norway)	• Being overly rank conscious. Scandinavians pay relatively little attention to a person's rank in the hierarchy.

ASIA

All Asian countries	• Pressuring an Asian job applicant or employee to brag about his or her accomplishments. Asians feel self-conscious when boasting about individual accomplishments; they prefer to let the record speak for itself. In addition, they prefer to talk about group rather than individual accomplishment.
Japan	• Shaking hands or hugging Japanese (as well as other Asians) in public. Japanese consider these practices to be offensive.
	• Not interpreting "We'll consider it" as a no when spoken by a Japanese businessperson. Japanese negotiators mean no when they say "We'll consider it."
	• Not giving small gifts to Japanese when conducting business. Japanese are offended by not receiving these gifts.
	• Giving your business card to a Japanese businessperson more than once. Japanese prefer to give and receive business cards only once.
China	• Using black borders on stationery and business cards, because black is associated with death.
	• Giving small gifts to Chinese when conducting business. Chinese are offended by these gifts.
	• Making cold calls on Chinese business executives. An appropriate introduction is required for a first-time meeting with a Chinese official.
Korea	• Saying no. Koreans feel it is important to have visitors leave with good feelings.
India	• Telling Indians you prefer not to eat with your hands. If the Indians are not using cutlery when eating they expect you to do likewise.

MEXICO AND LATIN AMERICA

Mexico	• Flying into a Mexican city in the morning and expecting to close a deal by lunch. Mexicans build business relationships slowly.
Brazil	• Attempting to impress Brazilians by speaking a few words of Spanish. Portuguese is the official language of Brazil.
Most Latin American countries	• Wearing elegant and expensive jewelry during a business meeting. Latin Americans think people should appear more conservative during a business meeting

Note: A cultural mistake for Americans to avoid when conducting business in most countries outside the United States and Canada is to insist on getting down to business quickly. North Americans in small towns also like to build a relationship before getting down to business. The preceding suggestions will lead to cross-cultural skill development if practiced in the right setting. During the next 30 days, look for an opportunity to relate to a person from another culture in the way described in these suggestions. Observe the reaction of the other person for feedback on your cross-cultural effectiveness.

OVERCOMING CROSS-CULTURAL COMMUNICATION BARRIERS

Learning Objective 3 ▶ We have already discussed the importance of overcoming communication barriers in Chapter 3. Cultural differences create additional barriers. Here are some guidelines for overcoming cross-cultural communication barriers.

1. **Be sensitive to the fact that cross-cultural communication barriers exist.** If you are aware of these potential barriers, you will be ready to deal with them. When you are dealing with a person in the workplace with a different cultural background than yours, solicit feedback in order to minimize cross-cultural barriers to communication. Being aware of these potential barriers will help you develop cultural sensitivity.

2. **Show respect for all workers.** The same behavior that promotes good cross-cultural relations in general helps overcome communication barriers. A widely used comment that implies disrespect is to say to another person from another culture, "You have a funny accent." Should you be transposed to that person's culture, you, too, might have a "funny accent."

3. **Use straightforward language and speak slowly and clearly.** When working with people who do not speak your language fluently, speak in an easy-to-understand manner. Minimize the use of idioms and analogies specific to your language. A computer analyst from Greece left confused after a discussion about a software problem with her manager. The manager said, "Let's talk about this another time because *I can't seem to get to first base with you.*" (The manager was referring to the fact that the conversation was headed nowhere because he couldn't come to an agreement with the analyst.) The computer analyst did not ask for clarification because she did not want to appear uninformed.

4. **Observe cultural differences in etiquette.** Violating rules of etiquette without explanation can erect immediate communication barriers. A major rule of etiquette in many countries is that people address superiors by their last name unless they have worked together for a long time. Or, the superior might encourage being on a first-name basis with him or her. Be aware that an increasing number of cultures are moving toward addressing each other and customers by using the first name only. Yet, it is best to error on the side of formality.

5. **Be sensitive to differences in nonverbal communication.** Stay alert to the possibility that a person from another culture may misinterpret your nonverbal signal. An engineer for a New Jersey company was asked a question by a German coworker. He signaled okay by making a circle with his thumb and forefinger. The German worker stormed away because in his country the same gesture is a personal insult and a vulgar gesture.

   Another key area of cross-cultural differences in nonverbal communication is the handshake. In some cultures, a woman is expected to extend her hand first to shake with a man. In other cultures, people, hug, embrace, or bow instead of shaking hands.[11] (With good cultural sensitivity and cultural intelligence you can figure out what to do when meeting another person.)

6. **Do not be diverted by style, accent, grammar, or personal appearance.** Although these superficial factors are all related to business success, they are difficult to interpret when judging a person from another culture. It is therefore better to judge the merits of the statement or behavior.[12] A brilliant individual from another culture may still be learning your language and thus make basic mistakes in speaking your language. Also, he or she might not yet have developed a sensitivity to dress style in your culture.

7. **Be attentive to individual differences in appearance.** A major cross-cultural insult is to confuse the identity of people because they are members of the same race or ethnic group. An older economics professor reared in China and teaching in the United States had difficulty communicating with students because he was unable to learn their names. The professor's defense was "So many of these Americans look alike to me." Recent research suggests that people have difficulty seeing individual differences among people of another race because they code race first, such as thinking "He has the nose of an African American." However, people can learn to search for more distinguishing features, such as a dimple or eye color.[13] In this way, individual differences are recognized.

BUSINESS IMPLICATIONS OF UNDERSTANDING CULTURAL DIFFERENCES

Top-level management at many companies emphasize cross-cultural understanding, including overcoming communication barriers, because such activities improve profits. If you establish rapport with people from other cultures—and avoid antagonizing them—they will most likely become and remain your customers. Similarly, if you establish good rapport with valuable employees from other cultures, they are more likely to stay with the company.

◀ Learning Objective 4

Establishing a culturally and demographically diverse organization has a proven record of enhancing hiring and retention (keeping employees).[14] The enhanced recruiting and retention takes place primarily among members of minority groups who feel more comfortable when a reasonable number of other people from their group are part of the workforce.

A woman who joined a printing firm as the only woman supervisor in the plant quit after six months. The problem was that she felt uncomfortable being singled out as the only female member of management. The woman joined a larger competitor where she was among five other women supervisors. She said she enjoyed being in her new work environment because her sex was not an issue.

Following are three examples of how cross-cultural understanding has improved profits, reduced costs, or enhanced employee satisfaction:

- Xerox Corporation has a longstanding reputation of reaching out to minorities and appreciating the contributions of people from diverse cultures. As a result, Xerox has been able to recruit and retain talented people from many cultural groups. One of many examples is Ursula Burns, the president of the company's United States Business Operations. Burns is one of the highest placed black women in American business.

- Several large automobile dealerships across the United States and Canada have deliberately cultivated a culturally diverse sales force. This type of cultural diversity often leads to much improved sales to the diverse cultural groups. A Cadillac dealer in New York City reported that sales to Asiatic Indians have quadrupled since he hired a sales representative raised in India. The same dealer reports that more cultural diversity in the service end of the business has also boosted sales to diverse ethnic and racial groups.

- For almost 15 years, the United States Postal Service has been committed to hiring, promoting, and retraining an inclusive workforce. Surveys taken regularly indicate that such diversity has contributed to positive employee perceptions of such factors as fairness/cooperation, job/organization satisfaction, supervision, discrimination, and work conditions.[15]

Back to the Opening Case

One year after recruiting a more culturally diverse workforce for sales and service, the president and marketing director at Superior Motors believed that they had strengthened their business considerably. For example, a young Chinese American hired as a sales rep proved to have excellent contacts with wealthy Chinese families, and many of these contacts resulted in sales for Superior Motors.

TECHNIQUES FOR IMPROVING CROSS-CULTURAL RELATIONS

Learning Objective 5 ▶ Many training programs have been developed to improve cross-cultural relations and to help workers value diversity. All of the information presented so far in this chapter is likely to be included in such programs. In this section we describe programs for improving cross-cultural relations including cultural training, cultural intelligence training, language training, and diversity training. A skill-building exercise accompanies a description of three of the programs. We will also describe some precautions regarding how diversity training can sometimes backfire.

CULTURAL TRAINING

cultural training A set of learning experiences designed to help employees understand the customs, traditions, and beliefs of another culture.

For many years, companies and government agencies have prepared their workers for overseas assignments. The method most frequently chosen is **cultural training,** a set of learning experiences designed to help employees understand the customs, traditions, and beliefs of another culture. In today's diverse business environment and international marketplace, learning about individuals raised in different cultural backgrounds has become more important. Many industries therefore train employees in cross-cultural relations.

Cultural training is also important for helping people of one culture understand their customers from another culture in particular, such as Chinese people learning to deal more effectively with their American customers. For example, in one training program Chinese businesspeople are taught how to sprinkle their e-mail with English phrases like "How are you?" "It was great to hear from you" and "Can we work together?"[16]

The Job-Oriented Interpersonal Skills in Action box describes how cultural training can improve the effectiveness of establishing call centers overseas.

To practice improving your cross-cultural relations, do Skill-Building Exercise 6-3.

CULTURAL INTELLIGENCE TRAINING

A new development in assisting people work more effectively with workers in other cultures is *cultural intelligence training,* a program based on the principles of cultural intelligence described earlier in this chapter. A key part of the training is to learn the three contributors to CQ—head, heart, and body. Instead of learning a few simple guidelines for working effectively with people from another culture, the trainee is taught strategies for sizing up the environment to determine which course of action is best. The culturally intelligent overseas worker would learn how to determine how much humor to interject into meetings, what kind of handshake is most appropriate, and so forth. The following excerpt will give you a feel for what is involved in cultural intelligence training:

A Canadian manager is attempting to interpret a "Thai smile." First, she needs to observe the various cues provided in addition to the smile gesture

Job-Oriented Interpersonal Skills in Action

INDIAN CALL CENTER WORKERS LEARN TO THINK AND ACT LIKE AMERICANS

In a sleek new office building, two dozen young Indians are studying the customs of a place none of them have ever seen. One by one, the students present their conclusions about this fabled land. "Americans eat a lot of junk food. Table manners are very casual," says Ritu Khanna. "People are self-centered. The average American has 13 credit cards," says Nerissa Dcosata.

The Indians, who range in age from 20 to 27, have been hired to take calls from cranky or distraught Americans whose computers have gone haywire. To do this, they need to communicate in a language that is familiar but a culture that is foreign. "We're not saying India is better or America is better," says their trainer, Alefiya Rangsala. "We just want to be culturally sensitive so there's no disconnect when someone phones for tech support."

Call centers took root in India during the 2001 recession, when U.S. companies were struggling to reduce expenses. At first, training was simple. The centers gave employees names that were acceptable to American ears, with *Arjun* becoming *Aaron* and *Sangita* becoming *Susan*. The new hires were instructed to watch American television shows to get an idea of American folkways.

But whether Aaron and Susan were repairing computers, selling long-distance service, or fulfilling orders for diet tapes, problems immediately cropped up. The American callers often wanted a better deal or an impossibly swift resolution, and were aggressive and sometimes abrasive about saying so. The Indians responded according to their deepest natures: They were silent when they didn't understand, and they often committed to more than their employers could deliver. They would tell the Americans that someone would get back to them tomorrow to check on their problems, and no one would.

Customer satisfaction plummeted. The U.S. clients grew alarmed. Some even returned their business to U.S. call centers. Realizing that the multibillion-dollar industry with 150,000 employees was at risk, Indian call centers have recently embarked on more comprehensive training. New hires are taught how to express empathy, strategies to successfully open and close conversations, and above all how to be assertive, however unnatural it might feel.

Khanna, Dcosata, and their new colleagues work for Sutherland Global Services, an upstate New York firm that is one of the larger outsourcing companies in India. They've been put through a three-week training session where they research hot-button issues, and pretend they are American anchors reporting the latest news, and imitate celebrities.

On the students' last day of cultural and voice training, Rangsala warns them that at least half a dozen are still speaking incomprehensibly and might wash out. As they slip away one by one to make a short recording that will test their pronunciation skills, K. S. Kumar, Sutherland's director of operations for India, gives a little graduation speech. "You're shortchanging yourself if you don't stick with this." (The shift work and difficult work goals contribute to high turnover.)

Originally, the ever-agreeable Indian agents had a hard time getting people to pay bills that were six months overdue. Too often, says trainer Deepa Nagraj, the calls would go like this:

"Hi," the Indian would say. "I'd like to set up a payment to get your account current. Can I help you do that?"

"No," the American responds.

"OK, let me know if you change your mind," the Indian says and hangs up.

Now, says Nagraj, the agents take no excuses.

Like Sutherland, Mphasis is basing a lot of its hopes on training. Indrandiel Ghosh, an Mphasis trainer, gives refresher courses to reps who handle customer-service accounts for a big credit-card company. One rep says he recently was helping a customer change his card data because his wife left him. When the rep expressed sympathy, the man cut him short, saying he hadn't really liked his wife.

"In case you empathize and then you see they don't want your empathy, move on," Ghosh advises. "This is someone from another culture. That increases the complexity tenfold."

Questions

1. What do you see as a major cultural difference between Indians and Americans that make the call center job so challenging for Indians?

2. Some of the call center representatives in India are instructed to identify themselves as students in Salt Lake City, in addition to giving them American first names. What is your take on the ethics of these disguises?

Source: From David Streitfeld, "A Crash Course on Irate Calls," August 2, 2004. *Los Angeles Times.* Reprinted with permission.

82

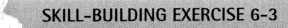

CROSS-CULTURAL RELATIONS ROLE-PLAY

One student plays the role of Ritu, a call center representative in Bombay, India. Her specialty is helping customers with cell phone problems. Another student plays the role of Todd, an irate American. His problem is that he cannot get his camera-equipped cell phone to transmit his photos over e-mail. He is scheduled to attend a party in two hours, and wants to take loads of photos with his cell phone. Todd is impatient, and in the eyes of Ritu, somewhat overbearing. Ritu is good natured and pleasant, but feels she must help Todd solve his problem without being bullied by him. Because Ritu is instructed to spend the minimum time necessary to resolve the problem, she spends about five minutes on this problem.

The observers should make note of how well Ritu has made the necessary cross-cultural adaptations.

itself (e.g., other facial or bodily gestures, significance of others who may be in proximity, the source of the original smile gesture) and to assemble them into a meaningful whole and make sense of what is really experienced by the Thai employee. Second, she must have the requisite motivation (directed effort and self-confidence) to persist in the face of confusion, challenge, or apparently mixed signals. Third, she must choose, generate, and execute the right actions to respond appropriately.

If any of these elements is deficient she is likely to be ineffective in dealing with the Thai employee. A high CQ manager has the capability with all three facets as they action in unison.[17]

As the example illustrates, to be culturally intelligent you need to apply cognitive skills, have the right motivation, and then put your knowledge and confidence into action. Armed with such skills you would know, for example, whether to greet a Mexican worker on a business trip to Texas with a handshake, a hug, or a kiss on both cheeks.

LANGUAGE TRAINING

Learning a foreign language is often part of cultural training, yet it can also be a separate activity. Knowledge of a second language is important because it builds better connections with people from other cultures than does relying on a translator. Building connections with people is still important even if English has become the international language of business. Many workers, aside from international business specialists, also choose to develop skills in a target language. Speaking another language can help build rapport with customers and employees who speak that language. As mentioned earlier, it is easier to sell to customers when using their native language.

Almost all language training has elements similar to taking a course in another language or self-study. Companies invest heavily in helping employees learn a target language because it facilitates conducting business in other countries. For this reason companies that offer language training and translation services are currently experiencing a boom. Medical specialists, police officers, and firefighters also find second language skills to be quite helpful because clients under stress, such as an injured person, are likely to revert to their native tongue. Learning a second language is particularly important when many of your customers and employees do not speak your country's official language. For example, Casa Rio, in San Antonio, Texas, found that its English-speaking managers were unable to communicate with Spanish-speaking employees regarding benefits and other issues.[18]

SKILL-BUILDING EXERCISE 6-4

USING THE INTERNET TO HELP DEVELOP
FOREIGN LANGUAGE SKILLS

A useful way of developing skills in another language, and learning more about another culture, is to create a computer "bookmark" or "favorite" written in your target language. In this way, each time you go to the Internet on your own computer, your cover page will contain fresh information in the language you want to develop.

Enter a search word such as "Italian newspaper" or "Spanish language newspaper" in the search probe. After you find a suitable choice, enter the edit function for "Favorites" or "Bookmarks" and insert that newspaper as your front page. For example, imagine that French is your target language and culture. The search engine might have brought you to the site *http://www.france2.fr.* This Web site keeps you abreast of French and international news, sports, and cultural events—written in French. Every time you access the Internet you can spend five minutes on your second language, thereby becoming multicultural. You can save a lot of travel costs and time using the Internet to help you become multicultural, including developing proficiency in another language.

As with any other skill training, investments in language training can pay off only if the trainee is willing to work hard at developing the new skill outside the training sessions. Allowing even 10 days to pass without practicing your target language will result in a sharp decline in your ability to use that language.

Skill-Building Exercise 6-4 presents a low-cost, pleasant method of enhancing your foreign language and cross-cultural skills.

DIVERSITY TRAINING

The general purpose of cultural training is to help workers understand people from other cultures. Understanding can lead to dealing more effectively with them as work associates or customers. **Diversity training** has a slightly different purpose. It attempts to bring about workplace harmony by teaching people how to get along better with diverse work associates. Quite often the program is aimed at minimizing open expressions of racism and sexism. Diversity training takes a number of forms. Nevertheless, all center on increasing awareness of and empathy for people who are different in some noticeable way from oneself.

Training sessions in appreciating cultural diversity focus on the ways that men and women or people of different races reflect different values, attitudes, and cultural backgrounds. These sessions can vary from several hours to several days. Training sessions can also be held over a long period of time. Sometimes the program is confrontational, sometimes not.

An essential part of relating more effectively to diverse groups is to empathize with their points of view. To help training participants develop empathy, representatives of various groups explain their feelings related to workplace issues. A representative segment of a training program designed to enhance empathy took the following format. A minority group member was seated at the middle of a circle. First, the coworkers listened to a Vietnamese woman explain how she felt excluded from the in-group composed of whites and African Americans in her department. "I feel like you just tolerate me. You do not make me feel that I am somebody important." The next person to sit in the middle of the circle was a Muslim. He complained about people wishing him Merry Christmas. "I would much prefer that my coworkers stop to think that I do not celebrate Christian holidays. I respect your religion, but it is not my religion."

diversity training
Training that attempts to bring about workplace harmony by teaching people how to get along better with diverse work associates.

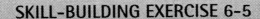

DEVELOPING EMPATHY FOR DIFFERENCES

Class members come up to the front of the room one by one and give a brief presentation (perhaps even three minutes) of any way in which they have been perceived as different, and how they felt about this perception. The difference can be of any kind, relating to characteristics such as ethnicity, race, choice of major, physical appearance, height, weight, hair color, or body piercing. After each member of the class (perhaps even the instructor) has presented, class members discuss what they learned from the exercise. It is also important to discuss how this exercise can improve relationships on the job.

A recent trend in diversity training is cross-generational diversity, or relating effectively to workers much older or younger than you. Wendy's International Inc., with the help of a consultant, has developed training programs that raise awareness of generational issues. Allen Larson, director of management resources, says "Since generational cohorts help form people's attitudes toward work, employees of different generations who must work together may find that their work styles conflict with those of coworkers."[19]

Cross-generational awareness training is one component in the corporate training program. The premise behind the program is that after acquiring cognitive knowledge, engaging in dialogue, and role-playing, employees will learn to accept people's differences, some of which are age driven. For example, younger employees might feel less guilty than would seniors when calling in sick just to have a day's vacation.

Skill-Building Exercise 6-5 provides you an opportunity to simulate an empathy-building experience in a diversity training program.

Diversity training has frequently improved cross-cultural relationships in the workplace. Yet such programs can also create ill will and waste time. One problem is that participants are sometimes encouraged to be too confrontational and express too much hostility. Companies have found that when employees are too blunt during these sessions, it may be difficult to patch up interpersonal relations in the work group later on.

A negative consequence of diversity training is that it sometimes results in perpetuating stereotypes about groups, such as people from Latin America not placing much value on promptness for meetings. A related problem is that diversity training might focus too much on differences instead of similarities.[20] For example, even if people are raised with different cultural values they must all work harmoniously together to accomplish work. Although a worker believes that relationships are more important than profits, he or she must still produce enough to be a good investment for the company.

SUMMARY

Today's workplace has become more culturally diverse, and business has become increasingly international. As a result, to succeed one must be able to relate effectively to people from different cultural groups from within and outside one's country. The true meaning of valuing diversity is to respect and enjoy a wide range of cultural and individual differences. The diversity umbrella continues to include more people as the workforce encompasses a greater variety of people.

The groundwork for developing effective cross-cultural relations is to understand cultural differences. Six key aspects of understanding cultural differences are

(1) cultural sensitivity, (2) cultural intelligence, (3) respect for all workers and all cultures, (4) cultural fluency—the ability to conduct business in a diverse, international environment, (5) differences in cultural values, and (6) avoidance of cultural bloopers. Cultural intelligence is based on cognitive, emotional/motivational, and physical (taking action) factors.

Countries differ in their national values, leading to differences in how most people from a given country will react to situations. The values studied here are (1) individualism versus collectivism, (2) acceptance of power and authority, (3) materialism versus concern for others, (4) formality versus informality, (5) urgent time orientation versus casual time orientation, and (7) high-context versus low-context cultures.

An effective way of being culturally sensitive is to minimize actions that are likely to offend people from another culture based on their values. These cultural bloopers can take place when working in another country or when dealing with foreigners in one's own country. Studying potential cultural bloopers is helpful, but recognize also that individual differences may be of significance.

Communication barriers created by cultural differences can often be overcome by the following: (1) be sensitive to the fact that these barriers exist; (2) show respect for all workers; (3) use straightforward language and speak slowly and clearly; (4) observe cultural differences in etiquette; (5) be sensitive to differences in nonverbal communication; (6) do not be diverted by style, accent, grammar, or personal appearance; and (7) be attentive to individual differences in appearance.

Improved cross-cultural understanding can improve profits through attracting and retaining diverse customers. Similarly, establishing good rapport with valuable employees from other cultures can improve employee recruitment and retention.

Cultural training is a set of learning experiences designed to help employees understand the customs, traditions, and beliefs of another culture. In today's diverse business environment and international marketplace, learning about individuals raised in different cultural backgrounds has become more important. Cultural intelligence training includes developing strategies for sizing up the environment to determine which course of action is best. Learning a foreign language is often part of cultural training, yet it can also be a separate activity.

Diversity training attempts to bring about workplace harmony by teaching people how to get along better with diverse work associates. Most forms of diversity training center on increasing awareness of and empathy for people who are different in some noticeable way from yourself.

QUESTIONS FOR DISCUSSION AND REVIEW

1. How can a person demonstrate to others on the job that he or she is culturally fluent (gets along well with people from other cultures)?

2. Several well-known companies conduct awareness weeks to celebrate selected diverse groups such as Hispanics or gays and lesbians. What is your opinion of the effectiveness of such activities for bringing about workplace harmony?

3. Some companies, such as Singapore Airlines, make a deliberate effort for customer-contact personnel to all be of the same ethnic group (Singapore natives). How justified is this practice in an era of cultural diversity and valuing differences?

4. A major purpose of diversity programs is to help people celebrate differences. Why should people celebrate a difference such as being a wheelchair user?

5. Provide an example of cultural insensitivity of any kind that you have seen, read about, or could imagine.

6. Why is knowing the language of the other person more important when selling to rather than buying from that person?

7. How could you use the information presented in Table 6-1, comparing U.S. values to those of other countries, to help you succeed in business?

8. If you were a supervisor, how would you deal with a group member who had a very low acceptance of power and authority?

9. The cultural bloopers presented in Skill-Building Exercise 6-2 all dealt with errors people make in regard to people who are not American. Give an example of a cultural blooper a person from another country might make in the United States.

10. Many people speak loudly to other people who are deaf, blind, and those who speak a different language. Based on the information presented in this chapter, what mistakes are these people making?

GO TO THE WEB

http://www.DiversityInc.com
(Extensive information about cultural diversity in organizations)

http://www.berlitz.com
(Information about language training and cultural training in countries throughout the world. Investigate in your second language to enhance the cross-cultural experience.)

AN INTERPERSONAL RELATIONS CASE PROBLEM

RALPH LAUREN SEEKS RACIAL HARMONY

Fashion magnate Ralph Lauren says he first became aware of racial tension within his company after an incident in 1997 at a Long Island sportswear boutique. A regional manager with Polo Ralph Lauren Corp. dropped by the new Polo Sport store in anticipation of an inspection by an important visitor: Jerome Lauren, Ralph's older brother and the executive overseeing Polo menswear. The mall where the boutique was located attracts a middle-class, racially integrated clientele. But the regional manager concluded that the store's ambiance was too "urban," meaning black, former Polo officials said.

The manager ordered two black and two Hispanic sales associates off the floor and back into the stock room, so they wouldn't be visible to Lauren. The sales associates followed orders, but they later hired a lawyer and threatened to sue Polo for discrimination. The company reached confidential settlements with the four.

Ralph Lauren says he learned about the incident several weeks after it happened and "was just sick" about it. The regional manager, Greg Ladley, was ordered to undergo racial-relations training but wasn't fired. A company spokesperson says that Ladley's recollection is that some sales associates working on inventory were asked to move to the stock room because they weren't "dressed appropriately."

After the episode, Ralph Lauren told subordinates, "We have to correct this. Let's make a change." But executives who worked at Polo at the time say their boss didn't make clear what changes they wanted.

AIR OF EXCLUSIVENESS

Polo, like some of its rivals, presents a multiracial face to the world, with black models in some of its ads, and a following of young black consumers wearing its familiar logo of a horse rider wielding a polo mallet. Yet internally, big fashion houses tend to exude an exclusiveness that is uninviting to many nonwhites. Few blacks or Hispanics have penetrated the upper ranks of major clothes manufacturers and retailers.

In response to complaints that have flared up at Polo, Lauren has met with lawyers, hired lieutenants to overhaul company personnel practices, and embraced diversity training. But he says he has left the details to others, as he is usually preoccupied with design work at his headquarters studio.

The Polo aura of Anglo-Saxon elitism is the elaborate creation of Polo's founder, Ralph Lauren, 62 years old, who remade himself as he rose from modest roots in the Bronx, to become the chair and CEO of a fashion powerhouse. Polo retail supervisors routinely tell salespeople to think Hollywood. "Ralph is the director," the instruction goes, "and you are the actors, and we are here to make a movie." But some black and Hispanic employees say the movie seems to lack parts for them.

COLOR-BLIND?

Lauren says he is color-blind when it comes to hiring talent. He frequently points out the wide visibility he has given Tyson Beckford, the striking shaven-headed black fashion model who has appeared in Polo ads since 1994. "Tyson is not just in jeans," Lauren says. "We put him in a pinstripe suit, in our best Purple Label brand. Tyson is in the annual report, in our advertisements on TV."

Lauren says Polo "is a leader to do the right things to bring in the people who are the best in the industry." Some of his subordinates complain, however, that it is difficult to find black and Hispanic applicants with the credentials for design jobs coming out of the New York fashion schools where Polo usually recruits.

A Polo staffer recommended in 1998 that Lauren meet Lacey Moore, a 20-year-old African American from Brooklyn, who had taken some college-level communications courses and had aspirations to be in the music business. Since high school, Moore had worn Polo Oxford shirts and knit tops with flashy gold chains and a hip-hop attitude: precisely the sort of hybrid image Lauren hoped would draw younger customers. "Lacy is edgy—he gets it," Lauren recalls thinking, snapping his fingers for effect. He hired the young man as a design assistant.

The new recruit's rap-influenced personal style and lingo confounded his coworkers. Moore felt isolated. He says he understood that in any competitive workplace "there are people who don't like you." But in Polo's cliquish and overwhelmingly white Madison Avenue headquarters, he says coworkers made it clear he wasn't welcome. "I kept getting this bad vibe," he says. He quit in 2000.

Shocked, Lauren telephoned Moore at home. "Lacey, I want you to come back," he recalls saying. After listening to Moore's complaints, Lauren says he made it clear to the young man's white coworkers, "I want you all to work this out." A couple of weeks later, Moore returned, but warily.

ADVICE AND PRESSURE

Polo has received advice and pressure on the race issue from a variety of outside counselors and advocates. A civil rights authority advised Lauren that achieving a truly diverse workforce requires hiring more than a few black employees. A black activist minister met with Polo officials and helped some minority workers reach confidential settlements with the company.

Today Moore (the young design assistant) says his colleagues seem friendlier. The human resource vice president has given Moore reassurance. "You feel there is someone looking out for you," says the young assistant, who helps prepare for fashion shows and consults on clothing design.

Lauren says he is paying more attention to what he sees at work. For example, he recalls that at a company Christmas party in 2000, he was surprised that a group of blacks and Hispanics had congregated in a separate room. "Why is this happening?" he wondered. "What's not welcoming to those employees?"

According to Lauren he didn't approach his workers to ask them, however, and is still wondering about the answers to those questions.

Case Questions

1. What advice can you offer Lauren to achieve fuller workplace diversity at Polo?

2. Is the Christmas (holiday) party incident a symptom of an organizational problem? Or were the black and Hispanic employees just behaving as they chose?

3. Does Ralph Lauren "get it" as a leader with respect to cultural diversity in the workplace?

Source: Adapted from Teri Agins, "Color Line: A Fashion House with an Elite Aura Wrestles with Race," *The Wall Street Journal,* August 19, 2002, pp. A1, A9.

INTERPERSONAL RELATIONS CASE PROBLEM

THE TRANSGENDER PHARMACIST

Kim Dower has held a pharmacist position at King Soopers in Denver for almost 10 years. Dower is biologically and physiologically male, yet is undergoing gender transformation and wants to wear women's clothes at work. According to Dower, management at King Soopers will not allow the cross-dressing. "I want to see King Soopers change their policy so other people like me can't be discriminated against," said Dower, 50, who is recently separated and has two children from a previous marriage. "I have struggled with this most of my life."

Dower hired a lawyer to represent him, and filed a complaint with the Equal Employment Opportunity Commission. "Our feeling is this is a very important case," said Dower's attorney, Betty Tsamis. King Soopers declined to comment on the charge, as is standard practice for a company facing a formal complaint.

Twelve months ago, Dower said, she informed a store manager that she was undergoing gender transformation. In March, she asked if she could begin to wear women's clothing while on the job. The manager took that request to a higher level of management, Dower said. The answer came back negative—no dressing as a woman while working as a pharmacist.

"There was no talking about it," Dower said. "They never contacted me. They never said, 'Let's talk about this.'"

Dower wants to eventually undergo sex reassignment surgery—a change of gender (sex) characteristics from male to female. However, her physician won't perform the surgery until she has lived as her target gender (female) around the clock for a year. Dower says she currently dresses as a man for only two occasions: work and visits with her father, who has Alzheimer's disease.

Editor's note: In cases of gender transition, the Denver Post respects preferred gender in pronoun use.

Case Questions

1. What would you recommend that management at King Soopers do about Dower's request to dress like a woman while on the job?

2. What business excuse might management at King Soopers offer for turning down Dower's request to wear women's clothing?

3. What compromise can you offer to satisfy the positions of both Kim Dower and management at the King Soopers?

4. What has this case got to do with cultural diversity in the workplace?

Source: Kelly Pate Dwyer, "Transsexual Charges Soopers Bias," July 7, 2004. The Denver Post. Reprinted with permission.

CHAPTER
5

Handling Conflict and Being Assertive

Learning Objectives

After studying the information and doing the exercises in this chapter, you should be able to:

◆ Identify reasons why conflict between people takes place so often

◆ Pinpoint several helpful and harmful consequences of conflict

◆ Choose an effective method of resolving conflict

◆ Improve your negotiating skills

◆ Improve your assertion skills

◆◆◆◆◆◆◆◆◆◆◆◆◆◆

A manager was so concerned about a problem facing her in the office that she wrote to a business columnist, "I am a manager in a small office. My problem is that one of the staff people (a man who is 12 years older than I) is verbally harassing me, telling me that I don't know what I'm doing and that I'm incompetent. A lot of times, I just avoid dealing with him. Instead of saying something I'll regret, I figure I'm better off walking away.

This man doesn't report directly to me. He reports to someone else, but I have authority over his work. What are my rights here? How should I handle this?"

The columnist, who consulted several human relations specialists, responded, "What a tense situation! And what obnoxious remarks! You're probably dreading the thought of any direct confrontation with this man. Unfortunately, however, that's exactly what the experts want you to do—talk directly with the offender about his behavior."[1]

The situation just described illustrates a reality about the workplace and personal life. Conflict takes place frequently, and being able to manage it well contributes to your feeling of well-being. **Conflict** is a condition that exists when two sets of demands, goals, or motives are incompatible. For example, if a person wants a career in retailing yet also wants to work a predictable eight-hour day with weekends off, that person faces a conflict. He or she cannot achieve both goals. When two people have differences in demands, it often leads to a hostile or antagonistic relationship between them. A conflict can also be considered a dispute, feud, or controversy. The two people described above are in conflict because the man wants to insult the woman and the woman wants a peaceful relationship.

Unless workers learn how to resolve conflict effectively, it will be difficult to achieve a workplace in which people collaborate. When the work environment is filled with collaboration and caring, the organization will be more productive, and workers will experience less negative stress. Organizational psychologist James Campbell Quick observes, "When competition and competitive behavior go to an extreme, it becomes dysfunctional and destructive. Over-the-top competition and stress can tear down individuals and organizations."[2]

A major purpose of this chapter is to describe ways of resolving conflict so that a win-win solution is reached. Both sides should leave the conflict feeling that their needs have been satisfied without having to resort to extreme behavior. Both parties get what they deserve yet preserve the dignity and self-respect of the other side. Another purpose of this chapter is to explain assertiveness because being assertive helps prevent and resolve conflict.

▲ WHY SO MUCH CONFLICT EXISTS

Many reasons exist for the widespread presence of conflict in all aspects of life. All these reasons are related to the basic nature of conflict—the fact that not every person can have what he or she wants at the same time. As with other topics in this book, understanding conflict helps you develop a better understanding of why people act as they do. Here we describe six key sources of conflict.

COMPETITION FOR LIMITED RESOURCES

A fundamental reason you might experience conflict with another person is that not everybody can get all the money, material, supplies, or human help they want. Conflict also ensues when employees are asked to compete for prizes such as bonuses based on individual effort or company-paid vacation trips. Because the number of awards is so limited, the competition becomes intense enough to be regarded as conflict. In some families, two or more children are pitted in conflict over the limited resources of money available for higher education.

Conflict stemming from limited resources has become prevalent as so many companies attempt to reduce expenses. Many units of the organization have to compete for the limited money available to hire new people or purchase new technology. An individual might be in conflict who says to the manager, "You expect higher and higher productivity, yet I am not authorized to purchase the most advanced software."

THE GENERATION GAP AND PERSONALITY CLASHES

Various value and personality differences among people contribute to workplace conflict. Differences in age, or the generation gap, can lead to conflict because members of one generation may not accept the values of another. Some observers see a clash between baby boomers and Generation X and Generation Y. (Recall the discussion in Chapter 2 about need differences among the three generations.) The baby boomers are typically considered people born between 1946 and 1964, Generation X between 1965 and 1987, and Generation Y between 1978 and 1984. Another workforce group with values of its own are veterans, born between 1922 and 1943.

According to the stereotype, baby boomers see members of Generation X and Generation Y as disrespectful of rules, not willing to pay their dues, and being disloyal to employers. Generation X and Generation Y members see baby boomers as worshiping hierarchy (layers of authority), being overcautious, and wanting to preserve the status quo. Baby boomers, however, appreciate teamwork more than the veterans, who prefer the old-fashioned, militaristic style organization. The four groups, of course, see themselves in a favorable light. Members of Generation X and Generation Y believe that employers have been disloyal to them, and baby boomers believe that the search for job security is highly sensible. Veterans believe in a centralized authority and a heroic attitude about work.[3] An example follows of a conflict based on generational differences in habits and values:

> Hosting a retirement dinner for the boss at an expensive restaurant, a senior manager was appalled when not one of the young employees bothered to dress up. Although the office dress code is casual, he had assumed employees would know enough to freshen up for the occasion, if only as a sign of respect for the leader.[4]

Many disagreements on the job stem from the fact that some people simply dislike each other. A **personality clash** is thus an antagonistic relationship between two people based on differences in personal attributes, preferences, interests, values, and styles. People involved in a personality clash often have difficulty specifying why they dislike each other. The end result, however, is that they cannot maintain an amiable work relationship. A strange fact about personality clashes is that people who get along well may begin to clash after working together for a number of years. Many business partnerships fold because the two partners eventually clash.

Aggressive Personalities Including Bullies

Coworkers naturally disagree about topics, issues, and ideas. Yet some people convert disagreement into an attack that puts down other people and damages their self-esteem. As a result, conflict surfaces. **Aggressive personalities** are people who verbally and sometimes physically attack others frequently. Verbal aggression takes the form of insults, teasing, ridicule, and profanity. The aggression may also be expressed as attacks on the victim's character, competence, background, and physical appearance.[5]

Aggressive personalities are also referred to as *workplace bullies*. Among their typical behaviors are interrupting others, ranting in a loud voice, and making threats. A typical attitude of a bullying boss is "My way or the highway," sending the message that the employee's suggestions are unwelcome. One bullying manager would frequently ask people, "Are you going to be stupid the rest of your life?" Bullied workers complain of a range of psychological and physical ailments such as the following: anxiety, sleeplessness, headache, irritable bowel syndrome, skin problems, panic attacks, and low self-esteem.[6]

Aggressiveness can also take the extreme form of the shooting or knifing of a former boss or colleague by a mentally unstable worker recently dismissed from the company. Violence has become so widespread that homicide is the second-highest cause of workplace deaths, with about 1,000 workers murdered each year in the United States.[7] Most of these deaths result from a robbery or commercial crime. Many of these killings, however, are perpetrated by a disgruntled worker or former employee harboring an unresolved conflict. As companies have continued to reduce their workforce despite being profitable, these incidents have increased in frequency. Workplace violence is sometimes referred to as *desk rage*. The problem includes such diverse behaviors as distracting rudeness, attacks on trashcans, keyboards, and even coworkers.

CULTURALLY DIVERSE TEAMS

Conflict often surfaces as people work in teams whose members vary in many ways. William L. Ury, a negotiation expert, says, "Conflict resolution is perhaps the key skill needed in a diverse work force."[8] Ethnicity, religion, and gender are three of the major factors that lead to clashes in viewpoints. Differing educational backgrounds and work specialties can also lead to conflict. Workers often shut out information that doesn't fit comfortably with their own beliefs, particularly if they do not like the person providing the information. When these conflicts are properly resolved, diversity lends strength to the organization because the various viewpoints make an important contribution to solving a problem. Groups that are reminded of the importance of effective communication and taught methods of conflict resolution can usually overcome the conflict stemming from mixed groups.[9]

COMPETING WORK AND FAMILY DEMANDS

Balancing the demands of work and family life is a major challenge facing workers at all levels. Yet achieving this balance and resolving these conflicts is essential for being successful in career and personal life. The challenge of achieving balance is particularly intense for employees who are part of a two-wage-earner family. **Work–family conflict** occurs when the individual has to perform multiple roles: worker, spouse or partner, and often parent. From the standpoint of the individual, this type of conflict can be regarded as work interfering with family life. From the standpoint of the employer, the same conflict might be regarded as family life interfering with work.

A team of researchers studying work interference with family life gathered data from approximately 501 employees in large companies. A major conclusion was that long hours at work increase work–family conflict, and that the conflict is related to depression and other stress-related health problems.[10]

Attempting to meet work and family demands is a frequent source of conflict because the demands are often incompatible. Imagine having to attend your child's championship soccer game and then being ordered at the last minute to attend a late-afternoon meeting. A survey revealed the following evidence of work–family conflict and the potential of such conflict:

- ◆ About 45 percent of students say their top consideration in selecting a first employer is the opportunity to achieve a balance between work and life outside of work.

- ◆ Approximately 80 percent of workers consider their effort to balance work and personal life as their first priority.

- ◆ More than one-third of employed Americans are working 10 or more hours a day, and 39 percent work on weekends.

- ◆ One-third of employees say that they are forced to choose between advancing in their jobs or devoting attention to their family or personal lives.[11]

The conflict over work versus family demands intensifies when the person is serious about both work and family responsibilities. The average professional working for an organization works approximately 55 hours per week, including five hours on weekends. Adhering to such a schedule almost inevitably results in some incompatible demands from work versus those from family members and friends. Conflict arises because the person wants to work sufficient hours to succeed on the job yet still have enough time for personal life.

Employers have taken major steps in recent years to help employees balance the competing demands of work and family. One reason for giving assistance in this area is that balancing work and family demands helps both the worker and the company. A survey of work and family strategies found that family-friendly business firms find big returns on their efforts. Absenteeism and turnover decrease, and productivity and profits increase.[12] Some employers have developed programs aimed directly at reducing the conflict that arises from competing work and family demands. A sampling of these programs and practices follows:

1. *Flexible work schedules.*   Many employers allow employees to work flexible hours, provided that they work the full 40-hour schedule and are present at certain core times. A related program is the compressed workweek, whereby the person works 40 hours in four days or less. Some employees prefer the compressed workweek because it gives them longer weekends with their families. Yet compressed workweeks can also be family unfriendly and create major conflicts. An example is that for some workers, having to work three 12-hour days in one week creates family problems.

2. *Dependent-care programs.*   Assistance in dealing with two categories of dependents, children and elderly parents, lies at the core of programs and policies to help employees balance the demands of work and family. At one end of child care assistance is a fully equipped nursery school on company premises. At the other end is simply a referral service that helps working parents find adequate childcare. Many companies offer financial assistance for childcare, including pretax expense accounts that allow employees to deduct dependent-care expenses.

3. *Compassionate attitudes toward individual needs.*   An informal policy that facilitates balancing work and family demands is for the manager to decide what can be done to resolve individual conflicts. Yet the manager cannot make arrangements with employees who would violate company policy. Being sensitive to individual situations could involve such arrangements as allowing a person time off to deal with a personal crisis. After the crisis is resolved, the employee makes up the lost time in small chunks of extra work time. In this way the manager helps the worker achieve success both on and off the job.

Sexual Harassment: A Special Type of Conflict

Many employees face conflict because they are sexually harassed by a supervisor, coworker, or customers. **Sexual harassment** is generally defined as unwanted sexually oriented behavior in the workplace that results in discomfort and/or interference with the job. It can include an action as violent as rape or as subdued as telling a sexually toned joke. In this way sexual harassment is defined in terms of its consequences to the victim. The harasser behaves in an aggressive and objectionable or offensive manner.

Sexual harassment creates conflict because the harassed person has to make a choice between two incompatible motives. One motive is to get ahead, keep the job, or have an unthreatening work environment. But to satisfy this motive, the person is forced to sacrifice the motive of holding on to his or her moral values or preferences. For example, a person might say, "I want to be liked by my coworkers and not be considered a prude. Yet to do this, must I listen to their raunchy jokes about the human anatomy?" Of even greater conflict, "I want a raise; but to do this, must I submit to being fondled by my boss?" Here we focus on the types and frequency of sexual harassment and guidelines for dealing with the problem.

Types and Frequency of Harassment

Two types of sexual harassment are legally recognized. Both are violations of the Civil Rights Acts of 1964 and 1991 and are therefore a violation of your rights when working in the United States. Other countries also have human rights legislation prohibiting sexual harassment. In quid pro quo sexual harassment, the individual suffers loss (or threatened loss) of a job benefit as a result of his or her response to a request for sexual favors. The demands of a harasser can be blatant or implied. An implied form of quid pro quo harassment might take this form: A manager casually comments to one of his or her employees, "I've noticed that workers who become very close to me outside of the office get recommended for bigger raises."

The other form of sexual harassment is hostile-environment harassment. Another person in the workplace creates an intimidating, hostile, or offensive working environment. No tangible loss or psychological injury has to be suffered under this form of sexual harassment.

A major problem in controlling sexual harassment in the workplace is that most workers understand the meaning and nature of quid pro quo harassment but are confused about what constitutes the hostile-environment type. For example, some people might interpret the following behaviors to be harassing, while others would regard them as friendly initiatives: (1) calling a coworker "sweetie" and (2) saying to a subordinate, "I love your suit. You look fabulous."

A group of researchers provided useful insights into the role of perception in deciding which behaviors of supervisors and coworkers constituted both types of harassment.[13] Typical harassment behaviors include physical contact, inappropriate remarks, a sexual proposition, a threat or promise associated with a job, comments on the other person's physical appearance, or a glaring stare at the person harassed. The setting for the survey was a manufacturing plant that had a strict policy against sexual harassment. Furthermore, supervisory and professional personnel had training in dealing with sexual harassment. Employee perceptions were compared to U.S. federal guidelines of sexual harassment—the basis for a "correct" response.

EXHIBIT 7-1

Accuracy of 114 Workers In Identifying Each Sexually Harassing Behavior

Supervisory Behaviors	*Correspondence with U.S. Federal Guidelines*	
If your supervisor did this, would you consider this sexual harassment?	Inaccurate	Accurate
1. Asks you to have sex with the promise that it will help you on the job.	18	96
2. Asks you to have sex with the threat that refusing to have sex will hurt you on the job.	17	97
3. Asks you to go out on a date with the promise that it will help you on the job.	18	96
4. Asks you to go out on a date with the promise that it will hurt you if you do not go.	16	98
5. Touches you on private parts of the body; for example, breasts, buttocks, etc.	22	92
6. Touches you on parts of the body not considered private; for example, shoulder, hand, arm, etc.	77	37
7. Looks at you in a flattering way.	75	39
8. Makes gestures (signs) of a flattering nature.	51	63
9. Makes comments about your dress or appearance that are meant to be complimentary.	96	18
10. Makes comments about your appearance meant to be insulting.	91	23
11. Makes sexually offensive comments.	49	65
12. Tells sexually oriented jokes.	75	39

SOURCE: Marjorie L. Icenogle, Bruce W. Eagle, Sohel Ahman, and Lisa A. Hanks, "Assessing Perceptions of Sexual Harassment Behaviors in a Manufacturing Environment," *Journal of Business and Psychology*, Summer 2002, p. 607.

Exhibit 7-1 presents the responses of the 114 participants in the survey with regard to supervisory behavior. (The perceptions of the accuracy versus inaccuracy in classifying coworker behavior as being harassing were essentially the same.) The responses indicated that the majority of workers can accurately identify behaviors frequently associated with quid pro quo harassment. However, the same workers had difficulty identifying behaviors that are used to establish evidence of a hostile work environment. Male workers had a slight edge in the accuracy of their perceptions about what constitutes harassment, and women in white-collar jobs were more accurate than women in blue-collar jobs.

An employee who is continually subjected to sexually suggestive comments, lewd jokes, or requests for dates is a victim of hostile-environment harassment. When the offensive behavior stems from customers or vendors, it is still harassment. Although the company cannot readily control the actions of customers or vendors, the company may still be liable for such harassment. According to several legal decisions, it is a company's job to take action to remedy harassment problems involving employees.

Surveys as well as the opinions of human resource professionals suggest that somewhere between 50 and 60 percent of women are sexually harassed at least once in their career. Aside from being an illegal and immoral act, sexual harassment has negative effects on the well-being of its victims. The harassed person may experience job stress, lowered morale, severe conflict, and lowered productivity. A study with both business and university workers found that even at low levels of frequency, harassment exerts a significant impact on women's psychological well-being and productivity. High levels of harassment, however, had even more negative effects.[14]

A related study of the long-term effects of sexual harassment indicated that the negative effects remained two years after the incident. For example, 24 months after an incident of sexual harassment, many women still experienced stress, a decrease in job satisfaction, and lowered productivity.[15]

GUIDELINES FOR PREVENTING AND DEALING WITH SEXUAL HARASSMENT

A starting point in dealing with sexual harassment is to develop an awareness of the type of behaviors that are considered sexual harassment. Often the difference is subtle. Suppose, for example, you placed copies of two nudes painted by Renoir, the French painter, on a coworker's desk. Your coworker might call that harassment. Yet if you took that same coworker to a museum to see the originals of the same nude paintings, your behavior would usually not be classified as harassment. Education about the meaning of sexual harassment is therefore a basic part of any company program to prevent sexual harassment. The situation and your tone of voice, as well as other nonverbal behavior, contribute to perceptions of harassment. For example, the statement "You look wonderful" might be perceived as good natured versus harassing, depending on the sender's voice tone and facial expression.

The easiest way to deal with sexual harassment is to speak up before it becomes serious. The first time it happens, respond with statements such as, "I won't tolerate that kind of talk." "I dislike sexually oriented jokes." "Keep your hands off me." Write the harasser a stern letter shortly after the first incident. Confronting the harasser in writing dramatizes your seriousness of purpose in not wanting to be sexually harassed. If the problem persists, say something to the effect, "You're practicing sexual harassment. If you don't stop, I'm going to exercise my right to report you to management." Additional suggestions for dealing with sexual harassment are presented in Exhibit 7-2.

EXHIBIT 7-2

Tips on Harassment

Here are some tips on dealing with sexual harassment from the New York State Division of Human Rights:

- Don't leave any room for doubt that the behavior or words you heard were unwelcome.

- If the behavior continues, report your complaint to a higher authority or the person your company or organization has designated to handle such complaints.

- Put the complaint in writing to reduce the chances of confusion.

- Keep concise yet accurate notes of incidents.

- If the matter isn't resolved internally, see a lawyer promptly for advice. The person can steer you through various legal options, possibly through federal or state court.

▲ THE GOOD AND BAD SIDES OF CONFLICT

Conflict over significant issues is a source of stress. We usually do not suffer stress over minor conflicts such as having to choose between wearing one sweater or another. Since conflict is a source of stress, it can have both positive and negative consequences to the individual. Like stress in general, we need an optimum amount of conflict to keep us mentally and physically energetic.

You can probably recall an incident in your life when conflict proved to be beneficial in the long run. Perhaps you and your friend or spouse hammered out an agreement over how much freedom each one has in the relationship. Handled properly, moderate doses of conflict can be beneficial. Some of the benefits that might arise from conflict can be summarized around these key points:

1. *Talents and abilities may emerge in response to conflict.* When faced with a conflict, people often become more creative than they are in a tranquil situation. Assume that your employer told you that it would no longer pay for your advanced education unless you used the courses to improve your job performance. You would probably find ways to accomplish such an end.

2. *Conflict can help you feel better because it satisfies a number of psychological needs.* By nature, many people like a good fight. As a socially acceptable substitute for attacking others, you might be content to argue over a dispute on the job or at home.

3. *As an aftermath of conflict, the parties in conflict may become united.* Two warring supervisors may become more cooperative toward each other in the aftermath of confrontation. A possible explanation is that the shared experience of being in conflict with each other *sometimes* brings the parties closer.

4. *Conflict helps prevent people in the organization from agreeing too readily with each other, thus making some very poor decisions.* Groupthink is the situation that occurs when group members strive so hard to get along that they fail to critically evaluate each other's ideas.

Despite the positive picture of conflict just painted, it can also have detrimental consequences to the individual, the organization, and society. These harmful consequences of conflict make it important for people to learn how to resolve conflict:

1. *Prolonged conflict can be detrimental to some people's emotional and physical well-being.* As a type of stress, prolonged conflict can lead to such problems as heart disease and chronic intestinal disorders. President Lyndon B. Johnson suffered his first heart attack after an intense argument with a young newspaper reporter.

2. *People in conflict with each other often waste time and energy that could be put to useful purposes.* Instead of fighting all evening with your roommate, the two of you might fix up your place. Instead of writing angry e-mail messages back and forth, two department heads might better invest that time in thinking up ideas to save the company money.

3. *The aftermath of extreme conflict may have high financial and emotional costs.* Sabotage—such as ruining machinery—might be the financial consequence. At the same time, management may develop a permanent distrust of many people in the workforce, although only a few of them are saboteurs.

4. *Too much conflict is fatiguing, even if it does not cause symptoms of emotional illness.* People who work in high-conflict jobs often feel spent when they return home from work. When the battle-worn individual has limited energy left over for family responsibilities, the result is more conflict. (For instance, "What do you mean you are too tired to visit friends?" or "If your job is killing your interest in having friends, find another job.")

5. *People in conflict will often be much more concerned with their own interests than with the good of the family, organization, or society.* A married couple in conflict might disregard the welfare of their children. An employee in the shipping department who is in conflict with his supervisor might neglect to ship an order. And a gang in conflict with another might leave a park or beach strewn with broken glass.

6. *Workplace violence erupts, including the killing of managers, previous managers, coworkers, customers, as well as spouses and partners.* The number of violent incidents at work causing death or serious injury has risen dramatically in recent years, as mentioned previously.[16] Disgruntled employees, such as those recently fired, may attempt revenge by assassinating work associates. People involved in an unresolved domestic dispute sometimes storm into the partner's workplace to physically attack him or her. Unresolved conflict and frustration from financial, marital, or other domestic problems increase the odds of a person "going ballistic" at work.

▲ TECHNIQUES FOR RESOLVING CONFLICTS

Because of the inevitability of conflict, a successful and happy person must learn effective ways of resolving conflict. An important general consideration is to face conflict rather than letting conflict slide or smoothing over it. Ignoring or smoothing over conflict does little to resolve the real causes of conflict and seldom leads to an effective long-term solution.[17] Here we concentrate on methods of conflict resolution that you can use on your own. Most of them emphasize a collaborative or win-win philosophy. Several of the negotiating and bargaining tactics to be described may be close to the competitive orientation.

CONFRONTATION AND PROBLEM SOLVING LEADING TO WIN-WIN

The most highly recommended way of resolving conflict is **confrontation and problem solving.** It is a method of identifying the true source of conflict and resolving it systematically. The confrontation in this approach is gentle and tactful rather than combative and abusive. It is best to wait until your anger cools down before confronting the other person, to avoid being unreasonable. Reasonableness is important because the person who takes the initiative in resolving the conflict wants to maintain a harmonious working relationship with the other party. Also, both parties should benefit from the resolution of the conflict.

Assume that Jason, the person working at the desk next to you, whistles loudly while he works. You find the whistling to be distracting and annoying; you think Jason is a noise polluter. If you don't bring the problem to Jason's attention, it will probably grow in proportion with time. Yet you are hesitant to enter into an argument about something a person might regard as a civil liberty (the right to whistle in a public place).

An effective alternative is for you to approach Jason directly in this manner:

You: Jason, there is something bothering me that I would like to discuss with you.

Jason: Go ahead, I don't mind listening to other people's problems.

You: My problem concerns something you are doing that makes it difficult for me to concentrate on my work. When you whistle, it distracts me and grates on my nerves. It may be my problem, but the whistling does bother me.

Jason: I guess I could stop whistling when you're working next to me. It's probably just a nervous habit. Maybe I can find a less disruptive habit, such as rolling my tongue inside my mouth.

An important advantage of confrontation and problem solving is that you deal directly with a sensitive problem without jeopardizing the chances of forming a constructive working relationship in the future. One reason that the method works so effectively is that the focus is on the problem at hand and not on the individual's personality.

Another approach to confrontation and problem solving is for each side to list what the other side should do. The two parties then exchange lists and select a compromise that both sides are willing to accept. Laying out each side's demands in writing is an effective confrontation technique, especially if the items on the list are laid out factually without angry comments included. Items causing a woman's conflict with her boyfriend might be as follows:

- "Please don't introduce me as 'my current girlfriend.' It makes our relationship sound temporary."
- "Turn off the television set when we talk on the phone."
- "At least once in a while, give me priority over your family when we are scheduling a social event together."
- "Please open and close the car door for me when we are driving in your car."

All these items relate to consideration and respect, so they are part of the same conflict. The partner can then point out where he can grant concessions. Of course, he will have his chance to produce a list.

The intent of confrontation and problem solving is to arrive at a collaborative solution to the conflict. The collaborative style reflects a desire to fully satisfy the desires of both parties. It is based on an underlying philosophy of **win-win,** the belief that after conflict has been resolved, both sides should gain something of value. The user of win-win approaches is genuinely concerned about arriving at a settlement that meets the needs of both parties or at least that does not badly damage the welfare of the other side. When collaborative approaches to resolving conflict are used, the relationships among the parties are built on and improved.

Here is an example of a win-win approach to resolving conflict. A manager granted an employee a few hours off on an occasional Friday afternoon because she was willing to be on call for emergency work on an occasional weekend. Both parties were satisfied with the outcome, and both accomplished their goals.

Human Relations Skill-Building Exercise 7-1 gives you an opportunity to practice the win-win approach to conflict resolution. Confrontation and problem solving typically paves the way for getting to win-win.

DISARM THE OPPOSITION

The armament your criticizer has is valid negative criticism of you. The criticizer is figuratively clobbering you with knowledge of what you did wrong. If you deny that you have made a mistake, the criticism intensifies. A simple technique has been developed to help you deal with this type of manipulative criticism. **Disarm the opposition** is a method of conflict resolution in which you disarm the criticizer by agreeing with his or her criticism of you. The technique assumes that you have done something wrong. Disarm

---

HUMAN RELATIONS SKILL-BUILDING EXERCISE 7-1

Win-Win Conflict Management

The class is organized into groups of six, with each group being divided into conflict resolution teams of three each. The members of the team would like to find a win-win solution to the issue separating each side. The team members are free to invent their own pressing issue or choose among the following:

- Management wants to control costs by not giving cost-of-living adjustments in the upcoming year. The employee group believes that a cost-of-living adjustment is absolutely necessary.

- The marketing team claims it could sell 250,000 units of a toaster large enough to toast bagels if the toasters could be produced at $15 per unit. The manufacturing group says it would not be feasible to get the manufacturing costs below $20 per unit.

- Starbucks Coffee would like to build in a new location, adjacent to a historic district in one of the oldest cities in North America. The members of the town planning board would like the tax revenue and the jobs that the Starbucks store would bring, but they still say they do not want a Starbucks store adjacent to the historic district.

After the teams have developed win-win solutions to the conflicts, the creative solutions can be shared with teammates.

---

the opposition generally works more effectively than counterattacking a person with whom you are in conflict.

Agreeing with criticism made of you by a manager or team leader is effective because, by so doing, you are in a position to ask that manager's help in improving your performance. Most managers and team leaders recognize that it is their responsibility to help employees to overcome problems, not merely to criticize them. Imagine that you have been chronically late in submitting reports during the last six months. It is time for a performance review and you know you will be reprimanded for your tardiness. You also hope that your boss will not downgrade all other aspects of your performance because of your tardy reports. Here is how disarming the situation would work in this situation:

Your boss: Have a seat. It's time for your performance review, and we have a lot to talk about. I'm concerned about some things.

You: So am I. It appears that I'm having a difficult time getting my reports in on time. I wonder if I'm being a perfectionist. Do you have any suggestions?

Your boss: I like your attitude. I think you can improve on getting your reports in on time. Maybe you are trying to make your reports perfect before you turn them in. Try not to figure out everything to four decimal places. We need thoroughness around here, but we don't want to overdo it.

HUMAN RELATIONS SKILL-BUILDING EXERCISE 7-2

Disarming the Opposition

In each of these two scenarios, one person plays the role of the person with more power in the situation. The other person plays the role of the individual attempting to disarm the criticizer.

◆ A representative from a credit organization telephones you at work to inform you that you are 60 days behind schedule on your car payment. The agent wants a settlement as soon as possible. Unfortunately, the credit agent is correct. Run this happy scenario for about five minutes.

◆ Your manager calls you into the office to discuss the 10-page report you just submitted. The boss says in a harsh tone, "Your report is a piece of trash. I counted 25 word-use mistakes such as writing *whether* for *weather* and *seen* for *scene*. [Your spell checker couldn't catch these errors.] Besides that, I can't follow many of your sentences, and you left out the table of statistics. I'm wondering if you are qualified for this job."

Human Relations Skill-Building Exercise 7-2 gives you an opportunity to practice disarming the opposition. Also, apply the technique the next time you are being criticized for something you actually did wrong.

COGNITIVE RESTRUCTURING

An indirect way of resolving conflict between people is to lessen the conflicting elements in a situation by viewing them more positively. According to the technique of **cognitive restructuring,** you mentally convert negative aspects into positive ones by looking for the positive elements in a situation. The original purpose of cognitive restructuring was to help people overcome automatic, negative thinking about themselves or situations. An example would be recognize that a challenging situation, such as making a presentation in front of a group, is not as bad as it first seems. The idea is to overcome unhealthy thoughts. How you frame or choose your thoughts can determine the outcome of a conflict situation. Your thoughts can influence your actions. If you search for the beneficial elements in a situation, there will be less area for dispute. Although this technique might sound like a *mind game* to you, it can work effectively.

Imagine that a coworker of yours, Jennifer, has been asking you repeated questions about how to carry out a work procedure. You are about ready to tell Jennifer, "Go bother somebody else, I'm not paid to be a trainer." Instead, you look for the positive elements in the situation. You say to yourself, "Jennifer has been asking me a lot of questions. This does take time, but answering these questions is valuable experience. If I want to become a manager, I will have to help group members with problems."

After having completed this cognitive restructuring, you can then deal with the conflict more positively. You might say to Jennifer, "I welcome the opportunity to help you, but we need to find a mutually convenient time. In that way, I can better concentrate on my own work."

APPEAL TO A THIRD PARTY

Now and then you may be placed in a conflict situation in which the other party either holds most of the power or simply won't budge. Perhaps you have tried techniques such as confrontation and problem solving or disarming the opposition, yet you cannot resolve your conflict. In these situations you may have to enlist the help of a third party with power—more power than you or your adversary has. Among such third parties are your common boss, union stewards, or human resource managers. Taking your opponent to court is another application of the third-party technique.

In some situations, just implying that you will bring in a third party to help resolve the conflict situation is sufficient for you to gain advantage. One woman felt she was repeatedly passed over for promotion because of her sex. She hinted that if she were not given fairer consideration, she would speak to the Equal Employment Opportunity Commission (EEOC). She was given a small promotion shortly thereafter. Many conflicts about sexual harassment, as well as ethnic and racial harassment, are resolved through third-party appeal.

THE GRIEVANCE PROCEDURE

The formal process of filing a complaint and resolving a dispute within an organization is the **grievance procedure.** It can also be regarded as a formal method of resolving conflict, in which a series of third parties are brought into the picture. The third-party appeal described above skips the step-by-step approach of a formal grievance procedure. In a unionized firm, the steps in the grievance procedure are specified in the written contract between management and labor. An example of a grievance about favoritism would be, "I get the worst assignments because I'm not one of the boss's fishing buddies." An example of a grievance about discrimination would be, "I didn't get the transfer to the receptionist job because I'm 55 years old."

The steps in the grievance procedure may vary from one to six, depending on the labor agreement or company procedures. A summary of the typical steps in a grievance procedure is presented next and outlined in Exhibit 7-3. If the company does not have a labor union, a specialist from the human resources department might serve as a third party.

Step 1. Initiation of the formal grievance. Suppose that an employee feels that he or she has been treated unfairly or that his or her rights have been violated in some way. The employee then files a grievance with the supervisor (or team leader). Most grievances end at step 1 by conversation among the employee,

EXHIBIT 7-3

The Grievance Procedure

Step 1: Initiation of formal grievance

> Employee files grievance, and discussion is held with employee, supervisor or team leader, and union steward.

If not settled

Step 2: Second-level manager

> Grievance now goes to next-highest level of management and must be documented in writing by both sides.

If not settled

Step 3: Higher-level manager and local union president

> Higher-level officials from both union and employer step in to settle dispute.

If not settled

Step 4: Arbitration

> Independent arbitrator is called in to settle the issue.

union steward, and the supervisor. At this stage, it makes sense to use some of the techniques for resolving conflict already described.

Step 2.   Second level of management. If the steward, supervisor or team leader, and employee cannot reach a satisfactory solution to the conflict, it goes to the next-highest level in the organization. At this point, the grievance must be documented in writing by both sides. Which people are involved at this level depends on the size of the firm. In a small firm, a high-ranking manager might be involved in step 2.

Step 3.   A higher-level manager and the local union president. If the grievance is not resolved at step 2, higher-level officials from both the union and the employer become involved in settling the dispute. A general principle is that at each higher step in the grievance process, comparable levels of management from both company and union face each other, or a higher-level representative from the human resources department might be involved.

Step 4. Arbitration. If the grievance cannot be settled at lower steps, an independent arbitrator may be called in to settle the issue. Only about 1 percent of grievances go all the way to arbitration. Arbitration is often used as an alternative to a strike. The arbitrator has the authority to settle the dispute and must be a person acceptable to both sides.

Mediation is often confused with arbitration. A mediator is a third party who enters a controversy but holds no power of decision. The mediator helps the two sides find a resolution to their conflict. Relatively few labor agreements allow for mediation, yet mediation might be used to settle a strike. A mediator works like a marriage counselor by helping both sides come to agreement by themselves.

A grievance procedure used in many firms without a union is the **jury of peers,** whereby unresolved grievances are submitted to a panel of coworkers. The panel chosen is similar to a jury in a criminal case. Panel members weigh evidence and, after group discussion, vote for or against the grievant. The jury-of-peers method works well when the jury members are knowledgeable about organizational justice.

The grievance processes just described are formal and legalistic. Nevertheless, to represent your interests well, it is helpful to use the informal conflict resolution techniques described above, such as confrontation and problem solving.

ENGAGE IN METACOMMUNICATION

Many conflict situations take the form of poor communications between the parties involved. In this way resolving conflict and overcoming communication barriers come together. When confronted with a conflict involving communications, one response is to work around the problem by using one of the techniques already described in this chapter or Chapter 6. A more typical response is to ignore the conflict or barrier by making no special effort to deal with it—a "take-it-or-leave-it" approach to communication. Another possibility is to **metacommunicate,** or communicate about the conflicting part of your communications to help overcome barriers or resolve a problem.

Suppose you are the team leader and one of the team members projects angry facial expressions and harsh gestures during your conversation about goals. You might say, "It looks like I'm not getting through to you. What do you dislike about our discussion?" The team member might say, "It's just that you're giving me tougher goals than the other team members. I think I'm being treated unfairly." By metacommunicating, you have laid the groundwork to resolve the conflict over goals.

You can also use metacommunication to take the initiative about aspects of your communication that might create conflict. As a team leader facing heavy deadline pressures, you might say to a team member, "I might appear brusque today and tomorrow. Please don't take it personally. It's just that I have to make heavy demands on you because the team is facing a gruesome deadline."

NEGOTIATION AND BARGAINING TACTICS

Conflicts can be considered situations calling for **negotiating and bargaining,** conferring with another person to resolve a problem. When you are trying to negotiate a fair price for an automobile, you are also trying to resolve a conflict. At first the demands of both parties seem incompatible. After haggling for a while, you will probably reach a price that is satisfactory to both sides.

Negotiation has many applications in the workplace, including buying, selling, arriving at a starting salary or raise, and deciding on a relocation allowance. Negotiation may also take place with coworkers when you need their assistance. For example, you might need to strike a bargain with a coworker to handle some of your responsibilities if you are faced with a temporary overload.

A sampling of negotiating tactics to help you resolve conflict is presented next. As with other techniques of resolving conflict already presented, choose those that best fit your style and the situation.

Create a Positive Negotiating Climate

Negotiation proceeds much more swiftly if a positive tone surrounds the session, so it is helpful to initiate a positive outlook about the negotiation meeting. A good opening line in a negotiating session is, "Thanks for fitting this meeting into your hectic schedule." Nonverbal communication such as smiling and making friendly gestures helps create a positive climate.

In negotiating with coworkers for assistance, a positive climate can often be achieved by phrasing demands as a request for help. Most people will be more accommodating if you say to them, "I have a problem that I wonder if you could help me with." The problem might be that you need the person's time and mental energy. By giving that person a choice of offering you help, you have established a much more positive climate than by demanding assistance.[18]

Allow Room for Compromise, but Be Reasonable

The basic strategy of negotiation is to begin with a demand that allows room for compromise and concession. Anyone who has ever negotiated the price of an automobile, house, or used furniture recognizes this vital strategy. If you are a buyer, begin with a low bid. (You say, "I'll give you $60 for that painting" when you are prepared to pay $90.) If you are the seller, begin with a high demand. (You say, "You can have this painting for $130" when you are ready to sell it for as low as $100.) As negotiations proceed, the two of you will

COMMON SENSE PROPELS MANY NEGOTIATORS
TO ALLOW **TOO MUCH** ROOM FOR COMPROMISE

probably arrive at a mutually satisfactory price. This negotiating strategy can also be used for such purposes as obtaining a higher starting salary or dividing property after a divorce or legal separation.

Common sense propels many negotiators to allow *too much* room for compromise. They begin negotiations by asking way beyond what they expect to receive or offering far less than they expect to give. As a result of these implausible demands, the other side may become hostile, antagonistic, or walk away from the negotiations. Assume you spotted a DVD/VCR that you really wanted in a retail store. The asking price was $298.95. In an attempt to negotiate the price, you offered the store manager $98.95 for the DVD/VCR. Most likely the store manager would move on to the next customer. However, if you began with a plausible offer such as $240, the store manager would take you seriously. Beginning with a plausible demand or offer is also important because it contributes to a positive negotiating climate.

Focus on Interests, Not Positions

Rather than clinging to specific negotiating points, keep your overall interests in mind and try to satisfy them. A negotiating point might be a certain amount of money or a concession that you must have. Remember that the true object of negotiation is to satisfy the underlying interests of both sides. Among the interests you and the other side might be trying to protect include money, lifestyle, power, or the status quo. For example, instead of negotiating for a particular starting salary, your true interests might be to afford a certain lifestyle. If the company pays all your medical and dental coverage, you can get by with a lower salary. Or your cost of living might be much lower in one city than in another. You can therefore accept a lower starting salary in the city with a lower cost of living.

Make a Last and Final Offer

In many circumstances, presenting a final offer will break a deadlock. You might frame your message something like this. "All I can possibly pay for your guitar is $250. You have my number. Call me when it is available at that price." Sometimes the strategy will be countered by a last and final offer from the other side: "Thanks for your interest. My absolute minimum price for this guitar is $300. Call us if that should seem OK to you." One of you will probably give in and accept the other person's last and final offer.

Role-Play to Predict What the Other Side Will Do

An advanced negotiating technique is to prepare in advance by forecasting what the other side will demand or offer. Two professors from New Zealand have discovered that when people role-play conflicts, their ability to predict outcomes jumps remarkably. The researchers presented 290 participants with descriptions of six actual conflicts and asked them to choose the most likely eventual decisions. The conflicts involved labor-management, commercial, and civil disputes. Five of these conflicts were chosen for role playing. Without the use of role playing, the participants did not much better than chance, with a 27 percent success ratio. Next, the researchers asked 21 international game theorists (specialist in predicting outcomes of events) to forecast the conflict outcomes. The game theorists were correct only 28 percent of the time. (Chance here would be 1/5, or 20 percent.)

Next, 352 students were instructed to role-play the conflicts in the five situations. The average correct decision was 61 percent versus 27 percent for the comparable group. The authors note that in over 40 years of studying forecasting, they have never seen a technique that led to such improvement in predictive accuracy.[19]

The implication for making you a better negotiator is to role-play with a friend in advance of the negotiating session you will be facing. The role play should help you predict what the other side and you will do so you will be better prepared. For example, if your role play suggests that the company would be willing to give you a 15 percent bonus for incredible performance, ask for a 15 percent bonus.

Allow for Face-Saving

We have saved one of the most important negotiating and conflict resolution strategies for last. Negotiating does not mean that you should try to squash the other side. You should try to create circumstances that will enable you to continue working with that person if it is necessary. People prefer to avoid looking weak, foolish, or incompetent during negotiation or when the process is completed. If you do not give your opponent an opportunity to save face, you will probably create a long-term enemy.

Face-saving could work in this way. A small-business owner winds up purchasing a network system for about twice what he originally budgeted. After the sale is completed, the sales rep says, "I know you bought a more professional networking rig than you originally intended. Yet I know you made the right decision. You will be able to do boost productivity enough with the networked PCs to pay back the cost of the networking system in two years."

▲ DEVELOPING ASSERTIVENESS

Several of the techniques for resolving conflict require assertiveness. Without being forthright, confrontation and problem solving could not be achieved. Effective negotiation would also be difficult because assertiveness is required to carefully explain your demands. Learning to express your feelings and make your demands known is also an important aspect of becoming an effective individual in general. Expressing your feelings helps you establish good relationships with people. If you aren't sharing your feelings and attitudes with other people, you will never get close to them.

Another benefit from being emotionally expressive and, therefore, assertive is that you get more of what you want in life. If you are too passive, people will neglect giving you what you want. Often it is necessary to ask someone when you want a raise, promotion, date, or better deal on a bank loan. Successful people usually make their demands known yet throw tantrums only for an occasional effect and rarely bully others. (Exceptions include flamboyant trial lawyers and athletic coaches.)

Let's examine the nature of assertiveness and then describe several techniques for building assertiveness. However, first take Human Relations Self-Assessment Quiz 7-1 to relate assertiveness to yourself.

Assertive, Nonassertive, and Aggressive Behavior

As implied above, **assertive** people state clearly what they want or how they feel in a given situation without being abusive, abrasive, or obnoxious. People who are assertive are open, honest, and "up front" because they believe that all people have an equal right to express themselves honestly. Assertive behavior can be understood more fully by comparing it to that shown by two other types of people. **Nonassertive** people let things happen to them without letting their feelings be known. **Aggressive** people are obnoxious and overbearing. They push for what they want with almost no regard for the feelings of others.

Another representative assertive behavior is to ask for clarification rather than contradicting a person with whom you disagree. The assertive person asks for clarification when another person says something irritating

HUMAN RELATIONS SELF-ASSESSMENT QUIZ 7-1

The Assertiveness Scale

Answer each question Mostly True or Mostly False as it applies to you.

	Mostly True	Mostly False
1. It is extremely difficult for me to turn down a sales representative when that individual is a nice person.	_____	_____
2. I express criticism freely.	_____	_____
3. If another person were being very unfair, I would bring it to that person's attention.	_____	_____
4. Work is no place to let your feelings show.	_____	_____
5. No use asking for favors; people get what they deserve on the job.	_____	_____
6. Business is not the place for tact; I say what I think.	_____	_____
7. If a person looked as if he or she were in a hurry, I would let that person go in front of me in a supermarket line.	_____	_____
8. A weakness of mine is that I'm too nice a person.	_____	_____
9. I answer any e-mail message right away, even if it means that I fall behind in my other work.	_____	_____
10. I have laughed out loud in public more than once.	_____	_____
11. I've been described as too outspoken by several people.	_____	_____
12. I have no misgivings about returning merchandise that has even the slightest defect.	_____	_____
13. I dread having to express anger toward a coworker.	_____	_____
14. People often say that I'm too reserved and emotionally controlled.	_____	_____
15. Nice guys and gals finish last in business.	_____	_____
16. I fight for my rights down to the last detail.	_____	_____
17. If I disagree with a grade on a test or paper, I typically bring my disagreement to my instructor's attention.	_____	_____
18. If I have had an argument with a person, I try to avoid him or her.	_____	_____
19. I insist on my spouse (or roommate or partner) doing his or her fair share of undesirable chores.	_____	_____
20. It is difficult for me to look directly at another person when the two of us are in disagreement.	_____	_____

(Continued)

21. I have cried among friends more than once. _____ _____

22. If someone near me at a movie kept up a conversation with another person, I would ask him or her to stop. _____ _____

23. I am able to turn down social engagements with people I do not particularly care for. _____ _____

24. It is in poor taste to express what you really feel about another individual. _____ _____

25. I sometimes show my anger by swearing at or belittling another person. _____ _____

26. I am reluctant to speak up in a meeting. _____ _____

27. I find it relatively easy to ask friends for small favors such as giving me a lift to work while my car is being repaired. _____ _____

28. If another person were talking very loudly in a restaurant and it bothered me, I would inform that person. _____ _____

29. I often finish other people's sentences for them. _____ _____

30. It is relatively easy for me to express love and affection toward another person. _____ _____

Scoring and Interpretation: Give yourself plus 1 for each of your answers that agrees with the scoring key. If your score is 16 or less, it is probable that you are currently a nonassertive individual. A score of 17 through 24 suggests that you are an assertive individual. A score of 25 or higher suggests that you are an aggressive individual. Retake this score about 30 days from now to give yourself some indication of the stability of your answers. You might also discuss your answers with a close friend to determine if that person has a similar perception of your assertiveness. Here is the scoring key.

1. Mostly False	11. Mostly True	21. Mostly True
2. Mostly True	12. Mostly True	22. Mostly True
3. Mostly True	13. Mostly False	23. Mostly True
4. Mostly False	14. Mostly False	24. Mostly False
5. Mostly False	15. Mostly True	25. Mostly True
6. Mostly True	16. Mostly True	26. Mostly False
7. Mostly False	17. Mostly True	27. Mostly True
8. Mostly False	18. Mostly False	28. Mostly True
9. Mostly False	19. Mostly True	29. Mostly True
10. Mostly True	20. Mostly False	30. Mostly True

EXHIBIT 7-4

Assertive, Nonassertive, and Aggressive Gestures

Assertive	Nonassertive	Aggressive
Well balanced	Covering mouth with hand	Pounding fists
Straight posture	Excessive head nodding	Stiff and rigid posture
Hand gestures, emphasizing key words	Tinkering with clothing or jewelry	Finger waving or pointing
Moderately loud voice	Constant shifting of weight	Shaking head as if other person isn't to be believed
	Scratching or rubbing head or other parts of body	Hands on hips
	Wooden body posture	Voice louder than needed, fast speech
	Voice too soft with frequent pauses	

---

rather than hurling insults or telling the other person he or she is wrong.[20] For example, assume someone says to you, "Your proposal is useless." Aggressively telling the person, "You have no right to make that judgment," shuts out any possible useful dialogue. You will probably learn more if you ask for clarification, such as "What is wrong with my proposal?"

Suppose a stranger invites you to a party and you do not wish to go with that person. Here are the three ways of responding according to the three-way classification under discussion:

Assertive: Thank you for the invitation, but I prefer not to go.
Nonassertive: I'm not sure, I might be busy. Could you call me again? Maybe I'll know for sure by then.
Aggressive: I'd like to go to a party, but not with you. Don't bother me again.

Gestures, as well as words, can communicate whether the person is being assertive, nonassertive, or aggressive. Exhibit 7-4 illustrates these differences.

BECOMING MORE ASSERTIVE AND LESS SHY

Shyness is widespread, and about 50 percent of the American population is shyer than they want to be. The personality trait of shyness has positive aspects, such as leading a person to think more deeply and become involved in ideas and things. (Where would the world be today if Bill Gates weren't shy as a youth?) However, shyness can also create discomfort and lower self-esteem.[21] There are a number of everyday actions a person can take to overcome being nonassertive or shy. Even if the actions described here do not elevate your assertiveness, they will not backfire and cause you discomfort. After reading the following six techniques, you might be able to think of others that will work for you.[22]

1. Set a goal. Clearly establish in your mind how you want to behave differently. Do you want to date more often? Speak out more in meetings? Be able to express dissatisfaction to coworkers? You can overcome shyness only by behaving differently; feeling differently is not enough.

2. Appear warm and friendly. Shy people often communicate to others through their body language that they are not interested in reaching out to others. To overcome this impression, smile, lean forward, uncross your arms and legs, and unfold your hands.

3. Make legitimate telephone calls to strangers. Telephone conversations with strangers that have a legitimate purpose can help you start expressing yourself to people you do not know well. You might call numbers listed in classified ads to inquire about articles listed for sale. Try a positive approach: "Hello, my name is _____. I'd like to know about the condition of that piano you have for sale." Call the gas and electric company to inquire about a problem with your bill. Make telephone inquiries about employment opportunities in a firm of your choice. Call the library with reference questions. Call the federal government bureau in your town with questions about laws and regulations. With practice, you will probably become more adept at speaking to strangers. You will then be ready for a more challenging self-improvement task.

4. Conduct anonymous conversations. Try starting a conversation with strangers in a safe setting such as a sporting event, the waiting room of a medical office, or a waiting line at the post office or supermarket. Begin the conversation with the common experience you are sharing at the time. Among them might be:

"How many people do you estimate are in the audience?"

"How long does it usually take before you get to see the doctor?"

"Where did you get that shopping bag? I've never seen one so sturdy before."

5. Greet strangers. For the next week or so, greet many of the people you pass. Smile and make a neutral comment such as "How ya doing?" or "Great day, isn't it." Since most people are unaccustomed to being greeted by a stranger, you may get a few quizzical looks. Many other people may smile and return your greeting. A few of these greetings may turn into conversations. A few conversations may even turn into friendships. Even if the return on your investment in greetings is only a few pleasant responses, it will boost your confidence.

HUMAN RELATIONS SKILL-BUILDING EXERCISE 7-3

Becoming More Assertive by Being Decisive

An important part of being assertive is to be decisive. To enhance your decisiveness, follow these steps:

1. Make a list of the requests people make of you that are a burden. Review the list and select one or two requests that you will refuse in the next week. Think about how you will politely but firmly inform someone of your need to say "no," then carry out your plan. What happened? Did you feel less guilty than you thought you would?

2. Review the requests you want to make of others to help you meet your own needs. Select one or two. Get clear in your mind what you specifically want. Formulate each request so that it is as reasonable as possible for the person you will ask, then make your request(s). Did you get a positive response? Are you happy with the support you obtained?

SOURCE: Adapted from Mel Silberman, with Freda Hansburg, *PeopleSmart: Developing Your Interpersonal Intelligence* (San Francisco: Berrett-Koehler Publishers, 2000), pp. 90–91.

6. Practice being decisive. An assertive person is usually decisive, so it is important to practice being decisive. Some nonassertive people are even indecisive when asked to make a choice from a restaurant memo. They communicate their indecisiveness by asking their friend, "What are you going to have?" or asking the server, "Could you please suggest something for me?" or "What's good?" Practice quickly sizing up the alternatives in any situation and reaching a decision. This will help you be assertive and also project an image of assertiveness. Human Relations Skill-Building Exercise 7-3 is designed to improve decisiveness.

▲ SUMMARY

Conflict occurs when two sets of demands, goals, or motives are incompatible. Such differences often lead to a hostile or antagonistic relationship between people. A conflict can also be considered a dispute, feud, or controversy.

Among the reasons for widespread conflict are (1) competition for limited resources; (2) the generation gap and personality clashes; (3) aggressive personalities including bullies; (4) culturally diverse teams; (5) competing work and family demands; and (6) sexual harassment. Many companies have programs to help their employees reduce work–family conflict including flexible work schedules and dependent care. Such programs increase productivity. Sexual harassment is of two types: quid pro quo (a demand for sexual favors in exchange for job benefits) and creating a hostile environment. It is important for workers to understand what actions and words constitute sexual harassment and how to deal with the problem.

The benefits of conflict include the emergence of talents and abilities, constructive innovation and change, and increased unity after the conflict is settled. Among the detrimental consequences of conflict are physical and mental health problems, wasted resources, the promotion of self-interest, and workplace violence.

Techniques for resolving conflicts with others include the following:

1. Confrontation and problem solving leading to win-win—get to the root of the problem and resolve it systematically. The intention of confrontation and problem solving is to arrive at a collaborative solution to the conflict.

2. Disarm the opposition—agree with the criticizer and enlist his or her help.

3. Cognitive restructuring—mentally converting negative aspects into positive ones by looking for the positive elements in a situation.

4. Appeal to a third party (such as a government agency).

5. The grievance procedure (a formal organizational procedure for dispute resolution).

6. Engage in metacommunications—talk about your conflict and differences in communication.

7. Use negotiation and bargaining tactics.

Negotiation and bargaining tactics include (1) creating a positive negotiating climate; (2) allowing room for compromise but being reasonable; (3) focusing on interests, not positions; (4) making a last and final offer; (5) role-playing to predict what the other side will do; and (6) allowing for face-saving.

Several of the techniques for resolving conflict require assertiveness, or stating clearly what you want and how you feel in a given situation. Being assertive also helps you develop good relationships with people and get more of what you want in life. People can become more assertive and less shy by using techniques such as (1) setting a goal; (2) appearing warm and friendly; (3) conducting legitimate phone conversations with strangers; (4) greeting strangers; and (5) practicing being decisive.

Questions and Activities

1. Why are conflict resolution skills considered so important in a culturally diverse workplace?

2. Give an example from your own life of how competition for limited resources can breed conflict.

3. Some conflicts go on for decades without being resolved, such as groups in North America fighting the government over the right to fish for lobsters where and when they want. Why is it so difficult to resolve such conflicts?

4. Many male managers who confer with a female worker in their offices leave the door open to avoid any charges of sexual harassment. Are these managers using good judgment, or are they being overly cautious?

5. Why is it that during a game, professional athletes touch, hug, and kiss each other yet such behavior is frowned on or forbidden in other workplaces, such as the office or factory?

6. Identify several occupations in which conflict resolution skills are particularly important.

7. How might a person use cognitive restructuring to help deal with the conflict of having received a below-average raise yet expecting an above-average raise?

8. What is your explanation of the research showing that role-playing a negotiation scenario helps people make more accurate predictions about the outcome of conflicts? (You might find some information in Chapter 6 about communications that would provide a possible clue.)

9. You are dining in an expensive restaurant with a special person in your life. A person seated at the next table starts making a series of calls, in a loud voice, on his cell telephone. You and your partner are upset about the calls interrupting your romantic dinner. Make up an assertive statement to tell the phone caller how you feel.

10. Ask a successful person how much conflict he or she experiences in balancing the demands of work and personal life. Be prepared to report your findings in class.

INTERNET SKILL BUILDER: Negotiating for a Raise or Other Benefit

To acquire several concepts that you might use to enhance your negotiating skills, visit www.negotiationskills.com/workplace.html. You will be advised to prepare for negotiation in the future by first building a good relationship with the boss and understanding your value to the organization. After reviewing the information about negotiating for a raise and negotiating a situation with a coworker, jot down two key points you have learned. How do these concepts compare to the ideas presented about negotiation in the text?

HUMAN RELATIONS CASE PROBLEM

Caught in a Squeeze

Heather Lopez is a product development specialist at a telecommunications company. For the last seven months she has worked as a member of a product development team composed of people from five different departments within the company. Heather's previously worked full time in the marketing department. Her primary responsibilities were to research the market potential of an idea for a new product. The product development team is now working on a product that will integrate a company's printers and copiers.

Heather's previous position in the marketing department was a satisfactory fit for her lifestyle. Heather thought that she was able to take care of her family responsibilities and her job without sacrificing one for the other. As Heather explains, "I worked about 45 predictable hours in my other job. My hours were essentially 8:30 A.M. to 4:30 P.M. with a little work at night and on Saturdays. But I could do the work at night and on Saturdays at home.

"Brad, my husband, and I had a smooth-working arrangement for sharing the responsibility for getting our son Christopher off to school and picking him up from the after-school child care center. Brad is a devoted accountant, so he understands the importance of giving high priority to a career yet still being a good family person."

In her new position as a member of the product-development team, Heather is encountering some unanticipated demands. Three weeks ago, at 3 P.M. on a Tuesday, Tyler Watson, Heather's team leader, announced an emergency meeting to discuss a budget problem with the new product. The meeting would start at 4 and probably end at about 6:30. "Don't worry folks," said the team leader, "if it looks like we are going past 6:30, we will order in some Chinese food."

With a look of panic on her face, Heather responded to Tyler, "I can't make the meeting. Christopher will be expecting me at about 5 at the child care center. My husband is out of town, and the center closes at 6 sharp. So count me out of today's meeting."

Tyler said, "I said that this is an emergency meeting and that we need input from all the members. You need to organize your personal life better to be a contributing member to this team. But do what you have to do, at least this once."

Heather chose to leave the office at 4:30 so she could pick up Christopher. The next day, Tyler did not comment on her absence. However, he gave her a copy of the minutes and asked for her input. The budget problem surfaced again one week later. Top-level management asked the group to reduce the cost of the new product and its initial marketing costs by 15 percent.

Tyler said to the team on a Friday morning, "We have until Monday morning to arrive at a reduced cost structure on our product development. I am dividing up the project into segments. If we meet as a team Saturday morning at 8, we should get the job done by 6 at night. Get a good night's rest so we can start fresh tomorrow morning. Breakfast and lunch will be on the company."

Heather could feel stress overwhelming her body, as she thought to herself, "Christopher is playing in the finals of his Little League soccer match tomorrow morning at 10. Brad has made dinner reservations for 6, so we can make it to the *Phantom*

(Continued)

of the Opera at 8 P.M. Should I tell Tyler he is being unreasonable? Should I quit? Should I tell Christopher and Brad that our special occasions together are less important than a Saturday business meeting?"

Questions

1. What type of conflicts is Heather facing?

2. What should Heather do to resolve her conflicts with respect to family and work responsibilities?

3. What should the company do to help deal with the type of conflict Heather is facing? Or should the company not consider Heather's dilemma to be their problem?

WEB CORNER

Cognitive restructuring:
www.garyflegal.com/cognitive_restructuring.htm

Shyness: www.shyness.com

HUMAN RELATIONS SKILL-BUILDING EXERCISE 7-4

Conflict Resolution

Imagine that Heather in the case just presented, decides that her job is taking too big a toll on her personal life. However, she still values her job and does not want to quit. She decides to discuss her problem with her team leader Tyler. From Tyler's standpoint, a professional person must stand ready to meet unusual job demands and cannot expect an entirely predictable work schedule. One person plays the role of Heather and another the role of Tyler as they attempt to resolve this incident of work–family conflict.

▲ REFERENCES

1. Kathleen Driscoll, "Manager Must Confront Disrespectful Employee, or Behavior Will Not Improve," *Rochester (NY) Democrat and Chronicle,* May 10, 1995, p. 1D.

2. Deborah Smith, "Strength in Collaboration," *Monitor on Psychology,* December 2001, p. 60.

3. Katharine Mieskowski, "Generation 8##@88##@!!, *Fast Company,* October 1999, pp. 106–108; Lynne C. Lancaster and David Stillman, *When Generations Collide: Who They Are, Why They Clash* (New York: HarperBusiness, 2002).

4. Stillman, *When Generations Collide,* as quoted in Andrea Sachs, "Generation Hex?" *Time,* March 2002, p. Y22.

5. Dominic A. Infante, *Arguing Constructively* (Prospects Heights, IL: Waveland Press, 1992).

6. Survey reported in Jessica Guynn, "Bullying Behavior Affects Morale as Well as Bottom Line," Knight-Ridder, November 2, 1998.

7. Gillian Flynn, "Employers Can't Look Away from Workplace Violence," *Workforce,* July 2000, p. 68.

8. Quoted in Sybil Evans, "Conflict Can Be Positive," *HR Magazine,* May 1992, p. 50.

9. Angela Pirisi, "Teamwork: The Downside of Diversity," *Psychology Today,* November/December 1999, p. 18.

10. Virginia Smith Major, Katherine J. Klein, and Mark G. Ehrhart, "Work Time, Work Interference with Family, and Psychological Distress," *Journal of Applied Psychology,* June 2002, pp. 427–436.

11. "When Work and Private Lives Collide," *Workforce,* February 1999, p. 27.

12. Keith H. Hammonds, "Balancing Work and Family," *BusinessWeek,* September 16, 1996, p. 75.

13. Majorie L. Icenogle, Bruce W. Eagle, Sohel Ahaman, and Lisa A. Hanks, "Assessing Perceptions of Sexual Harassment Behaviors in a Manufacturing Environment," *Journal of Business and Psychology,* Summer 2002, pp. 601–616.

14. Kimberly T. Schneider, Suzanne Swan, and Louise F. Fitzgerald, "Job-Related and Psychological Effects of Sexual Harassment in the Workplace: Empirical Evidence in Two Organizations," *Journal of Applied Psychology,* June 1997, p. 406.

15. Theresa M. Glomb, Liberty J. Munson, and Charles L. Hulin, "Structural Equation Models of Sexual Harassment: Longitudinal Explorations and Cross-Sectional Generalizations," *Journal of Applied Psychology,* February 1999, pp. 14–28.

16. Jennifer A. Sommers, Terry L. Schell, and Stephen J. Vodanovich, "Developing a Measure of Individual Differences in Organizational Revenge," *Journal of Business and Psychology,* Winter 2002, pp. 207–222.

17. "Right and Wrong Ways to Manage Conflict," *Manager's Edge,* October 2001, p. 5.

18. Joseph D'O'Brian, "Negotiating with Peers: Consensus, Not Power," *Supervisory Management,* January 1992, p. 4.

19. J. Scott Armstrong, "Forecasting in Conflicts: How to Predict What Your Opponents Will Do," *Knowledge@Wharton,* February 13, 2002.

20. "Use Assertiveness, Not Aggression," *Working Smart,* November 1998, p. 2.

21. Bernardo J. Carducci, *Shyness: A Bold Approach* (New York: Harper-Collins, 1999).

22. Philip Zimbardo, *Shyness: What It Is, What to Do about It* (Reading, MA: Addison-Wesley, 1977), pp. 220–226; Mel Silberman with Freda Hansburg, *PeopleSmart* (San Francisco: Berrett-Koehler Publishers, 2000), pp. 75–76.

▲ ADDITIONAL READING

Blackard, Kirk, and James W. Gibson. *Capitalizing on Conflict: Strategies for Turning Conflict to Synergy in Organizations.* Palo Alto, CA: Davies-Black, 2002.

Cloke, Kenneth, and Joan Goldsmith. *Resolving Conflicts at Work: A Complete Guide for Everyone on the Job.* San Francisco: Jossey-Bass, 2000.

Fisher, Roger, Elizabeth Kopelman, and Andrea Kupfer Schneider. *Beyond Machiavelli: Tools for Coping with Conflict.* Cambridge, MA: Harvard University Press, 2000.

Janove, Jathan W. "Sexual Harassment and the Three Big Surprises." *HR Magazine,* November 2001, pp. 123–130.

Landau, Sy, Barbara Landau, and Daryl Landau. *From Conflict to Creativity: How Resolving Workplace Disagreement Can Inspire Innovation and Productivity.* San Francisco: Jossey-Bass, 2002.

Magley, Vicki J., Charles L. Hulin, Louise F. Fitzgerald, and Mary Denardo. "Outcomes of Self-Labeling Sexual Harassment." *Journal of Applied Psychology,* June 1999, pp. 390–402.

Nugent, Patrick S. "Managing Conflict: Third-Party Interventions for Managers." *Academy of Management Executive,* February 2002, pp. 139–155.

Rosa, Antonio José, and Michael G. Pratt. "Transforming Work-Family Conflict into Commitment in Network Marketing Organizations." *Academy of Management Executive,* August 2003, pp. 395–418.

Segal, Jonathan A. "The 'I Hate You' Defense." *HR Magazine,* October 2002, pp. 125–133.

Winters, Jeffrey. "The Daddy Track: Men Who Take Family Leave May Get Frowned upon at the Office." *Psychology Today,* October 2001, p. 18.

CHAPTER 6

Customer Satisfaction Skills

Learning Objectives

After reading and studying this chapter and doing the exercises you should be able to

1. Enhance your ability to satisfy customers by using general principles of customer satisfaction.
2. Create bonds with present or future customers.
3. Have a plan for dealing effectively with customer dissatisfaction.
4. Understand the contribution of customer service training.

A s Tanya Polanski approached the receptionist counter at the hotel, she was tired, frustrated, and confused. "Everything has gone wrong for me the last two days," she explained to Kathy Chang, the receptionist. "My flight from Moscow arrived 10 hours late. I was delayed at customs for an hour. The man said they were doing a random inspection of passengers, even though I didn't look or act like a terrorist. When I tried to use my credit card at the airport, they told me the computer wasn't working so I had to come back a couple of hours later."

"You certainly have had a difficult couple of days, Ms. Polanski," said Chang. "After you are settled in your room, you will start to feel much better. Let me access your reservations." After checking her computer, Chang said, "There seems to be a little problem here. We do not have reservations for you."

In tears, Polanski said, "Has everything gone crazy in America? I made these reservations three months ago for the Holiday Inn right on this avenue."

"I understand why you are upset. Let's work out this problem together. Could it be that you made reservations at our other Holiday Inn, a little closer to downtown? It's on the same street. I will check into our worldwide reservation system right now."

"You're in luck, Ms. Polanski," said Chang after a few minutes at the terminal. "Your reservations are at our other Holiday Inn, just five blocks away.

I will have our van take you there right away, and I will phone ahead to make sure you get to the front of the line as soon as possible. Enjoy your stay in the United States, and we look forward to seeing you again."

"Thank you, thank you, you have saved my day," replied Polanski.

Discussion Question

1. Which approach to customer satisfaction does this hotel receptionist emphasize?

Maybe the hotel receptionist in question is naturally gifted in interpersonal skills, or maybe she combined the right personality traits with the right training to become a compassionate and helpful hotel receptionist. Either way she has a lesson for workers at all levels in many different types of jobs. Outstanding customer service enhances a company's reputation, and leads to repeat business. This chapter presents information and exercises that can enhance your ability to satisfy both external and internal customers at a high level.

External customers fit the traditional definition and include clients, guests, and patients. External customers can be classified as retail or industrial. The latter represents one company buying from another, such as purchasing steel or a gross of printer cartridges. *Internal customers* are the people you serve within the organization or those who use the output from your job. Also, everyone you depend upon is an internal customer. The emphasis in this chapter is on satisfying external customers. Much of the rest of the book deals with better serving internal customers, because improved interpersonal relationships enhance the satisfaction of work associates.

Customer satisfaction skills are necessary for all workers in contact with customers, including sales representatives, customer service representatives (those who back up sales and take care of customer problems), and store associates. Various aspects of developing customer satisfaction skills are divided into three parts in this chapter: following the general principles of customer satisfaction, bonding with customers, and dealing with customer dissatisfaction. To reflect on your attitudes toward satisfying customers, do Self-Assessment Quiz 12-1.

Learning Objective 1 ▶

FOLLOWING THE GENERAL PRINCIPLES OF CUSTOMER SATISFACTION

Knowing how to satisfy customers is a subset of effective interpersonal relations in organizations. Nevertheless, there are certain general principles that will sharpen your ability to satisfy customers and thereby improve customer retention. This section presents eight key principles for satisfying customers. Remember, however, that satisfaction is considered a minimum expectation. If you do an outstanding job of satisfying customers, they will experience delight, as shown in Figure 12-1.

Customer satisfaction is important for several reasons. Satisfied customers are likely to tell friends and acquaintances about their satisfactory experiences, helping a firm grow its business. In contrast, dissatisfied customers—especially those with an unresolved problem—are likely to tell many people about their dissatisfaction, thus dissuading a large number of people from becoming new customers. Studies indicate that an upset or angry customer tells an average of between 10 and 20 other people about an unhappy experience.[1] Customer satisfaction is also highly valued

SELF-ASSESSMENT QUIZ 12-1

THE CUSTOMER ORIENTATION QUIZ

Directions: Answer each of the following statements about dealing with customers as "mostly true" or "mostly false." The statements relate to your attitudes, even if you lack direct experience in dealing with customers. Your experiences as a customer will also be helpful in responding to the statements.

	Mostly True	Mostly False
1. All work in a company should be geared toward pleasing customers.	_____	_____
2. The real boss in any business is the customer.	_____	_____
3. Smiling at customers improves the chances of making a sale.	_____	_____
4. I would rather find a new customer than attempt to satisfy one who is difficult to please.	_____	_____
5. Dealing with customers is as (or more) rewarding than dealing with coworkers.	_____	_____
6. I enjoy (or would enjoy) helping a customer solve a problem related to the use of my product or service.	_____	_____
7. The best way to get repeat business is to offer steep discounts.	_____	_____
8. In business, your customer is your partner.	_____	_____
9. Dealing directly with customers is (or would be) the most boring part of most jobs.	_____	_____
10. If you have the brand and model the customer wants, being nice to the customer is not so important.	_____	_____
11. A good customer is like a good friend.	_____	_____
12. If you are too friendly with a customer, he or she will take advantage of you.	_____	_____
13. Now that individual consumers and companies can shop online, the personal touch in business is losing importance.	_____	_____
14. Addressing a customer by his or her name helps build a relationship with that customer.	_____	_____
15. Satisfying a customer is fun whether or not it leads to a commission.	_____	_____

Scoring and Interpretation: Give yourself a +1, for each of the following statements receiving a response of "mostly true": 1, 2, 3, 5, 6, 8, 11, 14, and 15. Give yourself a +1 for each of the following statements receiving a response of "mostly false": 4, 7, 9, 10, 12, and 13.

13–15 points: You have a strong orientation toward providing excellent customer service.

8–12 points: You have an average customer service orientation.

1–7 points: You have a below-average orientation toward providing excellent customer service.

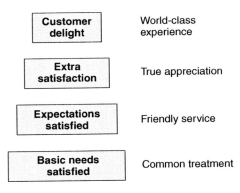

FIGURE 12-1 Levels of Customer Satisfaction

because it breeds customer loyalty, which in turn is very profitable. Repeat business is a success factor in both retail and industrial companies.

Another reason for satisfying customers is the humanitarian aspect. Satisfying people enhances their physical and mental health, whereas dissatisfaction creates negative stress. Have you ever been so angry at poor service that you experienced stress?

BE SATISFIED SO YOU CAN PROVIDE BETTER CUSTOMER SERVICE

Employees who are happy with their jobs are the most likely to satisfy customers. Treating employees well puts them in a better frame of mind to treat their customers well. For example, an extensive case history analysis of Sears found a strong relationship between employee and customer satisfaction. Employees who were satisfied influenced customers to be satisfied, resulting in more purchases and profits.[2] The first statement on the survey can be used to illustrate the basics of the process. The statement is "I like the kind of work I do."

> Employee feels, "I like the kind of work I do." → Smiles at customer and is courteous, → Customer feels positive about Sears → buys a new lawnmower and two pairs of jeans → improves profits for Sears.

Acting alone, you cannot improve company conditions that contribute to job satisfaction. What you can control to some extent, however, is your own attitudes that are related to job satisfaction. A checklist of attitudes and beliefs related to job satisfaction, and over which you can exert some control, follows:

- **Interest in the work itself.** Job satisfaction stems directly from being interested in what you are doing. People who love their work experience high job satisfaction and are therefore in the right frame of mind to satisfy customers.

- **A feeling of self-esteem.** If you have high self-esteem you are more likely to experience high job satisfaction. High-status occupations contribute more to self-esteem than do those of low status. Feelings of self-esteem also stem from doing work the individual sees as worthwhile. This perception is less influenced by external standards than it is the status associated with a particular job or occupation.

- **Optimism and flexibility.** An optimistic and flexible person is predisposed to be a satisfied employee. A pessimistic and rigid person will most likely be a dissatisfied employee. Every company has its share of "pills" who always find something to complain about. Some evidence suggests that a tendency toward optimism versus pessimism is inherited.[3] If you have a predisposition toward pessimism you can still become more optimistic with self-discipline. For example, you can look for the positive aspects of a generally unpleasant situation.

- **Positive self-image.** People possessing a positive self-image are generally more satisfied with their jobs than are those possessing a negative self-image. One explanation is that the people who view themselves negatively tend to view most things negatively. You have to like yourself before you can like your job.

- **Positive expectations about the job.** People with positive expectations about their jobs are frequently more satisfied than are those with low expectations. These expectations illustrate a self-fulfilling prophecy. If you expect to like your job, you will behave in such a way that those expectations will be met. Similarly, if you expect your job not to satisfy your needs, you will do things to make your expectations come true. Assume that a worker expects to earn low commissions in a sales job. The person's negativism may come through to customers and prospective customers, thereby ensuring low customer satisfaction and low commissions.

- **Effective handling of abuse from customers.** Customer service workers are often verbally abused by customers over such matters as products not working, merchandise returns not being acceptable, and the customer having been charged a late fee. Automated telephone-answering systems often force callers to hack through a thicket of prompts before reaching a human being. By the time a live person is reached, the customer is angry and ready to lash out at the customer service representative.[4] To prevent these oral tirades from damaging one's job satisfaction, it is essential to use effective techniques of dealing with criticism and resolving conflict as described in Chapter 7. The section of dealing with dissatisfied customers presented later in this chapter is also important.

High job satisfaction contributes to good customer service in another important way. Employees who are satisfied with their jobs are more likely to engage in service-oriented organizational citizenship behavior. As you will recall, *organizational citizenship behavior* relates to going beyond your ordinary job description to help other workers and the company. A customer service worker with high organizational citizenship behavior will go beyond ordinary expectations to find ways to solve a customer problem.[5] A member of the tech support staff in a consumer electronics store volunteered to drop by a customer's house to help him install a programmable DVD, even though such home visits were not required. As a result of the technician's kindness, the man purchased a $6,000 plasma screen TV receiver from the store.

RECEIVE EMOTIONAL SUPPORT FROM COWORKERS TO GIVE BETTER CUSTOMER SERVICE

Closely related to the idea that satisfied workers can better satisfy customers, is the finding that the emotional support of coworkers often leads to providing better customer service. According to a research study, the support of coworkers is even more important than supervisory support. The participants in the study were 354 customer service workers employed in service-based facilities. Customer satisfaction surveys were collected from 269 customers. The major finding was that employees who perceived their coworkers to be supportive, had a higher level of commitment to their customers.

The researchers concluded that it is important to have a supportive group of coworkers by your side to help you perform service-related duties. In this study, supervisory support was less important than coworker support in terms of bringing about a strong customer orientation. (A *customer service orientation* includes a desire to help customers, and a willingness to act in ways that would satisfy a customer. The hotel receptionist portrayed in the chapter opener exemplifies a service worker with a strong customer orientation.) Another important conclusion drawn from the study was that customer satisfaction was positively associated with the strength of the service worker's customer orientation.[6]

UNDERSTAND CUSTOMER NEEDS AND PUT THEM FIRST

The most basic principle of selling is to identify and satisfy customer needs. One challenge is that many customers may not be able to express their needs clearly. To help identify customer needs, you may have to probe for information. For example, the associate in a camera and video store might ask, "What uses do you have in mind for a video camera?" Knowing such information will help the associate identify which camcorder will satisfy the customer's needs.

The basic idea of satisfying customer needs continues to be expressed in different ways. Recent thinking suggests that highly competitive markets and abundant information (such as searching the Internet for prices) have caused a shift in power from suppliers to customers. Instead of being product centered, successful companies have become customer centered. The idea is to identify profitable customers and then anticipate their priorities.[7] If you satisfy customer needs, you are adding value for them. A person might be willing to pay $10 more per ticket to watch an athletic event if the extra $10 brought a better view and a chair instead of a backless bench. (The better view and more comfortable back add value for the spectator.)

After customer needs have been identified, the focus must be on satisfying those needs rather than the needs of oneself or the company. Assume that the customer says, "The only convenient time for me to receive delivery this week would be Thursday or Friday afternoon." The sales associate should not respond, "On Thursday and Friday our truckers prefer to make morning deliveries." Instead, the associate should respond, "I'll do whatever is possible to accommodate your request."

A major contributor to identifying customer needs is to listen actively to customers. Listening can take place during conversations with customers, and "listening" can also mean absorbing information sent by e-mail and written letters. A policy at Southwest Airlines is that if a customer (or employee) has an idea, a manager must respond instantaneously.[8] For example, Southwest obliged the customer suggestion that more reservation agents be Spanish speaking.

FOCUS ON SOLVING PROBLEMS, NOT JUST TAKING ORDERS

Effective selling uses sales representatives to solve problems rather than merely have them taking orders. An example is the approach taken by sales representatives for Xerox Corporation. Instead of focusing on the sale of photocopiers and related equipment, the sales reps look to help customers solve their information flow problems. The solution could involve selling machines, but it might also involve selling consulting services.

The focus on problem solving enables sales reps to become partners in the success of their customers' businesses. By helping the customer solve problems, the sales rep enhances the value of the supplier–customer relationship to the customer. The customer is receiving consulting services in addition to the merchandise or service being offered. In some situations, a store associate can capitalize on the same principle. If the customer appears unsure about a purchase, ask him or her which problem that the product should solve. The following scenario in a computer store illustrates this point:

Customer: I think I would like to buy this computer. I'm pretty sure it's the one I want. But I don't know too much about computers other than how to use them for word processing, e-mail, and basic search.

Store Associate: I am happy you would like to purchase a computer. But could you tell me what problems you are facing that you want a computer to help you solve?

Customer: Right now I feel I'm not capitalizing on the Internet revolution. I want to do more online, and get into digital photography so I can send cool photos to friends all over. I also want to purchase music online, so I can walk around with an MP3 player like my friends do.

Store Associate: To solve your problem you will need a more powerful computer than the one you are looking at. I would like you to consider another model that is about the same price as the one you have chosen. The difference is that it has the memory you need to e-mail photos and download music from a subscription service.

RESPOND POSITIVELY TO MOMENTS OF TRUTH

An effective customer contact person performs well during situations in which a customer comes in contact with the company and forms an impression of its service. Such situations are referred to as **moments of truth.** If the customer experiences satisfaction or delight during a moment of truth, the customer is likely to return when the need for service arises again. A person who is frustrated or angered during a moment of truth will often not be a repeat customer. A moment of truth is an important part of customer service because what really matters in a service encounter is the customer's perception of what occurred.[9] Visualize a couple that has just dined at an expensive restaurant as part of celebrating their anniversary. The food, wine, and music might have been magnificent, but the couple perceives the service as poor because one of them slipped on ice in the restaurant parking lot.

You can probably visualize many moments of truth in your experiences with service. Reflect on how a store associate treated you when you asked for assistance, the instructions you received when an airplane flight was canceled, or how you were treated when you inquired about financial aid. Each business transaction has its own moment of truth, yet they all follow the same theme of a key interaction between a customer and a company employee.

One way you can track moments of truth is to prepare a cycle-of-service chart, as shown in Figure 12-2. The **cycle-of-service chart** summarizes the moments of truth encountered by a customer during the delivery of a service.[10] To gain insight into these charts, do Skill-Building Exercise 12-1.

BE READY TO ACCEPT EMPOWERMENT

A major strategy for improving customer service is to empower customer contact employees to resolve problems. **Empowerment** refers to managers transferring, or sharing, power with lower ranking employees. In terms of customer relations it means pushing decision making and complaint resolution downward to employees who are in direct contact with customers. The traditional method of dealing with all but the most routine customer problems is for the customer contact worker to refer them to the manager. Many manufacturing firms and service firms now authorize customer contact workers to take care of customer problems within limits. For example, at the Hampton Inn, any worker can offer a guest a free night of lodging to compensate for a service problem.

moments of truth
Situations in which a customer comes in contact with a company and forms an impression of its service.

cycle-of-service chart
A method of tracking the moments of truth with respect to customer service.

empowerment The process of managers transferring, or sharing, power with lower ranking employees.

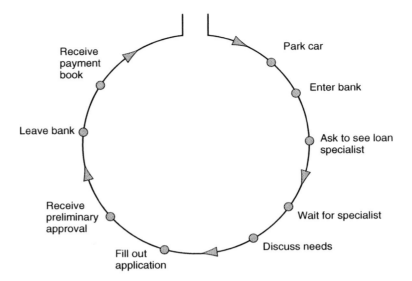

FIGURE 12-2 A Cycle-of-Service Chart for Obtaining a Car Loan at a Bank

Empowerment is not giving away the store, especially because limits are established to the customer contact worker's authority. Empowerment does involve taking a reasonable risk based on company principles to provide meaningful customer service. For empowerment to work, the company must grant decision-making latitude to employees. The employees, in turn, must be willing to accept empowerment (or decision-making authority).[11] Imagine yourself in a customer contact position. For empowerment to work effectively, you should be able to answer affirmatively to the following statements:

- I am willing to arrive at a quick decision as to whether the company or the customer is right.
- I would be willing to admit to a customer that the company has made a mistake.
- I would be willing to take the risk that at times I will lose money for the company on a given transaction.
- I would be comfortable making an out-of-the-ordinary decision about a customer problem without consulting a manager.

 **SKILL-BUILDING EXERCISE 12-1**

MOMENTS OF TRUTH

The class organizes into small groups to discuss what can go right versus what can go wrong during customer moments of truth. First refer to the cycle-of-service chart shown in Figure 12-2. Discuss what can go right or wrong at each moment of truth. Second, have the team develop its own cycle-of-service chart for another service, using its own experiences and imagination. After making the two analyses, discuss the usefulness of a cycle-of-service chart for improving customer satisfaction.

ENHANCE CUSTOMER SERVICE THROUGH INFORMATION TECHNOLOGY

Much has been said and written about how information technology has depersonalized customer service, such as having customers select from a long menu of choices on a telephone. Information technology, however, also plays an important role in recording customer preferences and individualizing service. A major contribution of information technology to enhancing customer service is to develop individualized appeals to customers. With the right software in place, you can make a direct appeal to customer preferences based on past purchases, and the habits of customers with similar preferences. If you have purchased online at a major e-tailer like Amazon.com, you may be familiar with this technology. Two examples follow:

1. Computerized information tells you immediately what the customer on the phone or online has bought in the past, so you may ask a question such as, "Two years ago you installed a centralized vacuum cleaning system. Do you need another set of bags by now?"

2. Speaking to the person, or sending an e-mail message to the customer, you may say, "Last year you purchased a heated doghouse for your Yorkshire terrier. Our information suggests that people who own a heated doghouse are also interested in dog sweaters. Please take a moment to look at our new line of dog sweaters for the canines who appreciate warmth."

Developing individualized appeals to customers is likely to be included in customer relationship management (CRM) software. The complex software is used to implement a strategy of interacting with your customers to bring them more value, and more profits to your firm. One of its basic purposes is to make the company easier for customers to do business with, including facilitating placing orders over the Internet.[112] As such, the individual customer service worker would not have the authority to install such a system. Yet the individual worker can always look for ways to apply the CRM system (such as that provided by Salesforce.com, or SAP) in a way that best serves the customer.

A major challenge in providing good customer service when using information technology is to preserve the human touch. Here are some hints for adding a personal touch to your electronic communications to help build customer loyalty.

Using voice mail

1. Vary your voice tone and inflection when leaving messages and in your greeting to avoid sounding bored or uninterested in your job and the company.

2. Smile while leaving your message—somehow a smile gets transmitted over the telephone wires or optic fibers!

3. Use voice mail to minimize "telephone tag" rather than to increase it. If your greeting specifies when you will return, callers can choose to call again or to leave a message. When you leave a message, suggest a good time to return your call. Another way to minimize telephone tag is to assure the person you are calling that you will keep trying.

4. Place an informative and friendly greeting (outgoing message) on your voice mail. Used effectively, a voice-mail greeting will minimize the number of people irritated by not talking to a person.

5. When you respond to a voice-mail outgoing message, leave specific, relevant information. As in the suggestions for minimizing telephone tag, be specific about why you are calling and what you want from the person called. The probability of receiving a return call increases when you leave honest and useful information. If you are selling something or asking for a favor, be honest about your intent.

6. When leaving your message, avoid the most common voice-mail error by stating your name and telephone number clearly enough to be understood. Most recipients of a message dislike intensely listening to it several times to pick up identifying information.

Using e-mail

1. Use the customer's name. Begin the greeting, "Hello, Lisa King." Many companies now greet customers by their first name only, but some customers consider this practice to be rude. However, few people are likely to be offended when you use both their first and last names.

2. Choose a human e-mail address. Marysmith@kaset.com feels more personal than an odd sequence of numbers, letters, and dashes. To enhance your credibility and professional stature, avoid cool electronic addresses such as Steelabs@aol.com or Angellady42@gmail.com.

3. Be conversational. Mention events you have shared, such as "I enjoyed seeing you at the company meeting."

4. Sign your name. Don't neglect your signature. "Best regards, Jim Woods."[13]

AVOID RUDENESS AND HOSTILITY TOWARD CUSTOMERS

I have reserved the most frequently violated principle of good customer service for last: Avoid being rude or hostile to customers. Although rudeness to customers is obviously a poor business practice, the problem is widespread. Rudeness by customer contact personnel is a major problem from the employer's standpoint. Rude treatment creates more lost business than does poor product quality or high prices. Several years ago McDonald's franchises were facing a downturn in sales. Surveys indicated that one of the problems facing McDonald's Corporation was the indifferent and rude behavior by many frontline workers. McDonald's then increased the training of store employees and upgraded the menu, to achieve a substantial rebound in sales. The Bojangles restaurant chain uses a direct appeal to employees to prevent and reduce rudeness. To remind employees who really pays their salaries, the restaurant prints this on every paycheck: "This is possible thanks to satisfied customers."[14]

Rudeness is sometimes a form of hostility because rudeness, such as grimacing at a customer, stems from anger. Being outright hostile toward customers can be a bigger problem than rudeness, which is more subtle. The impact of service provider hostility on customer satisfaction was explored by studying 142 naturally occurring service interactions at a telephone service center of a bank. A typical interaction would be a customer phoning the bank to inquire about an account balance. Service interactions usually lasted about two minutes. Customers were later contacted to complete a quality survey about their transaction. Hostility was measured through raters' judgment of the tone of the service providers' voices.

A major finding of the study was that when the technical performance (for example, providing the information needed) was low, hostility by the service provider lowered customer satisfaction considerably. When the technical performance of the service provider was good, hostility had a less negative impact on service quality.[15] When you get the information you need from a service provider, you are willing to put up with a few angry tones! The overall message supports a human relations perspective: Being hostile toward customers lowers their perception of the quality of service.

To elevate your awareness level about rudeness among customer contact personnel, do Self-Assessment Quiz 12-2.

SELF-ASSESSMENT QUIZ 12-2

AM I BEING RUDE?

Directions: Following is a list of behaviors that would be interpreted as rude by many customers. Check "Yes" if you have engaged in such behavior in your dealings with customers or if you would be *likely* to do so if your job involved customer contact, and "No" if you would not engage in such behavior.

	Yes	No
1. I talk to a coworker while serving a customer.	___	___
2. I conduct a telephone conversation with someone else while serving a customer.	___	___
3. I address customers by their first names without having their permission.	___	___
4. I address customers as "You guys."	___	___
5. I chew gum or eat candy while dealing with a customer.	___	___
6. I laugh when customers describe an agonizing problem they are having with one of our company's products or services.	___	___
7. I minimize eye contact with customers.	___	___
8. I say the same thing to every customer, such as "Have a nice day," in a monotone.	___	___
9. I accuse customers of attempting to cheat the company before carefully investigating the situation.	___	___
10. I hurry customers when my breaktime approaches.	___	___
11. I comment on an attractive customer's appearance in a flirtatious, sexually oriented way.	___	___
12. I sometimes complain about or make fun of other customers when I am serving a customer.	___	___
13. I sometimes use my cell phone to talk to another person while serving a customer.	___	___

Interpretation: The more of these behaviors you have engaged in, the ruder you are and the more likely it is that you are losing potential business for your company. If you have not engaged in any of these behaviors, even when faced with a rude customer, you are an asset to your employer. You are also tolerant.

CREATING A BOND WITH YOUR CUSTOMER ◀ Learning Objective 2

Another key perspective on achieving customer satisfaction and delight is to create a bond—or emotional relationship—with customers. The rationale is that if you form warm, constructive relationships with your customers, they will keep buying. Staying focused on the importance of customers will help provide the motivation for forming such a bond. The willingness to form a bond with the customer is part of having a strong customer orientation, defined as "a set of basic individual predispositions and an inclination to provide service, to be courteous and helpful in dealing with customers and associates."[16] You may recall Self-Assessment Quiz 12-1 about customer orientation at the outset of the chapter. Service-oriented organizational citizenship behavior relates to the same idea of focusing on customer needs.

Creating a bond is aimed at increasing sales, but it also enhances service. If the customer relies on and trusts the sales representative, the customer will perceive the service to be of high quality. Similarly, people perceive medical and legal services to be of high quality if they trust the physician or lawyer. Virtually all of the principles and techniques presented in this chapter will help form a bond with customers. However, six key principles are as follows:

1. Create a welcoming attitude, including a smile.
2. Provide exceptional service.
3. Show care and concern.
4. Make the buyer feel good.
5. Build a personal relationship.
6. Invite the customer back.

CREATE A WELCOMING ATTITUDE, INCLUDING A SMILE

An effective starting point in creating a customer bond is to use enthusiastic expressions, including a smile, when greeting customers. Attempt to show a sincere, positive attitude that conveys to customers and prospects, "I'm here to make you happy."[17] In addition to being an effective greeting, smiling is also a natural relationship builder and can help you bond with your customer. Smile several times at each customer meeting, even if your customer is angry at your product or service. A camcorder is a useful device for getting feedback on the quality of your smile. Practicing your smile in a mirror might feel a little less natural, but it is still helpful. Smiling at customers has a potential disadvantage, despite its general effectiveness. If your smile is too friendly and inviting, the customer might think that you want to get to know him or her outside the business relationship.

PROVIDE EXCEPTIONAL SERVICE

It's definitely a profitable strategy. When a customer comes in and the person behind the counter says hello, and maybe greets you by name, you feel a connection you don't find with most retailers anymore. It makes you feel welcome, and it makes you want to come back.
—Dave Pace, Starbucks executive vice president of partner resources, quoted in *Workforce Management,* February 2005, p. 30

The best-accepted axiom about keeping customers is to provide exceptional service. Many successful companies contend that their competitive advantage is good service. An important part of the comeback of Burger King in 2005 was a subtle way of providing top service to the company's most profitable demographic group, males between the ages of 18 and 34 who visit the stores three to four times a week. These "Super Fans" want indulgent, fat-laden, high-caloric, tasty food. So Burger King served up the Enormous Omelet Sandwich. CEO Greg Brenneman says he gives his customers what they want, not what others (such as nutritionists and physicians) think they should have.[18]

Exceptional service includes dozens of customer transactions, including prompt delivery, a fair-returns policy, accurate billing, and prompt attention to a customer's presence. Exceptional service also includes giving customers good advice about using the product or service. As shown in Figure 12-1, providing exceptional service leads to customer delight.

SHOW CARE AND CONCERN

During contacts with the customer, the sales representative should show concern for the customer's welfare. The rep should ask questions such as: "How have you enjoyed the optical scanner you bought awhile back?" "How much time and money have you saved since you installed the new system?" After asking the questions, the sales rep should project a genuine interest in the answer.

MAKE THE BUYER FEEL GOOD

A fundamental way of keeping a relationship going is to make the buyer feel good about himself or herself. In addition, the customer should be made to feel good because of having bought from the representative. Offer compliments about the customer's appearance or about a report that specified vendor requirements clearly. An effective feel-good line is: "I enjoy doing business with you."

BUILD A PERSONAL RELATIONSHIP

Building a good working relationship with a customer often leads to a positive personal relationship. A bold approach is to do the reverse—build a working relationship based on an authentic personal relationship. You gather personal facts about the interests of your customers and then appeal to those interests. A case history of a bank manager, Jack Foxboro, shows the potential effectiveness of this technique.

> *Several years ago Foxboro was a commercial loan officer. He acquired a base of existing accounts from the previous officer and gradually increased his base. Jack invested considerable time telephoning and sending e-mails to existing loan holders. He collected facts about them, such as birthdays, the names of family members, golf handicaps, hobbies, and favorite sports teams. Jack entered all this information into a database.*
>
> *Jack would send cards to customers in recognition of their birthdays and special accomplishments. When a customer visited the bank to talk about an existing loan or to apply for a new one, he would retrieve relevant personal facts from the database. Jack's clients were so impressed that he enlarged existing accounts and received substantial referral business.*

A high-tech way of building relationships with large numbers of customers is to interact with them through company *blogs,* or Web logs. The company representative is authorized to chat with hundreds of customers and potential customers by placing informal comments on the Web log in a manner similar to a personal diary. The worker lets out tidbits of information to customers without betraying company confidences or making defamatory statements about the company. However, the blog entries are not usually as positive as advertisements, which help form bonds with the customers. Many customers post replies and swap ideas with the company rep. Company-approved blogs are growing rapidly, as customers demand information presented in a more unvarnished way. A major advantage of blogs is that they humanize large organizations, such as the company representative mentioning a favorite recipe as well as chatting about a new product.[19]

Back to the Opening Case

The hotel receptionist appears to be doing everything right in terms of satisfying this frazzled guest. She shows care and concern for the customer's problem, and then engages in mutual problem solving.

INVITE THE CUSTOMER BACK

The southern U.S. expression "Y'all come back, now!" is well suited for bonding with customers. Specific invitations to return may help increase repeat business. The more focused and individualized the invitation, the more likely it will have an impact on customer behavior. ("Y'all come back, now!" is sometimes used too indiscriminately to be effective.) Pointing out why you enjoyed doing business with the customer, and what future problems you could help with, is an effective technique.

SKILL-BUILDING EXERCISE 12-2

BONDING WITH CUSTOMERS

Role-players in this exercise will demonstrate two related techniques for bonding with customers: show care and concern and make the buyer feel good.

Scenario 1: Show Care and Concern. A sales representative meets with two company representatives to talk about installing a new information system for employee benefits. One of the company reps is from the human resources department and the other is from the information systems department. The sales rep will attempt to show care and concern for both company representatives during the same meeting.

Scenario 2: Make the Buyer Feel Good. A couple, played by two role-players, enter a new-car showroom to examine a model they have seen advertised on television. Although they are not in urgent need of a new car, they are strongly interested. The sales representative is behind quota for the month and would like to close a sale today. The rep decides to use the tactic "make the buyer feel good" to help form a bond.

An industrial cleaning company supervisor might say, "Our crew enjoyed cleaning such a fancy office. Keep us in mind when you would like your windows to sparkle."

Despite the importance of forming a bond with your customer, getting too personal can backfire. Most customers want a business relationship with the company, and are not looking for a personal relationship with a company representative. As Daniel Askt observes, "Most customers want value and service without contending that a salesman who insists that he wants to be like family to you. Chances are you've already got a family, and for most of us, one is enough."[20]

Skill-Building Exercise 12-2 gives you an opportunity to practice techniques for bonding with customers.

Learning Objective 3 ▶

DEALING WITH CUSTOMER DISSATISFACTION

Most companies put honest effort into preventing customer dissatisfaction. In addition to employing many of the principles and techniques already cited, many companies routinely survey customers to detect problem areas that could lead to dissatisfaction. A representative survey is shown in Figure 12-3. Despite all these efforts to achieve total customer satisfaction, some customer dissatisfaction is inevitable. One reason is that mistakes in serving customers are almost inevitable; for example, a piece of equipment may have a faulty component unknown to the seller. A second reason is that some customers have a predisposition to complain. They will find something to complain about with respect to any product or service.

Dealing openly with dissatisfaction and complaints can improve both customer retention and sales. One study found that 63 percent of dissatisfied customers who fail to complain will not buy from the company again. Given a chance to complain and have their problem resolved, 90 percent will remain loyal customers.[21]

An important point to remember in dealing with dissatisfied customers is that the negative personality traits of customers can bring down your level of customer service.

How are we doing?
Dick's Clothing & Sporting Goods

Name (optional) _____   Address _____

Phone number _____   City _____

Date and time of visit _____   Name of associate who helped you _____

	Excellent	Good	Average	Needs improvement	Poor
Prompt and courteous greeting	☐	☐	☐	☐	☐
Knowledgeable salespeople	☐	☐	☐	☐	☐
Store cleanliness	☐	☐	☐	☐	☐
Store displays	☐	☐	☐	☐	☐
Prices	☐	☐	☐	☐	☐
Speedy checkouts	☐	☐	☐	☐	☐
How do you rate us overall?	☐	☐	☐	☐	☐

	Newspaper	TV	Radio	Other
What brought you to Dick's?	☐	☐	☐	☐

Did you make a purchase? _____

Items you wanted that we did not have? _____

General comments: _____

FIGURE 12–3 A Retail Store Customer Satisfaction Survey

Source: Dick's Clothing and Sporting Goods. Customer satisfaction survey. Reprinted with permission.

For example, a study conducted in two major fast-food chains in Singapore found that customers who scored high on the trait of agreeableness, tended to bring out positive emotion by the service personnel. In contrast, customers who scored high on negative affectivity (being disagreeable) brought out negative emotion among customer service personnel.[22] A service worker cannot change the personality traits of customers, yet a little self-management of emotion is in order. The service worker might say to himself or herself, "I won't let this nasty customer get me down. I will do my best to do my job without overreacting." Be careful not to fake your emotion too frequently because it can create stress. Instead be assertive with a comment like, "I want to help you, but might you tell me what you want in a more positive way?"

The next subsections describe three approaches to handling customer dissatisfaction: dealing with complaints and anger, involving the customer in working out a problem, and handling an unreasonable request.

DEAL CONSTRUCTIVELY WITH CUSTOMER COMPLAINTS AND ANGER

In an era when customer satisfaction is so highly valued, both retail and industrial customers are likely to be vocal in their demands. When faced with an angry customer, use one or more of the following techniques recommended by customer satisfaction specialists.[23]

1. **Acknowledge the customer's point of view.** Make statements such as "I understand," "I agree," and "I'm sorry." Assume, for example, a customer says, "The accounts payable department made a $1,000 overcharge on my account last month. I want this fixed right away." You might respond, "I understand how annoying this must be for you. I'll work on the problem right away."

2. **Avoid placing blame on the customer.** Suggesting that the customer is responsible for the problem intensifies the conflict. With the customer who claims to have been overcharged, refrain from saying: "Customers who keep careful account of their orders never have this problem."

3. **Use six magic words to defuse anger.** The magic words are *I understand* [that this is a problem], *I agree* [that it needs to be solved], and *I'm sorry* [that this happened to you].

4. **Apologize for the problems created by you or your company.** To recover from a breakdown in customer service, it is best to acknowledge an error immediately. Apologies are most effective when stated in the first person (such as "I created the problem"). The corporate "we're sorry" sounds less sincere than when one specific person accepts responsibility for what went wrong. Professional workers at the Kaiser Permanente HMO receive training in how to apologize to patients for medical errors. It has been found that sincere apologies can significantly reduce the cost of settling lawsuits, and may even convince unhappy patients not to sue at all. A sincere apology includes a statement of what the apologizer is going to do to fix the problem.[24]

5. **Take responsibility, act fast, and be thorough.** This technique is a simplified framework for managing customer dissatisfaction. As illustrated by Mark Delp, the manager of a fleet maintenance service, "Suppose a customer calls about an oil leak after Fleet Response services a car. I have the car immediately picked up from his office and clean any oil spots that may have been left on the driveway. I make sure there are no further leaks. Furthermore, I apologize and accept full responsibility, even if the problem is not our fault, such as when a part fails."[25]

6. **Tell the difficult customers how much you value them.** Quite often customers with problems feel unappreciated. Just before resolving the problem of a difficult customer, explain how important he or she is to your firm. You might say, "We value your business, so I want to correct this for you quickly."[26] (Of course, you would value the customer even more after he or she becomes less difficult.)

7. **Follow up on the problem resolution.** Following up to see whether the resolution to the problem is satisfactory brings closure to the incident. The follow-up also helps the service deliverer know that he or she can rebound from an episode of customer dissatisfaction. One useful form of follow-up is to telephone or send an e-mail to the customer whose problem was solved. For example, a representative from the service department of an automobile dealership might telephone a customer whose new car required substantial warranty repairs. "Hello, this is Jill Gordon from Oak Automotive. We replaced your original transmission last month. How is the new transmission working?"

A less personal, and usually less effective, form of follow-up is to send a customer satisfaction questionnaire to the person with the problem. The questionnaire will often be interpreted as a company procedure that does not reflect specific concern about the individual's problem.

INVOLVE THE CUSTOMER IN WORKING OUT THE PROBLEM

Mistakes and problems in serving customers are inevitable regardless of how hard service workers strive for perfection. To minimize the perception of poor service, the customer must be involved in deciding what should be done about the problem. By being involved in the solution to the problem, the customer is more likely to accept a deviation from the service promised originally. The ideal condition is for the customer service representative and dissatisfied customer to work as partners in resolving the problem. The following case history illustrates the technique of customer involvement and partnering.

> *Seth Bradbury is a sales promotion specialist at an advertising agency. A furniture store hired the agency to prepare and mail 3,000 postcards advertising a new line of furniture. One side of the postcard contained a photograph of the furniture, and the other side contained product details and space for addressing and stamping the card. After the cards were mailed, Seth received an urgent call from the client. "The photograph of the furniture is printed vertically. It looks horrible. We agreed on a horizontal shot. This means 3,000 cards have been mailed with a mistake."*
>
> *After allowing the client to finish his complaint, Seth responded, "You're right, it is a vertical shot. Perhaps we misinterpreted your directions. However, I think your furniture still looks beautiful. The extra white space the vertical shot provides creates an interesting effect. It's unfortunate that the cards have already been mailed. What would you like us to do? It's important that you are satisfied."*
>
> *The client responded, "I guess there is nothing we can do to change the photograph. Would you be willing to give us a discount off the price we agreed on?"*

ANTICIPATE HOW TO HANDLE AN UNREASONABLE REQUEST

No matter how hard the customer contact worker attempts to provide outstanding customer service, at some point a customer comes along with an unreasonable request—or the customer may raise an unfair objection. Speak to any experienced store associate to obtain a case history of a "customer from Hell." For example, a small-business owner demanded that a store associate grant him exchange credit for six printer cartridges. The cartridges were purchased four years previously and were now obsolete.

Recognize that the customer who makes an unreasonable demand is usually aware of the unreasonableness. The customer may not expect to be fully granted the request. Instead, the customer is bargaining by beginning with an unreasonable demand. The small-business owner who brought in the cartridges was probably looking to salvage whatever he could.

Sales representatives and other customer contact workers who stand their ground with dignity and courtesy generally will not lose customers with unreasonable requests. These suggestions will help you deal with unreasonable demands while retaining the customer's business.[27]

- Let your customers retain their dignity by stating your position politely and reasonably.

- Avoid arguing with an upset customer. As the adage says, "You never win an argument with a customer."

- Appeal to your customer's sense of fair play and integrity. Explain that your intention is to do what is right and fair.

- Be firm by repeating the facts of the situation, but keep your temper under control.

- Accept responsibility for your decision rather than blaming company policy or your manager. Making somebody else the villain may intensify the problem.
- Be willing to say no to a customer when it is justifiable. Saying yes to an outrageous demand opens the door for a series of outrageous demands.

MAINTAIN A REALISTIC CUSTOMER RETENTION ATTITUDE

Some customers are too unreasonable, and therefore may not be worth keeping.[28] A realistic goal is to retain as many profitable customers as possible. An extreme example of a customer not worth keeping is the airline passenger who engages in *air rage*. Symptoms of air rage include (1) insisting on being served more alcoholic beverages than permissible by airline regulations, (2) sexually harassing or physically attacking flight attendants or other passengers, (3) refusing to fasten their seat belts, (4) using electronic gear such as cell phones and laptop computers when not allowed by regulations, (5) smoking in the lavatory, and (6) using the aisles for a lavatory.

It is best to set limits for unruly customers and see if their behavior changes. If the customer insists on creating disturbances, it is best to suggest the customer never return. Another problem is that some customers require so much service, or demand such high discounts, that they are unprofitable to retain. Good service to these customers means there is less time available to respond to the needs of profitable customers.

Dealing diplomatically and effectively with difficult customers requires an awareness of the types of tactics described in the previous several pages. Practice on the firing line is indispensable. The type of experience provided by Skill-Building Exercise 12-3 is helpful.

 **SKILL-BUILDING EXERCISE 12-3**

DEALING WITH DIFFICULT CUSTOMERS

The following scenarios require one person to play the role of the customer contact worker and another person to play the difficult customer. As usual, the role-players project their feelings into the role-play by imagining how they would behave in the situation.

Scenario 1: One person is a store associate in a high-fashion women's clothing store. A woman who bought a $1,000 gown the previous week brings back the gown today. She claims that she is returning the gown because it doesn't fit comfortably. The store associate strongly suspects the woman bought the gown originally with the intent of wearing it for a special occasion and then returning it.

Scenario 2: One person plays the role of a customer service representative in a consumer-electronics store. Another person plays the role of a customer who purchased a $3,500 giant-screen television receiver three months ago. He comes up to the service rep's counter ranting about the store's ineptitude. The customer claims that the TV has broken down three times. After the first repair, the TV worked for two weeks and then broke down again. The second repair lasted two weeks, only for the TV to break down during a Super Bowl party at his house. The customer is red in the face and shouting loudly. The service rep wants to resolve the customer's problem and prevent him from bad-mouthing the store.

CUSTOMER SERVICE TRAINING AT A LUXURY HOTEL CHAIN

◀ Learning Objective 4

The information and exercises already presented in this chapter have provided you with an appreciation of the nature of customer service training. (Such training should result in the development of customer satisfaction skills.) To help reinforce this information, portions of an interview follow with Leonardo Inghilleri, the senior vice president of human resources for the Ritz-Carlton Hotel Company.[29] The company attributes much of the success of its 35 hotels to rigorous customer service training. Observe also how the Ritz-Carlton takes into account individual and cultural differences in achieving excellent customer service.

Author: Why does Ritz-Carlton feel it's important that every one of its nearly 16,000 employees undergo rigorous customer service training?

Inghilleri: Customers who come to our hotel pay a premium for perfection. We have the tremendous challenge to meet and exceed customer expectations. That's why we discuss customer service every single day of our lives. It starts with how we select our employees. We use scientific interviews to understand if an individual has the necessary behavioral traits to make him or her successful in our company. Only 1 of every 10 applicants is hired.

Author: What sort of traits? And how do you "scientifically" determine if a prospective employee has these traits?

Inghilleri: A person who works for us has to be hospitable, quality oriented, attentive to details, and so on. We've identified the top performers by job (waiters, chefs, housekeepers, etc.), and with the help of a psychological test we're able to determine the ideal profile for each specific job. If you want to be a successful housekeeper, for example, you have to have certain talents; and if you don't have these traits, you're not going to be hired. There also has to be the desire to use your talents, which a lot of people don't have. We interview each one of our employees in a scientific way to understand if that person possesses specific talents.

Author: How are the 120 hours of customer service training actually divvied up?

Inghilleri: It depends. Our entire training system is a combination of two key elements: technical skills and the Ritz-Carlton customer service philosophy. By technical training I mean how to serve in a fine-dining restaurant or how to make a bed according to standards. There may be 19 steps to making a bed. Until you make those beds perfectly, you're not going to earn a certification.

Customer service training is a little more complicated. We train our people how to resolve guest challenges. After all, it's an imperfect business we're in, and a lot of things that can go wrong will go wrong. A television at a certain point might break down. You have to train your people to instantly pacify our guests.

Author: What sort of financial and time commitments are we talking about here?

Inghilleri: It's a huge investment on our side. Think about it: Every employee spends 15 minutes every day in a meeting. Some might see this as a 15-minute loss of productivity, but we believe these are the most valuable 15 minutes of the day. We use this time to recognize and celebrate people, and create a sense of belonging.

Author: What exactly do your employees come away with after 120 or more hours of customer service training?

Inghilleri: From the training, they become professionals in the hospitality industry. In this industry, you're either a professional or you're a servant.

Making beds and cleaning toilets and serving meals are professions if they are done with pride. We create professional employees who have the desire to provide exceptional customer service, and who want to be part of our company.

Author: Does the fact that you have 35 hotels all over the world cause any sort of cultural problems when hiring and training employees in a customer service industry?

Inghilleri: We had to focus a lot on the cultural aspects. Every single culture has its own sense of hospitality. In Bali, we will not ask our ladies and gentlemen to say good morning and good afternoon. Instead, they'll greet in the traditional way by joining hands and bowing. We try to identify what makes that specific country special from a hospitality point of view. And then we adapt to its citizens' way of being hospitable.

Every Ritz-Carlton worker learns to "own the problem." This translates into each worker being empowered to spend up to $2,000 at any time to address any customer's complaint.

The type of customer service training just described is a vehicle for achieving customer satisfaction. Customer service training in other industries, such as retailing or telecommunications, might have different content, but the principles are similar.

SUMMARY

Many companies today emphasize total customer satisfaction because it leads to goodwill, repeat business, and referrals. Customer satisfaction skills are necessary for all workers in contact with customers. Eight key principles for satisfying and delighting customers are as follows:

1. Be satisfied so you can provide better customer service. (Some of your own attitudes, such as optimism and flexibility, influence your job satisfaction.)
2. Receive emotional support from coworkers so you can give better customer service.
3. Understand customer needs and put them first.
4. Focus on solving problems, not just taking orders.
5. Respond positively to moments of truth (points at which the customer forms an impression of company service).
6. Be ready to accept empowerment. (Being empowered enables you to solve customer problems.)
7. Enhance customer service through information technology.
8. Avoid rudeness and hostility toward customers. (Rude and hostile treatment of customers creates lost business.)

Another key perspective on achieving customer satisfaction and delight is to create a bond—or emotional relationship—with customers. Almost any act of good customer service helps create a bond, but six principles are highlighted here:

1. Create a welcoming attitude, including a smile.
2. Provide exceptional service.
3. Show care and concern.
4. Make the buyer feel good.

5. Build a personal relationship.

6. Invite the customer back.

Despite the best efforts on the company's part, some customer dissatisfaction is inevitable. One approach to dealing with customer dissatisfaction is to deal constructively with customer complaints and anger. Tactics for achieving this end include the following:

1. Acknowledge the customer's point of view.

2. Avoid placing blame on the customer.

3. Use six magic words to defuse anger.

4. Apologize for the problem created by you or your company.

5. Take responsibility, act fast, and be thorough.

6. Tell the difficult customers how much you value them.

7. Follow up on the problem resolution.

Another approach to dealing with customer dissatisfaction is to involve the customer in working out the problem. The customer contact worker must sometimes deal with an unreasonable request. Remember that the customer probably recognizes that he or she is being unreasonable. Do not argue with an unreasonable customer, but at times you must say no. Maintain a realistic customer retention attitude, meaning that as hard as you try to please, some customers are not worth keeping.

Customer service training encompasses many of the ideas in this chapter. Providing a high level of customer service can be a competitive advantage for a company.

QUESTIONS FOR DISCUSSION AND REVIEW

1. For what reason is a satisfied employee more likely to provide better customer service?

2. Describe a situation in your life when you experienced customer delight. What made the experience delightful?

3. A couple walks into an automobile showroom and say they want a big safe vehicle for them and their three children, yet they are unsure about what vehicle they should purchase. Describe how you might identify customer needs in this situation.

4. Describe several customer moments of truth you have experienced this week. What made you classify them as moments of truth?

5. Visualize yourself as an executive at Target. Develop a policy to empower customer service desk associates to resolve customer problems, including the limits to their empowerment.

6. Identify several typical ways in which customers are rude to customer contact workers.

7. How ethical is it for Burger King to satisfy customers by selling them the Enormous Omelet Sandwich when it contains so much bad cholesterol?

8. What is your opinion of the impact of information technology on customer service? Offer at least two specifics in your answer.

9. Can you identify any ways in which a customer contact worker has made you feel good? If so, provide the details.

10. How effective is the principle "the customer is always right" when dealing with dissatisfied customers?

GO TO THE WEB

AN INTERPERSONAL RELATIONS CASE PROBLEM

REPEAT BUSINESS AT WHOPPER WASH

Jim McNamara worked for 25 years in a variety of sales and marketing positions for a large company. In his last position he was the manager of direct marketing (selling products directly to customers rather than through stores or other intermediaries). As part of a company downsizing, McNamara's position was consolidated with another department's and he was laid off.

McNamara said he was disappointed to lose a good job, but he recognized that dealing with drastic changes in one's life is part of the modern world. He also recognized that at age 50, he was still young enough to pursue a new career and a new lifestyle. McNamara and his wife, Gwen, discussed the situation for many days, and decided to work as partners in a franchise business. Gwen worked part time as a home health aid, so she could find time to help with the business. Many of the best known franchises seemed out of reach for the Mc-Namaras because of start-up prices as high as $500,000.

After several weeks of research the McNamaras decided to purchase a power washing franchise, Whopper Wash, for a start-up fee of $10,000. The company provided the training, including advice on marketing the program. Typical services for power washing would include cleaning house siding, swimming pools, and the sidewalks of small businesses. Jim and Gwen would do the work themselves, including climbing on high ladders to wash the second level of a house.

The McNamaras opened their business officially on June 1 one year later. They placed ads in local newspapers, and had a Web site of their own, *http://www.JimandGwenWhopperWash.com.* Their first 10 orders for power washes were from friends and relatives, with the average price of the wash being $300. The newspaper ads were the most effective in drawing new customers, with the Web site also attracting some customers.

The business grew slowly. In a typical scenario, the McNamaras would show up at the site, get the job done in about two hours, and then receive payment. When Gwen had a conflict in the schedule, Jim would do the job himself. The customer would typically thank them for the service, and then say goodbye. Given the opportunity, either Jim or Gwen would attempt to engage the customer in light conversation. Gwen developed a standard joke to suggest repeat business. If she noticed that a dog was on the premises, she asked, "Can we power wash your dog next?" Not all pet owners laughed at her comment.

As the McNamaras reviewed their business results after six months, they observed a shortcoming. After completing a job, they would typically recommend that the service be repeated in two years. However, two years is a long time between repeat calls to a customer, the couple thought.

Jim remarked, "We don't have any good way of getting repeat business. I could see that our business could dry up quickly after we take care of most people who want their home or small business power washed. What do you think we can say to customers to get more repeat business?"

Case Questions

1. In what way is this case about customer satisfaction?

2. How might the McNamaras form better bonds with their customers?

3. What can this Whooper Wash couple do to get more repeat business?

AN INTERPERSONAL RELATIONS CASE PROBLEM

THE TROUBLESOME BIG SCREEN

The Chavez nuclear family consists of Maria, an office manager at a hospital; Tony, an ambulance medic; and their daughter Jennifer, an eighth-grade student. A happy family, they share many activities. Among their joint activities is watching MTV (music television). The family regularly scrunches down to watch their favorite music shows on a 10-year-old, 13-inch color television.

One Thursday evening, Jennifer sighed, "Mom and Dad, I have a great idea. Let's do something exciting with some of your money. Let's buy a giant TV so we can have more fun watching the rock channel."

Maria and Tony thought that Jennifer's idea had merit. However, they both agreed that a giant-screen TV was a luxury item they could ill afford right now. Just before they fell asleep, the issue surfaced again. Maria said to Tony, "Deep down, we both agree with Jennifer. For less than $1,000 we could bring much joy into our home."

Friday night the Chavez family visited Appliance City to look at television sets. Maria spotted a 29-inch TV that seemed ideal. A store associate, however, convinced them that the model they were inspecting was of mediocre quality. Instead, he recommended a domestic brand with a 32-inch screen that he claimed was the highest quality model in its class. Spearheaded by Jennifer's exuberance, the Chavez family was convinced. The cost, including a three-year complete service warranty, was $1,157.

The television set was delivered Monday evening as scheduled. For several days the Chavez family enjoyed watching MTV and other favorite programs on their new big-screen set. Friday evening, however, Maria, Tony, and Jennifer were mystified by an image that appeared on their screen. Shortly after Jennifer punched the menu button, an advertisement appeared on the screen touting the features of the set. Among the messages was one indicating that if the owner of this set were in a noisy room, he or she could mute the audio and watch the video.

Tony laughed as he explained that the demonstration mode was somehow triggered, and that the solution would be to just punch a few buttons. Next, he and Maria punched every button on the receiver and the TV remote control. The demonstration mode remained. Tony then pulled the plug and reinserted it, only for the demonstration mode to reappear.

Maria, Tony, and Jennifer then searched the owner's manual, but they found no information about the problem. Maria telephoned the dealer and got through to the service department after six minutes of being placed on hold. The service department said they knew nothing about the problem, but that she should speak to the sales department. After Maria explained her problem to a sales associate, she was told to speak to the service department.

Maria called back the service department and explained the problem again. A customer service specialist said that the store relied on an outside TV-appliance-repair firm to handle such problems. She said she would call the repair firm on Monday and that the firm would contact the Chavez family. By Tuesday morning the Chavez family still had not heard from the repair firm.

In desperation, Tony scanned a customer information booklet that came with the TV receiver. He found a list of 10 authorized service centers throughout the United States and Canada that repaired his brand of television. Tony telephoned a service center in California. A cheerful woman answered the phone and listened to Tony's problem. With a sympathetic laugh, she said, "We get lots of calls like this. No problem. Just push the volume-up and volume-down buttons at the same time. The demo mode will disappear. The mode was activated when somebody pressed the menu up and down buttons at the same time." Tony raced into the living room, and triumphantly restored the TV set to normal functioning.

Friday, a representative from the local television repair shop called. She said, "This is Modern TV and Appliance. Do you still need service on your set?" With anger in her voice, Maria explained how the problem was finally resolved.

Later that night, as the family gathered to watch MTV, Maria said, "I guess we all love our new giant-screen TV, but I wouldn't go back to Appliance City to buy even an electric can opener."

Case Questions

1. What mistakes in customer satisfaction principles did Appliance City personnel make?

2. What mistakes in customer satisfaction principles did Modern TV and Appliance make?

3. What would you have done if you experienced a similar problem with an expensive TV receiver?

4. Should the manufacturer of the giant-screen TV set have any responsibility for the problem the Chavez family faced?

CHAPTER 7

Enhancing Ethical Behavior

Learning Objectives

After reading and studying this chapter and doing the exercises you should be able to

1. Recognize the importance of ethical behavior for establishing good interpersonal relationships in organizations.

2. Identify several character traits associated with being an ethical person.

3. Identify job situations that often present ethical dilemmas.

4. Use a systematic method for making ethical decisions and behaving ethically.

As owner of a Mr. Handyman franchise in Los Angeles, T. L. Tenenbaum has rigid guidelines for the best approach to difficult drywall and plumbing problems. He also has ground rules for other home hazards his workers might encounter—say a misplaced pair of racy underwear or, as once happened, a butcher knife found under a bed. "Avert your eyes and pretend it doesn't exist," Tenenbaum instructs his techs on day one. "Pretend everything you see is perfectly normal."

Another common land mine: feuding spouses who involve technicians in personal matters—such as asking whether a married man should be friends with an ex-girlfriend.

"Agree with everyone, and don't take sides. We are doctors for their homes, and—people feel—for their relationships as well," Tenenbaum notes.

Trade professionals have long faced unique challenges when conducting business in the privacy of their customers' homes, but how they handled them was generally up to the individual. Now, a fast-growing industry of branded, home-maintenance franchises with such names as House Doctors and Mr. Handyman are trying to hone protocols for prickly on-the-job scenarios from scantily clad customers to overeager kids who want to play with tools.[1]

Discussion Question

1. What do you think the major home-maintenance franchises might be doing to improve the chances that the technicians will behave with good etiquette and good ethics?

The scenario just described illustrates that ethical issues in the workplace are not just about big business and corporate executives. People performing all types of work need a good sense of ethics (and etiquette) to be successful. *Ethics* refers to what is good and bad, right and wrong, just and unjust, and what people should do. Ethics is the vehicle for turning values into action. If you value fair play, you will do such things as giving honest performance evaluations to members of your group.

We study ethics here because a person's ethical code has a significant impact on his or her interpersonal relationships. This chapter's approach will emphasize the importance of ethics, common ethical problems, and guidelines for behaving ethically. Self-Assessment Quiz 13-1 gives you the opportunity to examine your ethical beliefs and attitudes.

SELF-ASSESSMENT QUIZ 13-1

THE ETHICAL REASONING INVENTORY

Directions: Describe how well you agree with each of the following statements, using the following scale: disagree strongly (DS); disagree (D); neutral (N); agree (A); agree strongly (AS). Circle the number in the appropriate column.

	DS	D	N	A	AS
1. When applying for a job, I would cover up the fact that I had been fired from my most recent job.	5	4	3	2	1
2. Cheating just a few dollars in one's favor on an expense account is okay if a person needs the money.	5	4	3	2	1
3. Employees should report on each other for wrongdoing.	1	2	3	4	5
4. It is acceptable to give approximate figures for expense account items when one does not have all the receipts.	5	4	3	2	1
5. I see no problem with conducting a little personal business on company time.	5	4	3	2	1
6. Just to make a sale, I would stretch the truth about a delivery date.	5	4	3	2	1
7. I would fix up a purchasing agent with a date just to close a sale.	5	4	3	2	1
8. I would flirt with my boss just to get a bigger salary increase.	5	4	3	2	1
9. If I received $400 for doing some odd jobs, I would report it on my income tax return.	1	2	3	4	5
10. I see no harm in taking home a few office supplies.	5	4	3	2	1
11. It is acceptable to read the e-mail messages and faxes of coworkers, even when not invited to do so.	5	4	3	2	1
12. It is unacceptable to call in sick to take a day off, even if only done once or twice a year.	1	2	3	4	5

13. I would accept a permanent, full-time job even if I knew I wanted the job for only six months.   5 4 3 2 1

14. I would first check company policy before accepting an expensive gift from a supplier.   1 2 3 4 5

15. To be successful in business, a person usually has to ignore ethics.   5 4 3 2 1

16. If I felt physically attracted toward a job candidate, I would hire that person over a more qualified candidate.   5 4 3 2 1

17. On the job, I tell the truth all the time.   1 2 3 4 5

18. If a student were very pressed for time, it would be acceptable to either have a friend write the paper or purchase one.   5 4 3 2 1

19. I would authorize accepting an office machine on a 30-day trial period, even if I knew we had no intention of buying it.   5 4 3 2 1

20. I would never accept credit for a coworker's ideas.   1 2 3 4 5

Total Score _____

Scoring and Interpretation: Add the numbers you have circled to obtain your total score.

90–100 You are a strongly ethical person who may take a little ribbing from coworkers for being too straitlaced.

60–89 You show an average degree of ethical awareness, and therefore should become more sensitive to ethical issues.

41–59 Your ethics are underdeveloped, but you at least have some awareness of ethical issues. You need to raise your level of awareness of ethical issues.

20–40 Your ethical values are far below contemporary standards in business. Begin a serious study of business ethics.

Learning Objective 1 ▶ # WHY BE CONCERNED ABOUT BUSINESS ETHICS?

When asked why ethics is important, most people would respond something to the effect that "Ethics is important because it's the right thing to do. You behave decently in the workplace because your family and religious values have taught you what is right and wrong." All this is true, but the justification for behaving ethically is more complex, as described next.[2]

A major justification for behaving ethically on the job is to recognize that people are motivated by both self-interest and moral commitments. Most people want to maximize gain for themselves (remember the expectancy theory of motivation?). At the same time, most people are motivated to do something morally right. As one of many examples, vast numbers of people donate money to charity, although keeping that amount of money for themselves would provide more personal gain.

Many business executives want employees to behave ethically because a good reputation can enhance business. A favorable corporate reputation may enable firms to charge premium prices and attract better job applicants. A favorable reputation also helps attract investors, such as mutual fund managers who purchase stock in companies. Certain mutual funds, for example, invest only in companies that are environmentally friendly. Managers want employees to behave ethically because unethical behavior—for example, employee theft, lost production time, and lawsuits—is costly.

Behaving ethically is also important because many unethical acts are illegal as well, which can lead to financial loss and imprisonment. According to one estimate, the cost of unethical and fraudulent acts committed by U.S. employees totals $400 billion per year. A company that knowingly allows workers to engage in unsafe practices might be fined and the executives may be held personally liable. Furthermore, unsafe practices can kill people. In recent history, two employees burned to death in a fire they could not escape in a chicken processing plant. Management had blocked the back doors to prevent employees from sneaking chicken parts out of the plant. Low ethics have also resulted in financial hardship for employees as company executives raid pension funds of other companies they purchase, sharply reducing or eliminating the retirement funds of many workers.

A subtle reason for behaving ethically is that high ethics increases the quality of work life. Ethics provides a set of guidelines that specify what makes for acceptable behavior. Being ethical will point you toward actions that make life more satisfying for work associates. A company code of ethics specifies what constitutes ethical versus unethical behavior. When employees follow this code, the quality of work life improves. Several sample clauses from ethical codes are as follows:

- Demonstrate courtesy, respect, honesty, and fairness.
- Do not use abusive language.
- Do not bring firearms or knives to work.
- Do not offer bribes.
- Maintain confidentiality of records.
- Do not harass (sexually, racially, ethnically, or physically) subordinates, superiors, coworkers, customers, or suppliers.

To the extent that all members of the organization abide by this ethical code, the quality of work life will improve. At the same time, interpersonal relations in organizations will be strengthened.

COMMON ETHICAL PROBLEMS

◀ Learning Objective 2

To become more skilled at behaving ethically, it is important to familiarize yourself with common ethical problems in organizations. Whether or not a given situation presents an ethical problem for a person depends to some extent on its **moral intensity,** or how deeply others might be affected.[3] A worker might face a strong ethical conflict about dumping mercury into a water supply but would be less concerned about dumping cleaning fluid. Yet both acts would be considered unethical and illegal. Here we first look at why being ethical is not as easy as it sounds. We then look at some data about the frequency of ethical problems and an analysis of predictable ethical temptations, and also examine the subtle ethical dilemma of choosing between rights.

moral intensity In ethical decision making, how deeply others might be affected by the decision.

WHY BEING ETHICAL ISN'T EASY

As analyzed by Linda Klebe Treviño and Michael E. Brown, behaving ethically in business is more complex than it seems on the surface for a variety of reasons.[4] To begin with, ethical decisions are complex. For example, someone might argue that hiring children for factory jobs in overseas countries is unethical. Yet if these children lose their jobs, many would starve or turn to crime to survive. Second, people do not always recognize the moral issues involved in a decision. The home-maintenance worker who found a butcher knife under the bed might not think that he has a role to play in perhaps preventing murder. Sometimes language hides the moral issue involved, such as when the term "file sharing" music replaces "stealing" music.

Another complexity in making ethical decisions is that people have different levels of moral development. At one end of the scale some people behavior morally just to escape punishment. At the other end of the scale, some people are morally developed to the point that they are guided by principles of justice and want to help as many people as possible. The environment in which we work also influences whether we behave ethically. Suppose a restaurant owner encourages such practices as serving customers food that was accidentally dropped on the kitchen floor. An individual server is more likely to engage in such behavior to obey the demands of the owner.

A SURVEY OF THE EXTENT OF ETHICAL PROBLEMS

The ethical misdeeds of executives have received substantial publicity in recent years. However, recent surveys show that ethical violations by rank-and-file employees are widespread, particularly with respect to lying. According to two separate surveys, more than one-third of U.S. workers admit to having fabricated about their need for sick days. More employees are stretching the reasons for taking time off. Job applicants reporting false or embellished academic credentials have hit a three-year high. Here are the major findings of a composite of several surveys:[5]

- 36 percent of employees call in sick when they are well.
- 34 percent of employees keep quiet when they see coworker misconduct.
- 19 percent of employees see coworkers lie to customers, vendors, and the public.
- 12 percent of employees steal from customers or the company.
- 12 percent of résumés contain at least some false information.

Although these findings might suggest that unethical behavior is on the increase, another explanation is possible. Workers today might be more observant of ethical problems, and more willing to note them on a survey.

FREQUENT ETHICAL DILEMMAS

Certain ethical mistakes, including illegal actions, recur in the workplace. Familiarizing oneself can be helpful in monitoring one's own behavior. The next subsections describe a number of common ethical problems faced by business executives as well as workers at lower job levels.[6]

Illegally Copying Software

A rampant ethical problem is whether or not to illegally copy computer software. According to the Business Software Alliance, approximately 35 percent of applications used in business are illegal.[7] Figure 13-1 offers details about and insight into this widespread ethical dilemma.

Treating People Unfairly

Being fair to people means equity, reciprocity, and impartiality. Fairness revolves around the issue of giving people equal rewards for accomplishing equal amounts of work. The goal of human resource legislation is to make decisions about people based on their qualifications and performance—not on the basis of demographic factors such as gender, race, or age. A fair working environment is where performance is the only factor that counts (equity). Employer–employee expectations must be understood and met (reciprocity). Prejudice and bias must be eliminated (impartiality).

Treating people fairly—and therefore ethically—requires a de-emphasis on political factors, or favoritism. Yet this ethical doctrine is not always easy to implement. It is human nature to want to give bigger rewards (such as fatter raises or bigger orders) to people we like.

Follow the **Platinum Rule:** *Treat people the way they wish to be treated.*
—Eric Harvey and Scott Airitam, authors of *Ethics 4 Everyone*

A flagrant unethical and **illegal** job behavior is unauthorized copying of software. When confronted with software pirating, people are quick to rationalize their actions. Here are the top ten defenses of software pirates. (None of them are likely to hold up if you are caught.)

1. **I'm allowed to make a backup disk in case something happens to the original, so it must be okay to use it on another machine.** A backup is strictly a backup to be used on the same computer. The original should be safely locked away, and the copy should be stored away only as a backup.
2. **I didn't copy it—a friend gave it to me.** Technically you are right. You would not be guilty of illegally copying software in this case, although your friend would. However, since illegally copied software is regarded as stolen property, you are just as guilty as you would be for stealing it in the first place.
3. **My boss (or department head, or instructor) told me to. It's that person's problem.** The defense "I was just following orders" is a weak one. Complying with your boss's demands to commit an illegal act does not get you off the hook. You could be fired for obeying an order to commit a crime.
4. **I bought the software; shouldn't I be able to do what I want with it?** Software is seldom ever sold to individuals. What is sold is a license to use the software, not full rights to do what you want. When you break open the package, the law assumes that you have agreed to abide by those terms.
5. **It's not like I'm robbing somebody.** Software is intellectual property just like a song, a book, an article, or a trademark. You are taking bread from the table of software engineers when you copy their work.
6. **It's OK if you're using the software for educational purposes.** If education were a justification for theft, driving instructors would be able to steal cars with impunity. There is a doctrine of **fair use** that allows some limited use of written materials in classrooms without permission from the copyright holder.
7. **I needed it, but the price was unreasonably high. If I had to actually pay for it, there is no way I could ever afford it.** Software prices are high for the same reason the price of houses is high: both require a lot of highly skilled labor to create. You cannot steal a DVD player just because you cannot afford one.
8. **I didn't know it was illegal.** Unauthorized duplication of software is a felony in many states and provinces. State and federal laws provide for civil and criminal penalties if you are convicted. It would be difficult to convince a judge or jury that you had no idea that unauthorized copying was illegal.
9. **It's only illegal if you get caught.** Criminal behavior is illegal whether or not you are caught. If you do get caught illegally copying software, you could face fines, imprisonment, and/or civil penalties. Some educational institutions take disciplinary action against software pirates, including suspension.
10. **Oh, come on, everyone is doing it.** This excuse has been used to justify everything from speeding to lynching. The popularity of a criminal act does not make it legal.

FIGURE 13-1 The Top Ten Reasons for Illegally Copying Software (and Why None of Them Are Good Enough)

Source: The Top Ten Reasons for Illegally Copying Software (and Why None of Them Are Good Enough). Rochester Institute of Technology. Reprinted with permission.

Sexually Harassing Coworkers

In Chapter 7 we looked at sexual harassment as a source of conflict and an illegal act. Sexual harassment is also an ethical issue because it is morally wrong and unfair. All acts of sexual harassment flunk an ethics test. Before sexually harassing another person, the potential harasser should ask, "Would I want a loved one to be treated this way?"

Facing a Conflict of Interest

Part of being ethical is making business judgments only on the basis of the merits or facts in a situation. Imagine that you are a supervisor who is romantically involved with a worker within the group. When it comes time to assign raises, it will be difficult for you to be objective. A **conflict of interest** occurs when your judgment or objectivity is compromised. Conflicts of interest often take place in the sales end of

conflict of interest A situation that occurs when a person's judgment or objectivity is compromised.

business. If a company representative accepts a large gift from a sales representative, it may be difficult to make objective judgments about buying from the rep. Yet being taken to dinner by a vendor would not ordinarily cloud one's judgment. Another common example of a conflict of interest is making a hiring decision about a friend who badly needs a job, but is not well qualified for the position.

Conflicts of interest have been behind some of the major business scandals in recent times, such as Enron Corporation auditors giving the company a favorable rating. Many outsiders dealing with Enron—including auditors, bankers, and even regulators—were tempted by a piece of the equity action.[8] The conflict occurs when one party paid to make objective judgments about the financial health of a second party has a personal interest in how profitable the second party looks to the public. An auditor might be hesitant to give a negative evaluation of the financial condition of a company if the auditor's firm also provides consulting services to that company. Some financial research analysts give glowing public reports about the fiscal condition of a company when that company is a client of the analyst's own firm. The analyst's firm sells services for issuing new stock and assisting with corporate mergers and acquisitions.

Dealing with Confidential Information

An ethical person can be trusted by others not to divulge confidential information unless the welfare of others is at stake. Suppose a coworker tells you in confidence that she is upset with the company and is therefore looking for another job. Behaving ethically, you do not pass along this information to your supervisor even though it would help your supervisor plan for a replacement. Now suppose the scenario changes slightly. Your coworker tells you she is looking for another job because she is upset. She tells you she is so upset that she plans to destroy company computer files on her last day. If your friend does find another job, you might warn the company about her contemplated activities.

The challenge of dealing with confidential information arises in many areas of business, many of which affect interpersonal relations. If you learned that a coworker was indicted for a crime, charged with sexual harassment, or facing bankruptcy, there would be a temptation to gossip about the person. A highly ethical person would not pass along information about the personal difficulties of another person.

Presenting Employment History

As noted above, many people are tempted to distort in a positive direction information about their employment history on their job résumé, job application form, and during the interview. Distortion, or lying, of this type is considered to be unethical and can lead to immediate dismissal if discovered. A well-known case in point is George O'Leary, who was dismissed after five days on the job as head coach of the Notre Dame football team. After his résumé distortions were uncovered, O'Leary resigned and admitted he falsified his academic and athletic credentials for decades. He had falsely claimed to have a master's degree in education and to have played college football for three years.[9] Shortly thereafter, O'Leary made good use of his network of professional contacts and was hired by the Minnesota Vikings professional football team in a coaching position. Despite being disgraced nationally, O'Leary's political skills provided him with a safety net.

Using Corporate Resources

A corporate resource is anything the company owns, including its name and reputation. If Jake Petro worked for Ford Motor Company, for example, it would be unethical for him to establish a body shop and put on his letterhead and Web site, "Jake Petro, Manufacturing Technician, Ford Motor Company." (The card and Web site would imply that the Ford Motor Co. supports this venture.) Other uses of corporate resources fall more into the gray area. It might be quite ethical to borrow a laptop computer for the weekend from your employer to conduct work at home. But it would be less ethical to borrow the laptop computer to prepare income taxes. In the

1. Do not use a computer to harm other people. Avoid all obscene, defamatory, threatening, or otherwise harassing messages. Take precautions against others developing repetitive motion disorders.
2. Do not interfere with other people's computer work. (This includes intentionally spreading computer viruses.)
3. Do not snoop around in other people's files.
4. Do not use a computer to steal.
5. Do not use a computer to bear false witness.
6. Do not use or copy software for which you have not paid (see Figure 13-1).
7. Do not use other people's resources without authorization.
8. Do not appropriate other people's intellectual output.
9. Do not use the employer's computer for the personal promotion of commercial goods or services, unless granted permission by the employer.
10. Do think about the social consequences of the program you write.
11. Do use a computer in ways that show consideration and respect.

FIGURE 13-2 Eleven Commandments for Computer Ethics

Source: Adapted and updated from Arlene H. Rinaldi and Florida Atlantic University, rinaldi@acc.fau.edu; "Code of Conduct for Computer and Network Use," *http://www.rit.edu/computerconduct.*

latter case you might be accused of using corporate resources for personal purposes. Loading personal software on company computers so you can access your bank account and so forth, also can be considered an ethical violation.

Ethically Violating Computers and Information Technology

As computers dominate the workplace, many ethical issues have arisen in addition to pirating software. One ethical dilemma that surfaces frequently is the fairness of tracking the Web sites a person visits and those he or she buys from. Should this information be sold, like a mailing list? Another issue is the fairness of having an employee work at a keyboard for 60 hours in one week when such behavior frequently leads to repetitive motion disorder. Figure 13-2 lists some major ethical issues involved in computer use.

You may have observed that these common ethical problems are not always clear-cut. Aside from obvious matters such as prohibitions against stealing, lying, cheating, and intimidating, subjectivity enters into ethical decision making. Skill-Building Exercise 13-1 provides an opportunity to try out your ethical reasoning.

CHOOSING BETWEEN TWO RIGHTS: DEALING WITH DEFINING MOMENTS

Ethical decision making usually involves choosing between two options: one we perceive to be right and one we perceive to be wrong. A challenging twist to ethical decision making is to sort through your values when you have to choose between two rights, or two morally sound choices. Joseph L. Badaracco, Jr., uses the term **defining moment** to describe choosing between two or more ideals in which we deeply believe.[10] If you can learn to work through defining moments, your ethical skills will be enhanced. Let's first take a nonwork example to illustrate a defining moment.

defining moment
Choosing between two or more ideals in which one deeply believes.

Imagine yourself as a basketball referee in a league for boys 10 years old and younger. Luis, the smallest boy on the team, has a self-confidence problem in general, and he has not scored a basket yet this season. This is the final game of the season. The other team is ahead by 10 points with one minute to go. Luis lets fly with a shot that goes into the basket, but his right heel is on the line. If the goal is allowed, Luis will experience one of the happiest moments in his life, and his self-confidence might increase. You strongly believe in helping people grow and develop. Yet you also strongly believe in following the rules of sports. What should you do?

SKILL-BUILDING EXERCISE 13-1

THE ETHICS GAME

Citicorp (now part of Citigroup) has developed an ethics game, The Work Ethic.[11] The game teaches ethics by asking small teams of employees to confront difficult scenarios such as those that follow. Discuss these ethical problems in teams. As you discuss the scenarios, identify the ethical issues involved.

Scenario 1: One of your assignments is to find a contractor to conduct building maintenance for your company headquarters. You invite bids for the job. High-Performance cleaners, a firm staffed largely by teenagers from troubled families who have criminal records, bids on the job.

Many of these teenagers also have severe learning disabilities and cannot readily find employment. High-Performance Cleaners proves to be the second-highest bidder. You:

A. advise High-Performance Cleaners that its bid is too high for consideration and that your company is not a social agency.

B. award the bid to High-Performance Cleaners and justify your actions with a letter to top management talking about social responsibility.

C. falsify the other bids in your report to management, making High-Performance Cleaners the low bidder—and thus the contract winner.

D. explain to High-Performance Cleaners that it lost the bid, but you will award the company a piece of the contract because of its sterling work with teenagers in need.

Scenario 2: You live in Texas and your company sends you on a three-day trip to New York City. Your business dealings in the Big Apple will keep you there Wednesday, Thursday, and Friday morning. You have several friends and relatives in New York, so you decide to stay there until Sunday afternoon. Besides, you want to engage in tourist activities such as taking a boat tour around Manhattan and visiting Radio City Music Hall. When preparing your expense report for your trip, you request payment for all your business-related costs up through Friday afternoon, plus

A. your return trip on Sunday.

B. the return trip and the room cost for Friday and Saturday nights.

C. the return trip, one-half of your weekend food expenses, and two extra nights in the hotel.

D. the return trip and your food costs for the weekend (which you justify because you ate at fast-food restaurants on Wednesday, Thursday, and Friday).

Scenario 3: You are the leader of a self-managing work team in a financial services company. The work of your team has expanded to the point where you are authorized to hire another team member. The team busily interviews a number of candidates from inside and outside the company. The other team members agree that one of the candidates (Pat) has truly outstanding credentials. You agree that Pat is a strong candidate, yet you don't want Pat on the team because the two of you were emotionally involved for about a year. You think that working with Pat would disrupt your concentration and bring back hurtful memories. You decide to

A. tell the group that you have some negative information about Pat's past that would disqualify Pat for the job.

B. telephone Pat and beg that Pat find employment elsewhere.

C. tell the group that you agree Pat is qualified, but explain your concerns about the disruption in concentration and emotional hurt.

D. tell the group that you agree Pat is right for the position, and mention nothing about the past relationship.

Scoring and Observation: Scenario 1, about High-Performance Cleaners, raises dozens of ethical questions, including whether humanitarian considerations can outweigh profit concerns. Teams that chose "a" receive 0 points; "b", 20 points; "c", −10 points; "d", 10 points. (Answer "d" is best here because it would not be fair to give the bid to the second-highest bidder. However, you are still finding a way to reward the High-Performance Cleaners for its meritorious work in the community. Answer "c" is the worst because you would be outright lying.)

Scenario 2 raises ethical issues about using company resources. Teams that chose "a" receive 20 points; "b", −10 points; "c", −15 points; "d", 0 points. (Answer "a" is fairest because the company would expect to reimburse you for your roundtrip plus the expenses up through Friday afternoon. Answer "c" is the worst because it would be unjustified for you to be reimbursed for your vacation in New York.)

Scenario 3 raises issues about fairness in making selection decisions. Teams that chose "a" receive −20 points; "b", −10 points; "c", 15 points; "d", 0 points. (Answer "c" is the most ethical because you are being honest with the group about the reason you do not wish to hire Pat. Answer "a" is the most unethical because you are telling lies about Pat. Furthermore, you might be committing the illegal act of libel.)

You may have recognized that a defining moment is a role conflict in which you have to choose between competing values. A CEO might deeply believe that she has an obligation to the stockholders to make a profit, and also believe in being generous and fair toward employees. However, to make a profit this year she will be forced to lay off several good employees with long seniority. The CEO now faces a moment of truth. Badaracco suggests that the individual can work through a defining moment by discovering "Who am I?" You discover who you are by soul searching answers to three questions:

1. What feelings and intuitions are coming into conflict in this situation?
2. Which of the values that are in conflict are the most deeply rooted in my life?
3. What combinations of expediency and shrewdness, coupled with imagination and boldness, will help me implement my personal understanding of what is right?

Skill-Building Exercise 13-2 gives you an opportunity to deal with defining moments. The three questions just asked could help you find answers, but do not be constrained by these questions.

GUIDELINES FOR BEHAVING ETHICALLY
◄ Learning Objective 3

Following guidelines for ethical behavior is the heart of being ethical. Although many people behave ethically without studying ethical guidelines, they are usually following guidelines programmed into their minds early in life. The Golden Rule exemplifies a guideline taught by parents, grandparents, and kindergarten teachers. In this section we approach ethical guidelines from five perspectives: (1) developing the right character traits; (2) following a guide to ethical decision making; (3) developing strong relationships with work associates; (4) using corporate ethics programs; and (5) following an applicable professional code of conduct.

DEVELOPING THE RIGHT CHARACTER TRAITS

Character traits develop early in life, yet with determination and self-discipline many people can modify old traits or develop new ones. A **character trait** is an enduring characteristic of a person that is related to moral and ethical behavior. For example, if a

Character trait An enduring characteristic of a person that is related to moral and ethical behavior.

SKILL-BUILDING EXERCISE 13-2

DEALING WITH DEFINING MOMENTS

The toughest ethical choices for many people occur when they have to choose between two rights. The result is a defining moment, because we are challenged to think in a deeper way by choosing between two or more ideals. Working individually or in teams, deal with the two following defining moments. Explain why these scenarios could require choosing between two rights, and explain the reasoning behind your decisions.

Scenario 1:   You are the manager of a department in a business firm that assigns each department a fixed amount of money for salary increases each year. An average-performing member of the department asks you in advance for an above-average increase. He explains that his mother has developed multiple sclerosis and requires the services of a paid helper from time to time. You are concerned that if you give this man an above-average increase, somebody else in the department will have to receive a below-average increase.

Scenario 2:   You are the team leader of an e-tailing (retail selling over the Internet) group. In recent months each team member has been working about 60 hours per week, with little prospect of the workload decreasing in the future. Since the e-tailing project is still losing money, higher management insists that one person be dropped from the team. One member of the team, Mildred, is willing to work only 45 hours per week because she spends considerable time volunteering with autistic children. Mildred's work is satisfactory, but her output is the lowest in the group because of her shorter number of working hours. You must make a decision about whether to recommend that Mildred be dismissed.

person has the character trait of untruthfulness, he or she will lie in many situations. Conversely, the character trait of honesty leads to behaving honestly in most situations.

The Character Counts Coalition is an organization formed to encourage young people to develop fairness, respect, trustworthiness, responsibility, caring, and good citizenship. The Coalition has developed a list of 10 key guidelines as a foundation for character development.[12] If you develop, or already have, these traits, it will be easy for you to behave ethically in business. As you read the following list, evaluate your own standing on each character trait. Remember, however, that extra effort is required to evaluate one's character traits because most people have an inflated view of their honesty and integrity.

1. **Be honest.** Tell the truth consistently, be sincere, avoid misleading or withholding information in relationships of trust, and do not steal.

2. **Show integrity.** Stand up for your beliefs about what you think is right and wrong, and resist pressures from others to do wrong.

3. **Follow through on promises.** Stick to your word and honor your commitments; pay your debts and return borrowed money or objects.

4. **Be loyal.** Support family, friends, employers, community, and country, and do not talk about people behind their backs.

5. **Be responsible.** Think before you act, consider the consequences of your actions, and be accountable for what you do.

6. **Pursue excellence.** Do your best with your talents, and persist in pursuing your goals.

7. **Be kind and caring.** Demonstrate that you care through generosity and compassion; avoid being selfish or mean.

8. **Treat all people with respect.** Be courteous and polite to everybody you meet. Judge all people on their merits rather than on superficial aspects of behavior. Be tolerant, appreciative, and accepting of individual differences.

9. **Be fair and just.** Treat all people fairly (how they deserve to be treated) and be open-minded. Listen attentively to others and try to understand what they are saying and feeling.

10. **Be a good citizen.** Obey the law and respect authority of appointed or elected officials, vote in local and national elections, do volunteer work, and protect the environment.

If you score high on all of the preceding character traits and behaviors, you are an outstanding member of your company, community, and school. Your ethical behavior is superior.

FOLLOWING A GUIDE TO ETHICAL DECISION MAKING ◀ Learning Objective 4

A powerful strategy for behaving ethically is to follow a guide for ethical decision making. Such a guide for making contemplated decisions includes testing ethics. **Ethical screening** refers to running a contemplated decision or action through an ethics test. Such screening makes the most sense when the contemplated action or decision is not clearly ethical or unethical. If a sales representative were to take a favorite customer to Pizza Hut for lunch, an ethical screen would not be necessary. Nobody would interpret a "veggie super" to be a serious bribe. Assume, instead, that the sales rep offered to give the customer an under-the-table gift of $600 for placing a large offer with the rep's firm. The sales representative's behavior would be so blatantly unethical that conducting an ethical screen would be unnecessary.

ethical screening
Running a contemplated decision or action through an ethics test.

Several useful ethical screens, or guides to ethical decision making, have been developed. A guide developed by Treviño and Nelson is presented here because it incorporates the basic ideas in other ethical tests.[13] After studying this guide, you will be asked to ethically screen three different scenarios. The eight steps to sound ethical decision making follow.

1. Gather the facts. When making an important decision in business it is necessary to gather relevant facts. Ask yourself the following questions: "Are there any legal issues involved here?" "Is there precedent in our firm with respect to this type of decision?" "Do I have the authority to make this decision?" "Are there company rules and regulations governing such a decision?"

The manager of a child-care center needed to hire an additional child-care specialist. One of the applicants was a 55-year-old male with experience as a father and grandfather. The manager judged him to be qualified, yet she knew that many parents would not want their preschool children to be cared for by a middle-aged male. Many people perceive that a younger woman is better qualified for child care than an older man. The manager therefore had to gather considerable facts about the situation, including facts about job discrimination and precedents in hiring males as child-care specialists.

2. Define the ethical issues. The ethical issues in a given decision are often more complicated than a first glance suggests. When faced with a complex decision, it may be helpful to talk over the ethical issues with another person. The ethical issues might involve character traits such as being kind and caring and treating others with respect. Or the ethical issues might relate to some of the common ethical problems described earlier in the chapter. Among them are facing conflict of interest, dealing with confidential information, and using corporate resources.

The manager of the child-care center is facing such ethical issues as fairness, job discrimination, and meeting the demands of customers at the expense of job applicants. The manager is also facing a diversity issue: Should the workforce in a child-care center be culturally diverse, or do we hire only young women?

3. Identify the affected parties. When faced with a complex ethical decision it is important to identify all the affected parties. Major corporate decisions can affect thousands of people. If a company decides to shut down a plant and outsource the manufacturing to a low-wage country, thousands of individuals and many different parties are affected. Workers lose their jobs, suppliers lose their customers, the local government loses out on tax revenues, and local merchants lose many of their customers. You may need to brainstorm with a few others to think of all the parties affected by a given decision.

The parties affected by the decision about hiring or not hiring the 55-year-old male include: the applicant himself, the children, the parents, and the board of directors of the child-care center. The government might also be involved if the man were rejected and filed charges of age and sex discrimination.

4. Identify the consequences. After you have identified the parties affected by a decision, the next step is to predict the consequences for each party. It may not be necessary to identify every consequence, yet it is important to identify the consequences with the highest probability of occurring and those with the most negative outcomes. The problem is that many people can be harmed by an unethical decision, such as not fully describing the possible side effects of a diet program.

Both short-term and long-term consequences should be specified. A company closing a plant might create considerable short-term turmoil, but in the long term the company might be healthier. People participating in a diet program might achieve their short-term objective of losing weight. Yet in the long term, their health might be adversely affected because the diet is not nutritionally balanced.

The *symbolic* consequences of an action are important. Every action and decision sends a message (the decision is a symbol of something). If a company moves manufacturing out of a community to save on labor costs, it means that the short-term welfare of domestic employees is less important than profit or perhaps the company surviving.

We return to the child-care manager and the job applicant. If the applicant does not get the job, his welfare will be adversely affected. He has been laid off by a large employer and cannot find work in his regular field. His family will also suffer because he will not be able to make a financial contribution to the family. Yet if the man is hired, the child-care center may suffer. Many traditionally minded parents will say, "Absolutely not. I do not want my child cared for by a middle-aged man. He could be a child molester." (It may be unethical for people to have vicious stereotypes, yet they still exist.) If the child-care center does hire the man, the act will symbolize the fact that the owners of the center value diversity.

5. Identify the obligations. Identify the obligations and the reasons for each obligation when making a complex decision. The manufacturer of automotive brakes has an obligation to produce and sell only brakes that meet high safety standards. The obligation is to the auto manufacturer who purchases the brakes and, more important, to the ultimate consumer whose safety depends on effective brakes. The reason for the obligation to make safe brakes is that lives are at stake. The child-care center owner has an obligation to provide for the safety and health of the children at the center. She must also provide for the peace of mind of the parents and be a good citizen of the community in which the center is located. The decision about hiring the candidate in question must be balanced against all these obligations.

6. Consider your character and integrity. A core consideration when faced with an ethical dilemma is how relevant people would judge your character and integrity.

What would your family, friends, significant others, teachers, and coworkers think of your actions? To refine this thinking even further, how would you feel if your actions were publicly disclosed in the local newspaper or over e-mail? Would you want the world to know that you gave an under-the-table kickback or that you sexually harassed a frightened teenager working for you? If you would be proud for others to know what decision you made when you faced an ethical dilemma, you are probably making the right decision.

The child-care center manager might ponder how she would feel if the following information were released in the local newspaper or on the Internet.

> The manager of Good Times Child Care recently rejected the application of a 55-year-old man for a child-care specialist position. She said that although Mr. _____ was well qualified from an experience and personality standpoint, she couldn't hire him. She said that Good Times would lose too much business because many parents would fear that Mr. _____ was a child molester or pedophile.

7. Think creatively about potential actions. When faced with an ethical dilemma, put yourself in a creative-thinking mode. Stretch your imagination to invent several options rather than thinking you have only two choices—to do or not do something. Creative thinking may point toward a third, and even fourth, alternative. Imagine this ethical dilemma: A purchasing agent is told that if her firm awards a contract to the sales representative's firm, she will find a leather jacket of her choice delivered to her door. The purchasing agent says to herself, "I think we should award the contract to the firm, but I cannot accept the gift. Yet if I turn down the gift, I will be forfeiting a valuable possession that the company simply regards as a cost of doing business."

The purchasing agent can search for another alternative. She may say to the sales rep, "We will give the contract to your firm because your products fit our requirements. I thank you for the offer of the leather jacket, but instead I would like you to give the jacket to the Salvation Army."

A creative alternative for the child-care manager might be to offer the applicant the next position that opened for an office manager or maintenance person in the center. In this way she would be offering a qualified applicant a job, but placing him in a position more acceptable to parents. Or do you feel this is a cop-out?

8. Check your intuition. So far we have emphasized the rational side of ethical decision making. Another effective way of conducting an ethical screen is to rely on your intuition. How does the contemplated decision feel? Would you be proud of yourself or would you hate yourself if you made the decision? Imagine how you would feel if you took money from the handbag of a woman sleeping in the park. Would you feel the same way if you took a kickback, sold somebody a defective product, or sold an 80-year-old man an insurance policy he didn't need? How will the manager of the child-care center feel if she turns down the man for the child-care specialist position?

You are encouraged to use the guide for ethical decision making when you next face an ethical dilemma of consequence. Skill-Building Exercise 13-3 gives you an opportunity to practice using the eight steps for ethical decision making.

DEVELOPING STRONG RELATIONSHIPS WITH WORK ASSOCIATES

A provocative explanation of the causes of unethical behavior emphasizes the strength of relationships among people.[14] Assume that two people have close professional ties to each other, such as having worked together for a long time or knowing each other both on and off the job. As a consequence they are likely to behave ethically toward one another on the job. In contrast, if a weak professional

SKILL-BUILDING EXERCISE 13-3

ETHICAL DECISION MAKING

Working in small groups, take one or more of the following ethical dilemmas through the eight steps for screening contemplated decisions. If more than one group chooses the same scenario, compare your answers for the various steps.

Scenario 1: To Recycle or Not.   Your group is the top management team at a large insurance company. Despite the movement toward digitizing all records, your firm still generates tons of paper each month. Customer payments alone account for truckloads of envelopes each year. The paper recyclers in your area claim they can hardly find a market any longer for used paper, so they will be charging you just to accept your paper for recycling. Your group is wondering whether to recycle.

Scenario 2: The Hole in the Résumé.   Emily has been working for the family business as an office manager for five years. Because the family business is being sold, Emily has started a job hunt. She also welcomes the opportunity to work in a larger company so she could learn more about how a big company operates. As she begins preparing her job résumé, she ponders how to classify the year of unemployment prior to working at the family business. During that year she worked a total of 10 weeks in entry-level jobs at three fast-food restaurants. Otherwise she filled her time with such activities as walking in the park, watching daytime television shows, surfing the Internet, playing video games, and pursuing her hobby of visiting graveyards. Emily finally decides to tack that year onto the five years in the family business. She indicates on her résumé that she has been working *six* years at the family business. As Emily says, "It's a tight job market for office managers, and I don't want to raise any red flags." Evaluate the ethics of Emily's decision to fill in the year off from work, and perhaps offer her some advice.

Scenario 3: The High-Profit Toys.   You are a toy company executive starting to plan your holiday season line. You anticipate that the season's hottest item will be Robo-Woman, a battery-operated crime fighter and super-heroine. Robo-Woman should wholesale for $25 and retail for $45. Your company figures to earn $15 per unit. You receive a sales call from a manufacturing broker who says he can produce any toy you want for one-third of your present manufacturing cost. He admits that the manufacturer he represents uses prison labor in China, but insists that his business arrangement violates no law. You estimate you can earn $20 per unit if you do business with the manufacturing broker. Your decision is whether to do business with him.

relationship exists between two people, either party is more likely to engage in an unethical relationship. The owner of an auto service center is more likely to behave unethically toward a stranger passing through town than toward a long-time customer. (The section in Chapter 11 about building relationships with coworkers and work associates provides suggestions for developing strong relationships.) The opportunity for unethical behavior between strangers is often minimized because individuals typically do not trust strangers with sensitive information or valuables.

The ethical skill-building consequence of information about personal relationships is that building stronger relationships with people is likely to enhance ethical behavior. If you build strong relationships with work associates, you are likely to behave more ethically toward them. Similarly, your work associates are likely to behave more ethically toward you. The work associates I refer to are all your contacts, both internal and external customers.

USING CORPORATE ETHICS PROGRAMS

Many organizations have various programs and procedures for promoting ethical behavior. Among them are committees that monitor ethical behavior, training programs in ethics, and vehicles for reporting ethical violations. The presence of these programs is designed to create an atmosphere in which unethical behavior is discouraged and reporting on unethical behavior is encouraged.

Ethics hotlines are one of the best established programs to help individuals avoid unethical behavior. Should a person be faced with an ethical dilemma, the person calls a toll-free line to speak to a counselor about the dilemma. Sometimes employees ask questions to help interpret a policy, such as "Is it okay to ask my boss for a date?" or "Are we supposed to give senior citizen discounts to customers who qualify but do not ask for one?" At other times, a more pressing ethical issue might be addressed, such as "Is it ethical to lay off a worker just five months short of his qualifying for a full pension?"

Sears, Roebuck and Co. has an ethics hotline the company refers to as an "Assist Line" because very few of the 15,000 calls it receives per year represent crises. Often the six full-time ethics specialists who handle the calls just listen; at other times they intervene to help resolve the problem. The Assist Line is designed to help with these kinds of calls: guidance about company policy; company code of conduct issues; workplace harassment and discrimination; selling practices; theft; and human resource issues. Employees and managers are able to access information and guidance without feeling they are facing a crisis. So the Assist Line is kind of a cross between "911" and "411" calls. At times an ethical problem of such high moral intensity is presented that employee confidentiality cannot be maintained. However, the Ethics Office handles the inquiries in as confidential a manner as practical and assigns them case identification numbers for follow-up.[15]

Wells Fargo & Co., a mammoth bank, emphasizes both a code of conduct and ethics training. Its Code of Ethics and Business Conduct specifies policies and standards for employees, covering a variety of topics from maintaining accurate records to participating in civic activities. Each year, employees also participate in ethics training. Any Wells Fargo employee may ask questions or report ethical breaches anonymously using an ethics hotline or dedicated e-mail address. The company will fire violators, dismissing about 100 people a year for misconduct ranging from conflicts of interest to cheating on incentive plans.

Patricia Callahan, executive vice president and director of human resources at the bank says, "I'm the biggest soft touch in the world. But when someone lies or cheats, you can't have people like that representing us to our customers, whose trust is all we have."[16]

The link between the programs just described and individual ethical skills is that these programs assist a worker's skill development. For example, if you become comfortable in asking about ethical issues, or turning in ethical violators, you have become more ethically skilled.

Back to the Opening Case

During their orientation at Handyman Matters (a major franchiser in the field) technicians must sit through a two-hour video about in-home conduct. The company also operates "secret shopper calls" where it gives customers scripts and asks them to monitor techs on certain protocols.

FOLLOWING AN APPLICABLE PROFESSIONAL CODE OF CONDUCT

Professional codes of conduct are prescribed for many occupational groups including physicians, nurses, lawyers, paralegals, purchasing managers and agents, and real estate salespeople. A useful ethical guide for members of these groups is to follow the code of conduct for their profession. If the profession or trade is licensed by the state or province, a worker can be punished for deviating from the code of conduct specified by the state. The code of conduct developed by the profession or trade is separate from the legal code, but usually supports the same principles and practices. Some of these codes of conduct developed by the professional associations are 50 and 60 pages long, yet all are guided by the kind of ethical principles implied in the ethical-decision-making guide described earlier. Figure 13-3 presents a sampling of provisions from these codes of conduct.

Professional Organization	Sample of Ethical Guidelines and Regulations
Institute of Management Accountants	1. Maintain an appropriate level of professional competence by ongoing development of their knowledge and skills.
	2. Refrain from disclosing confidential information acquired in the course of their work and monitor their activities to assure the maintenance of that confidentiality.
	3. Actual or apparent conflicts of interest and advise all appropriate parties of any potential conflict.
National Association of Legal Assistants	1. A legal assistant (paralegal) must not perform any of the duties that attorneys only may perform nor take any actions that attorneys may not take.
	2. A legal assistant may perform any task which is properly delegated and supervised by an attorney, as long as the attorney is ultimately responsible to the client, maintains a direct relationship with the client, and assumes professional responsibility for the work product.
	3. A legal assistant must protect the confidences of a client and must not violate any rule or statute now in effect or hereafter enacted controlling the doctrine of privileged communications between a client and an attorney.
National Association of Purchasing Management	1. Avoid the intent and appearance of unethical or compromising practice in relationships, actions, and communications.
	2. Refrain from any private business or professional activity that would create a conflict between personal interests and the interest of the employer.
	3. Refrain from soliciting or accepting money, loans, credits, or prejudicial discounts, and the acceptance of gifts, entertainment, favors, or services from present or potential suppliers which might influence, or appear to influence purchasing decisions.

FIGURE 13-3 Excerpts from Professional Codes of Conduct

Sources: Institute of Management Accountants Code of Ethics; National Association of Legal Assistants Professional Standards; National Association of Purchasing Management Principles and Standards of Purchasing Practice.

SUMMARY

Ethics refers to what is good and bad, right and wrong, just and unjust, and what people should do. Ethics turn values into action. A person's ethical code has a significant impact on his or her interpersonal relationships.

Understanding ethics is important for a variety of reasons. First, people are motivated by self-interest and a desire to be morally right. Second, good ethics can enhance business and avoid illegal acts. Third, having high ethics improves the quality of work life.

Being ethical isn't always easy for several reasons including the complexity of ethical decisions, lack of recognition of the moral issues, poor moral development, and pressures from the work environment. Ethical violations in the form of lying are widespread in the workplace.

Commonly faced ethical dilemmas include illegally copying software; treating people unfairly, sexually harassing coworkers, facing a conflict of interest, dealing with confidential information, presenting employment history, using corporate resources, and ethically violating computers and information technology.

A challenging twist to ethical decision making is to sort through your values when you have to choose between two morally sound choices. A defining moment is when you have to choose between two or more ideals in which you deeply believe.

One strategy for behaving ethically is to develop the right character traits, as specified by the Character Counts Coalition. Among these traits are honesty, integrity, promise keeping, loyalty, responsibility, pursuit of excellence, kindness, respect for others, fairness, and good citizenship. A key strategy for behaving ethically is to follow the eight steps in making a contemplated decision:

1. Gather the facts.
2. Define the ethical issues.
3. Identify the affected parties.
4. Identify the consequences.
5. Identify the obligations (such as to customers and society).
6. Consider your character and integrity.
7. Think creatively about potential actions.
8. Check your intuition.

Another way to raise the level of ethical behavior is to form strong professional relationships with work associates. This is true because people tend to behave more ethically toward people who are close to them. At times using a corporate program such as an ethics hotline can help a person resolve ethical dilemmas. Following an applicable code of professional conduct, such as that for accountants, paralegals, and purchasing specialists, is another guide to behaving ethically.

QUESTIONS FOR DISCUSSION AND REVIEW

1. How can behaving ethically improve a person's interpersonal relationships on the job?
2. What would most likely be some of the specific behaviors of a manager who scored 20 points on the ethical reasoning inventory?
3. A widespread practice is for top management to outsource (or "offshore") work such as call centers to low-wage countries such as India, the Philippines, and lately, Africa. What ethical problems do you see with outsourcing of this type?

4. The major business scandals in recent years have involved financial manipulations such as executives profiting from selling company stock while encouraging employees to buy the stock. In what ways do these financial scandals affect people?

5. Give an example from your own experiences or the media in which a business executive did something of significance that was morally right.

6. Provide an example of an action in business that might be unethical but not illegal.

7. Virtually all accountants have studied ethics as part of their education, yet many business scandals involve accountants. What's their problem?

8. What "commandment" about computer use would you like to add to the list in Figure 13-2?

9. Based on your knowledge of human behavior, why do professional codes of conduct—such as those for doctors, paralegals, and realtors—not prevent all unethical behavior on the part of members?

10. What decision of ethical consequence have you made in the last year that you would not mind having publicly disclosed?

GO TO THE WEB

http://www.ethics.org
(Ethics Resource Center)

http://www.businessethics.ca/codes
(Articles and a survey about business ethics)

AN INTERPERSONAL RELATIONS CASE PROBLEM

"HELP, I'M A VICTIM OF CLICK FRAUD"

Nathan McKelvey began to worry about foul play when Yahoo Inc. refunded him $69.28 early last year. He grew more suspicious when a $16.91 refund arrived from Google Inc. The refunds were for "unusual clicks" and "invalid click activity" and they suggested someone was sabotaging McKelvey's advertising strategy. He pitches his charter-jet brokerage the way companies increasingly do: contracting with Yahoo and Google to serve up small text ads to anyone searching the Web using certain words, such as "private jet" or "air charter." He pays the companies a fee every time someone clicks on his ads.

But Yahoo and Google determined someone was clicking on CharterAuction.com Inc.'s ads with no intention of doing business, thus unfairly driving up the company's advertising costs. McKelvey, turning detective, combed through lists of Internet Protocol (IP) addresses, the identifying codes supplied by computers when they access Web sites. He found several suspicious clicks from one address and about 100 more from one that was similar. They belonged to a New York-based rival, Blue Star Jets LLC, McKelvey says.

He had run into "click fraud," a term the industry uses to describe someone clicking on a search ad with ill intent. A fraudulent clicker can exploit the way Web ads work to rack up fees for a business rival, boost the placement of his or her own ads, or make money for himself or herself. Some people even employ software that automatically clicks on ads multiple times.

Some people believe that about 20 percent of clicks are from people not necessarily interested in the product advertised, and therefore in the industry's view, fraudulent; others say the problem is less severe. What's clear is that if left unchecked, click fraud could damage the credibility of Google, Yahoo, and the search-ad industry that spurred their meteoric growth. Click fraud is "the biggest threat to the Internet economy," Google's chief financial officer, George Reyes, said during an investor's conference.

During his sleuthing, McKelvey discovered that his industry was rife with click manipulation. He and others in the jet-charter brokerage fields say Yahoo and Google have been slow to help and vague on how they're tackling the problem. Meanwhile, McKelvey has cut his search-ad spending to $1,000 a month from $20,000. "I'm skeptical of the whole thing now," he says. He shifted the remaining $19,000 into other outlets, including magazines and events. "I feel like I've been snookered," he says. "Am I willing to take the risk and stick my neck out there at maybe $15 or $20 a click? Not now."

From the start of his business, McKelvey, now 35 years old, advertised through search engines. When a consumer search used words related to the charter-jet industry, his ad would pop up, often first on the list. Business rushed in, McKelvey says, and he bid on about 200 phrases including "jet charter," "business jet," "executive jet," and "charter flights." The advertiser who wins the bid gets his or her company's ad placed high in the search lists.

McKelvey's Web-hosting company traced dozens of clicks to an address belonging to an Internet service provider called BridgeCom International Inc. The company had assigned the IP address in question to Blue Star Jets. That was a lucky break for McKelvey because Internet service providers typically keep such information private.

Howard Moses, chief marketing office for Blue Star Jets, says some of Blue Star's staff and salespeople might have clicked on rivals' search ads looking for information. He denies the company engaged in any widespread, malicious clicking. "It's a little bit amusing to think that our staff is concentrating on driving their search-advertising spending up by $100 or something like that," Moses says.

McKelvey thinks the problem costs him more than the refunds he received. He believes there are more bad clicks he hasn't discovered. He says Yahoo and Google haven't helped. He contacted the Massachusetts attorney general's office, which he says decided not to take up the matter.

Case Questions

1. Is this case more about crime than ethics? Or is it more about ethics than crime? Explain your reasoning.

2. What would you recommend that McKelvey do about using the Internet searches as a source of leads for his business?

3. How might a code of ethics for companies that advertise on the Internet help resolve the issues raised in this case?

Source: From Kevin J. Delaney, "In 'Click Fraud,' Web Outfits Have a Costly Problem," *The Wall Street Journal,* April 6, 2005, pp. A1, A6. Reprinted with permission.

AN INTERPERSONAL RELATIONS CASE PROBLEM

THE HIGHLY RATED, BUT EXPENDABLE MARSHA

Department manager Nicholas had thought for a long time that Marsha, one of his financial analysts, created too many problems. Although Marsha performed her job in a satisfactory manner, she required a lot of supervisory time and attention. She frequently asked for time off when her presence was needed the most because of a heavy workload in the department. Marsha sent Nicholas many long and complicated e-mail messages that required substantial time to read and respond. When Nicholas responded to Marsha's e-mail message, she would typically send another e-mail back asking for clarification.

Marsha's behavior during department meetings irritated Nicholas. She would demand more time than any other participant to explain her point of view on a variety of issues. At a recent meeting she took ten minutes

explaining how the company should be doing more to help the homeless and invest in the development of inner cities.

Nicholas coached Marsha frequently about the problems she was creating, but Marsha strongly disagreed with his criticism and concerns. At one time, Nicholas told Marsha that she was a high-maintenance employee. Yet Marsha perceived herself as a major contributor to the department. She commented once, "Could it be Nick, that you have a problem with an assertive woman working in your department?"

Nicholas developed a tactic to get Marsha out of the department. He would give her outstanding performance evaluations, emphasizing her creativity and persistence. Marsha would then be entered into the company database as an outstanding employee, thereby making her a strong candidate for transfer or promotion. Within six months, a manager in a new division of the company took the bait. She requested that Marsha be recruited into her department as a senior financial analyst. Nicholas said to the recruiting manager, "I hate to lose a valuable contributor like Marsha, but I do not want to block her career progress."

Two months later, Marsha's new manager telephoned Nicholas, and asked, "What's the problem with Marsha? She's kind of a pill to have working with us. I thought she was an outstanding employee."

Nicholas responded, "Give Marsha some time. She may be having a few problems adjusting to a new environment. Just give her a little constructive feedback. You'll find out what a dynamo she can be."

Case Questions

1. How ethical was Nicholas in giving Marsha a high performance evaluation for the purposes of attracting her to other departments?

2. What should the manager do who was hooked by Nicholas's bait of the high performance evaluation?

3. What might the company do to prevent more incidents of inflated performance evaluations for the purpose of transferring an unwanted employee?

INTERPERSONAL SKILLS ROLE-PLAY

Confronting the Ethical Deviant

One student plays the role of the manager who transferred Marsha into his or her department. The new manager has become suspicious that Nicholas might have manipulated Marsha's performance evaluations to make her appear like a strong candidate for transfer or promotion. In fact, the new manager thinks he may have caught an ethical deviant. Another student plays the role of Nicholas who wants to defend his reputation as an ethical manager. During the role play, pay some attention to ethical issues. As usual, other students will provide feedback on the effectiveness of the interaction they observed.

CHAPTER 8

Stress Management and Personal Productivity

Learning Objectives

After reading and studying this chapter and doing the exercises you should be able to

1. Explain many of the symptoms and consequences of stress, including burnout.

2. Describe personality factors and job factors that contribute to stress.

3. Manage your own stress effectively.

4. Reduce any tendencies you might have toward procrastination.

5. Identify attitudes and values that will enhance your productivity.

6. Identify work habits and skills that will enhance your productivity.

7. Pinpoint potential time wasters that drain your productivity.

The week between Christmas and New Year's is a slow one at hospital executive Elizabeth Dever's office. Dever, who is director of public relations and volunteers at the Shriners Hospital for Children in Los Angeles, intends to spend that week organizing her work space and her thoughts for the new year. She already has started a big desk cleanup and a filing system overhaul.

"December for me gets to be a little less busy, and then it starts back for me in January," says Dever. "I thought, 'It's going to be the new year coming up very soon. If I'm going to do this, now is the time.'"[1]

Discussion Question

1. How might organizing her desk have really paid off for Elizabeth Dever?

The hospital executive just described is performing one of the most basic tasks on the road to decreasing job stress and increasing personal productivity—organizing her work and her thoughts. Although this book is primarily about interpersonal skills, information about managing stress and enhancing personal productivity is relevant. Having your work under control and not being stressed out enables you to focus better on interpersonal relationships.

The first half of this chapter deals with the nature of stress and how it can be managed, whereas the second half describes various approaches to improving personal productivity. The two topics are as closely related as nutrition and health. When you effectively manage stress, you can be more productive. And when your work is under control, you avoid the heavy stress of feeling overwhelmed.

UNDERSTANDING AND MANAGING STRESS

A major challenge facing any worker who wants to stay healthy and have good interpersonal relationships is to manage stress effectively. Although *stress* is an everyday term, a scientific definition helps clarify its meaning. **Stress** is an adaptive response that is the consequence of any action, situation, or event that places special demands on a person. Note that stress, as used here, refers to a reaction to the situation, not the situation or force itself. A **stressor** is the external or internal force that brings about the stress.

Individual differences in the perception of an event play a key role in determining what events are stressful. Giving a presentation to management, for example, is stressful for some people but not for others. Some people perceive a presentation as a threatening and uncomfortable experience, while others might perceive the same event to be an invigorating challenge.

The term *special demands* is also critical because minor adjustments, such as a pencil point that breaks, are usually not perceived as stressful. Yet piling on of minor adjustments, such as having 10 small things go wrong in one day, is stressful. This is true because stress is additive: A series of small doses of stress can create a major stress problem.

This textbook's approach to understanding stress centers on its symptoms and consequences, personality and job factors that contribute to stress, and methods and techniques for stress management. Managing stress receives more emphasis because the same techniques can be used to combat a variety of stressors.

stress An adaptive response that is the consequence of any action, situation, or event that places special demands on a person.

stressor The external or internal force that brings about stress.

Learning Objective 1 ▶

SYMPTOMS AND CONSEQUENCES OF STRESS

The physiological changes that take place within the body in response to stress are responsible for most stress symptoms. These physiological changes are almost identical for both positive and negative stressors. Ski racing, romantic attraction, and being downsized can make you feel about the same physically. The experience of stress helps activate hormones that prepare the body to run or fight when faced with a challenge. This battle against the stressor is referred to as the **fight-or-flight response**. It helps you deal with emergencies.

The research of Shelley Taylor and her associates suggests the possibility that women, along with females of other species, react differently to major stressors. Instead of the fight-or-flight response typical of males, they *tend and befriend*. When stress levels mount, women are more likely to protect and nurture their children (tend) and turn to social networks of supportive females (befriend). Women use affiliation with others to relieve stress. The researchers speculate that the tend-and-befriend behavior became prevalent over the centuries because women who tended and befriended were more likely to have their offspring survive and pass on their mother's traits. Men may tend and befriend also, but to a lesser extent. The tend-and-befriend response

fight-or-flight response The body's physiological and chemical battle against a stressor in which the person tries to cope with the adversity head-on or tries to flee from the scene.

can be traced to a hormone, oxytocin, produced in the brain. Although this research may not be politically correct, it has stimulated the interests of many scientists.[2]

A modern explanation of the fight-or-flight response theory explains that, when faced with stress, the brain acts much like a thermostat. When outside conditions deviate from an ideal point, the thermostat sends a signal to the furnace to increase heat or air conditioning. The brain senses stress as damage to well-being and therefore sends out a signal to the body to cope. The purpose of coping is to modify the discrepancy between the ideal (low-stress) and actual (high-stress) conditions.[3] The brain is thus a self-regulating system that helps us cope with stressors.

Physiological Reactions

The activation of hormones when the body has to cope with a stressor produces a short-term physiological reaction. Among the most familiar reactions is an increase in heart rate, blood pressure, blood glucose, and blood clotting. To help you recognize these symptoms, try to recall your internal bodily sensations the last time you were almost in an automobile accident or heard some wonderful news. Less familiar changes are a redirection of the blood flow toward the brain and large muscle groups and a release of stored fluids from places throughout the body into the bloodstream.

If stress is continuous and accompanied by these short-term physiological changes, annoying and life-threatening conditions can occur. Damage occurs when stress levels rarely subside. A stressful life event usually leads to a high cholesterol level (of the unhealthy type) and high blood pressure. Other conditions associated with stress are cardiac disease, migraine headaches, ulcers, allergies, skin disorders, irritable bowel syndrome, and cancer. A study of 812 Swedish workers conducted over a 25-year period found that work stress doubles the risk of dying from a heart attack. Seventy-three of the workers died from cardiac disease during the study. The major type of stress studied was having high work demands with little control over the work, combined with being underpaid.[4]

To make matters worse, stress can hamper the immune system, thereby increasing the severity of many diseases and disorders. For example, people whose stress level is high recover more slowly from colds and injuries, and they are more susceptible to sexually transmitted diseases.

Stress symptoms vary considerably from one person to another. A general behavioral symptom of intense stress is for people to exaggerate their weakest tendencies. For instance, a person with a strong temper who usually keeps cool under pressure may throw a tantrum under intense pressure. Some common stress symptoms are listed in Figure 14-1.

Job Performance Consequences

Despite all the problems just mentioned, stress also plays a positive role in our lives. The right amount of stress prepares us for meeting difficult challenges and spurs us on to peak intellectual and physical performance. An optimum level of stress exists for most people and most tasks. In general, performance tends to be best under moderate amounts of stress. If the stress is too great, people become temporarily ineffective; they may freeze or choke. Under too little stress, people may become lethargic and inattentive. Figure 14-2 depicts the relationship between stress and job performance. An exception to this relationship is that certain negative forms of stress are likely to lower performance even if the stress is moderate. For example, the stress created by an intimidating supervisor or worrying about radiation poisoning—even in moderate amounts—will not improve performance.

Job stress can also lower job performance indirectly because distressed workers are more likely to be absent from the job thereby not accomplishing as much work. A study of 323 health service workers in the United Kingdom found that job-related psychological distress, particularly depression, was associated with more days absent, and a greater number of times absent.[5]

170

Mostly Physical and Physiological	
Shaking or trembling	Mouth dryness
Dizziness	Upper and lower back pain
Heart palpitations	Frequent headaches
Difficulty breathing	Low energy and stamina
Chronic fatigue	Stomach problems
Unexplained chest pains	Constant craving for sweets
Frequent teeth grinding	Increased alcohol or cigarette consumption
Frequent nausea	Frequent need to eliminate
Mostly Emotional and Behavioral	
Difficulty concentrating	Anxiety or depression
Nervousness	Forgetfulness
Crying	Restlessness
Anorexia	Frequent arguments with others
Declining interest in sex	Feeling high strung much of the time
Frequent nail biting or hair tugging	

FIGURE 14-1 A Variety of Stress Symptoms

Note: Anxiety is a general sense of dread, fear, or worry not linked to a specific event, such as being anxious about your future.

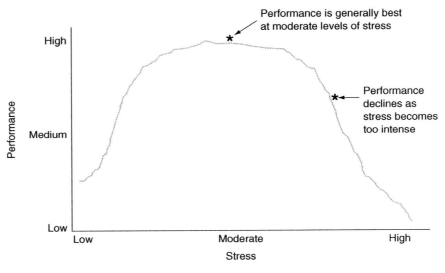

FIGURE 14-2 Relationship between Stress and Job Performance

The job performance impact of a stressor on the individual is influenced by a variety of personal and environmental factors. The research of Steve M. Jex indicates that decreases in performance are least likely when employees (1) understand clearly what to expect in their jobs, (2) have high self-esteem, (3) have high commitment to the organization, and (4) have low levels of Type A behavior.[6]

The optimum amount of stress is a positive force that is the equivalent of finding excitement and challenge. Your ability to solve problems and deal with challenge is enhanced when the right amount of adrenaline flows in your blood to guide you toward peak performance. In fact, highly productive people are sometimes said to be hooked on adrenaline.

Burnout and Stress
One of the major problems of prolonged stress is that it may lead to **burnout**, a condition of emotional, mental, and physical exhaustion in response to long-term stressors. Burnout is also referred to as work exhaustion because fatigue is usually

burnout A condition of emotional, mental, and physical exhaustion in response to long-term stressors.

involved. Burned-out people are often cynical. Burnout is a complex phenomenon, but it often occurs when people feel out of control. Other critical factors that contribute to burnout are insufficient recognition and reward, a lack of emotional support in the workplace, or an absence of fairness. Christina Maslach observes that "When the workplace does not recognize the human side of work, then the risk of burnout grows, carrying with it a high price and hurting all the parties involved."[7]

The key feature of burnout is the distancing that occurs in response to work overload. Burnout sufferers shift into a mode of doing the minimum as a way of protecting themselves. They start leaving work early and dehumanizing their clients, patients, or customers. People experiencing burnout may do their jobs, but their heart is not in it anymore.[8]

PERSONALITY AND JOB FACTORS CONTRIBUTING TO STRESS

◀ Learning Objective 2

Workers experience stress for many different reasons, including personal predispositions, factors stemming from the job, or the combined influence of both. If a person with an extreme negative predisposition has to deal with irate customers, he or she is most likely to experience substantial stress. Here we describe a sampling of important individual and organizational factors that contribute to job stress.

Personality Factors Predisposing People toward Stress

Individuals vary considerably in their susceptibility to job stress based on their personality traits and characteristics. Four such factors are described next.

Low Perceived Control. A key factor in determining whether workers experience stress is how much they believe they can control a given adverse circumstance. **Perceived control** is the belief that an individual has at his or her disposal a response that can control the negative aspects of an event. A survey of over 100 studies indicated that people with a high level of perceived control had low levels of physical and psychological symptoms of stress. Conversely, people with low perceived control are more likely to experience work stress.[9]

perceived control The belief that an individual has at his or her disposal a response that can control the negative aspects of an event.

Low Self-Efficacy. Self-efficacy, like perceived control, is another personal factor that influences susceptibility to stress. (Note that because self-efficacy is tied to a specific situation it is not strictly a personality trait.) When workers have both low perceived control and low self-efficacy the stress consequences may be much worse. However, having high self-efficacy (being confident in one's abilities) softens the stress consequences of demanding jobs.[10]

Two studies with about 2,300 U.S. Army soldiers each showed that respondents with strong self-efficacy were less stressed out mentally and physically by long work hours and work overload. A key conclusion of the studies is that high levels of self-efficacy may help employees cope more effectively with job stressors.[11] To illustrate, an active coping method would be to reorganize an overwhelming workload so it can be performed more efficiently.

Type A Behavior. A person with **Type A behavior** is demanding, impatient, and overstriving and is therefore prone to negative stress. Type A behavior has two main components. One is the tendency to try to accomplish too many things in too little time. This leads the Type A individual to be impatient and demanding. The other component is free-floating hostility. Because of this sense of urgency and hostility, trivial things irritate these people. People with Type A behavior are aggressive and hardworking.

Type A personalities frequently have cardiac diseases, such as heart attacks and strokes, at an early age, but only certain features of the Type A personality pattern may be related to coronary heart disease. The heart attack triggers are hostility,

Type A behavior A behavior pattern in which the individuals is demanding, impatient, and overstriving, and therefore prone to negative stress.

anger, cynicism, and suspiciousness, as contrasted to impatience, ambition, and being work driven. In fact, hostility is more strongly associated with coronary heart disease in men than smoking, drinking, overeating, or high levels of bad (LDL) cholesterol.[12] Note that the heart attack triggers also make for strained interpersonal relationships.

negative affectivity A tendency to experience aversive emotional states.

Negative Affectivity. A major contributor to being stress prone is **negative affectivity**, a tendency to experience aversive emotional states. In more detail, negative affectivity is a pervasive disposition to experience emotional stress that includes feelings of nervousness, tension, and worry. The same disposition also includes such emotional states as anger, scorn, revulsion, guilt, self-dissatisfaction, and sadness.[13] Such negative personalities seem to search for important discrepancies between what they would like and what exists. Poor interpersonal relationships often result from the frequent complaining of people with negative affectivity.

Job Sources of Stress

Almost any job situation can act as a stressor for some employees, but not necessarily for others. As just described, certain personality factors make it more likely that a person will experience job stress. Furthermore, other personal life stressors may spill over into the workplace, making it more likely that a person will experience job stress. Four frequently encountered job stressors are outlined in Figure 14-3 and described below.

role overload Having too much work to do.

Role Overload. Having too much work to do, **role overload**, can create negative stress in two ways. First, the person may become fatigued and thus be less able to tolerate annoyances and irritations. Second, a person subject to unreasonable work demands may feel perpetually behind schedule, a situation that is itself a powerful stressor. Downsizing often creates overload because fewer people are left to handle the same workload as before. (If work is carefully streamlined, role overload is minimized.) According to a Families and Work Institute survey, one in three American workers feels chronically overworked. People were found to be working longer and harder, yet younger workers in particular are finding ways to balance the demands by dividing their focus between the job and personal life. Many employers were found to be more flexible in helping workers achieve this balance, such as allowing flexible working hours.[14]

Role Conflict and Role Ambiguity. Role conflict, described in Chapter 7 as an important workplace conflict, is also a major workplace stressor. People experience stress when they have to choose between two sets of expectations. Suppose an accountant

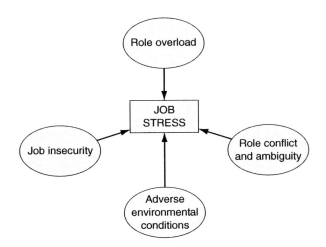

FIGURE 14–3 Four Significant Sources of Job Stress

is asked by her manager to state company earnings in a way that conflicts with the professional norms of accountants. If she complies with her manager, she will feel that she is betraying her profession. If she does not comply with her manager, she will enter into dispute with the manager. The woman is likely to experience job stress.

Role ambiguity is a condition in which the jobholder receives confusing or poorly defined expectations. Workers in many organizations are placed in situations in which they are unsure of their true responsibilities. Some workers who are placed on a self-managing work team experience role ambiguity because they are asked to solve many problems by themselves. It is less ambiguous to have the manager tell you what to do. Many people experience stress symptoms when faced with role ambiguity.

role ambiguity A condition in which the job holder receives confusing or poorly defined expectations.

Adverse Environmental Conditions. A variety of adverse organizational conditions are stressors, as identified by the National Institute for Occupational Safety and Health (NIOSH). Among these adverse organizational conditions are unpleasant or dangerous physical conditions, such as crowding, noise, air pollutions, or ergonomic problems. Enough polluted air within an office building can create a sick building in which a diverse range of airborne particles, vapors, molds, and gases pollute the indoor environment. The result can be headaches, nausea, and respiratory infections as well as the stress created by being physically ill.[15]

Ergonomic problems refer to a poor fit between the physical and human requirements of a job. Working at a computer monitor for prolonged periods of time can lead to adverse physical and psychological reactions. The symptoms include headaches and fatigue, along with eye problems. According to the Vision Syndrome Information Center, about 90 percent of people working on computers more than three hours a day have vision problems, with some 10 million a year seeking treatment. Common visual problems are dry eyes and blurred or double vision. Another vision-related problem is that people lean forward to scan the monitor, leading to physical problems such as back strain.

The repetitive-motion disorder most frequently associated with keyboarding and the use of optical scanners is **carpal tunnel syndrome**. The syndrome occurs when repetitive flexing and extension of the wrist causes the tendons to swell, thus trapping and pinching the median nerve. Carpal tunnel syndrome creates stress because of the pain and misery. About one in five computer users will suffer from carpal tunnel syndrome at some point.[16] The thoughts of having to permanently leave a job requiring keyboarding is another potential stressor. If ergonomic principles, such as erect posture, are incorporated into computer usage, these stress symptoms diminish.

carpal tunnel syndromé A condition that occurs when repetitive flexing and extension of the wrist causes the tendons to swell, thus trapping and pinching the median nerve.

Job Insecurity. Worrying about losing your job is a major stressor. Even when jobs are plentiful, having to search for another job and facing the prospect of geographic relocation are stressors for many people. Downsizing and corporate mergers (which usually result in downsizing) have contributed to job insecurity. The anticipation of layoffs among employees can increase negative stress and lower job performance. In addition, the survivors of a downsizing often experience pressure from the fear of future cuts, loss of friends, and worry about a sudden increase in workload.[17]

METHODS AND TECHNIQUES FOR STRESS MANAGEMENT

◀ Learning Objective 3

Unless stress is managed properly, it may lead to harmful long-term consequences, including disabling physical illness and career retardation. Managing stress refers to controlling stress by making it a constructive force in your life. Managing thus refers to both preventing and reducing stress. However, the distinction between methods of preventing and reducing stress is not clear-cut. For example, physical exercise not only reduces stress, it also contributes to a relaxed lifestyle that helps you prevent stress.

Coping with, or managing, stress includes hundreds of activities, with substantial individual differences in which technique is effective. Running is a case in point. For many people running or jogging is an excellent method of stress reduction. Others find that running creates new stressors, such as aching knees, shin splints, dizziness from breathing in vehicle exhausts, and worrying about being hit by vehicles. In general, coping efforts involve cognitions and behaviors aimed at managing the stressor and its associated emotions. For example, you might have to decrease the troublesome elements in your job (such as role overload) and also deal with the tension generated by overwork. The following subsections describe eight methods for managing stress, including a list of everyday stress busters.

Eliminate or Modify the Stressor

The most potent method of managing stress is to eliminate or modify the stressor giving you trouble. One value of relaxation techniques and tranquilizing medication is that they calm a person enough so that he or she can deal constructively with the stressor. A helpful way to attack the cause of stress is to follow the steps in problem solving and decision making. You clarify the problem, identify the alternatives, weigh the alternatives, and select one alternative. One difficulty, however, is that your evaluation of the real problem may be inaccurate. There is always a limit to self-analysis. For example, a person might think that work overload is the stressor when the true stressor is low self-efficacy.

Get Appropriate Physical Exercise

A moderate amount of physical exercise is a cornerstone of managing stress and achieving wellness. To manage stress it is important to select an exercise program that is physically challenging but does not lead to overexertion and muscle and bone injury. Competitive sports, if taken too seriously, can actually increase stress. Aerobic exercises are most beneficial because they make you breathe faster and raise your heart rate. Walking is highly recommended as a stress reducer because it is inherently relaxing, and offers many of the benefits of other forms of exercise with a minimum risk of physical danger. A major mental and emotional benefit of physical exercise stems from endorphins produced in the thalamus portion of the brain. The endorphins are associated with a state of euphoria referred to as "runner's high." Endorphins also work like pain killers, adding to their stress-reduction value.

Millions of people seek to reduce and prevent stress through yoga, which is both physical exercise and a way of developing mental attitudes that calm the body and mind. One of yoga's many worthwhile goals is to solder a union between the mind and body, thereby achieving harmony and tranquility. Another benefit of yoga is that it helps people place aside negative thoughts that act as stressors.[18]

Rest Sufficiently

Rest offers benefits similar to those of exercise, such as stress reduction, improved concentration, improved energy, and better tolerance for frustration. Achieving proper rest is closely linked to getting proper exercise. The current interest in adult napping reflects the awareness that proper rest makes a person less stress prone and enhances productivity. A growing number of firms have napping facilities for workers, and many workers nap at their desks or in their parked vehicles during lunch breaks. Naps of about 15 minutes duration taken during the workday are used both as energizers and as stress reducers. Napping can help a worker become more productive and less stressed. A rested brain is a more effective brain. To keep the effectiveness of workday napping in perspective, workers who achieve sufficient rest during normal sleeping hours have less need for a nap during working hours.[19]

Maintain a Healthy Diet

Another practical method of stress reduction and prevention is to maintain a well-balanced, and therefore healthy, diet. Nutritious food is valuable for physical and mental health, making it easier to cope with frustrations that are potential stressors. Some non-nutritious foods, such as those laden with caffeine or sugar, tend to enhance a person's level of stress. According to the Dietary Guidelines of the United States Department of Agriculture, a healthy diet is one that

- Emphasizes fruits, vegetables, whole grains, and fat-free or low-fat milk and milk products
- Includes lean meats, poultry, fish, beans, eggs, and nuts
- Is low in saturated fats, *trans* fats, cholesterol, salt (sodium), and added sugars.

These recommendations are for the general public over two years of age. Using MyPyramid, the government personalizes a recommended diet, taking into account our age, sex, and amount of physical exercise. Consult *http://www.mypyramid.gov*, as shown in Figure 14-4.

Build a Support Network

A **support network** is a group of people who can listen to your problems and provide emotional support. These people, or even one person, can help you through your difficult episodes. Members of your network can provide you with a sense of closeness, warmth, and acceptance that will reduce your stress. Also, the simple expedient of putting your feelings into words can be a healing experience. The way to develop this support network is to become a good listener so that the other person will reciprocate. A support network is therefore a method of stress management based squarely on effective interpersonal skills.

Practice Visualization

Perhaps the most effortless and enjoyable relaxation technique for managing stress is to visualize a pleasant experience, as explained in Skill-Building Exercise 14-1. Visualization, like so many stress-reduction techniques, including meditation, requires concentration. Concentrating helps slow down basic physiological processes such as the heartbeat and dissipates stress. Forcing yourself to concentrate is also valuable because a key stress symptom is difficulty in concentrating.

Practice Everyday Methods of Stress Reduction

The simple expedient of learning how to relax is an important method of reducing the tension and anxiety brought about by both positive and negative stress. Visualization of a pleasant experience is one such method. A sample of everyday

support network A group of people who can listen to your problems and provide emotional support.

The Food Groups

Grains

Vegetables

Fruits

Milk

Meat & Beans

Oils

FIGURE 14-4 Dietary Guidelines for Americans, developed by the U.S. Department of Agriculture. Access the pyramid to receive your personalized set of recommendations for a healthy diet.

Source: U.S. Department of Agriculture, *http://www.mypyramid.gov*.

SKILL-BUILDING EXERCISE 14-1

VISUALIZATION FOR STRESS REDUCTION

A standard, easy-to-use method for reducing stress symptoms is to visualize a pleasant and calm experience. If you are experiencing stress right now, try the technique. Otherwise, wait until the next time you perceive your body to be experiencing stress. In this context, visualization means to picture yourself doing something that you would like to do. Whatever fantasy suits your fancy will work, according to the advocates of this relaxation technique. Visualizations that work for some people include smiling at a loved one, floating on a cloud, caressing a baby, petting a kitten or puppy, and walking in the woods. Notice that all of these scenes are relaxing rather than exciting. What visualization would work for you?

To implement the technique, close your eyes and bring the pleasant image into focus in your mind. Think of nothing else at the moment (as in meditation). Imagine that a DVD of the pleasant experience is playing on the television screen in your brain. Breathe softly and savor the experience. Slowly return to reality, refreshed, relaxed, and ready to tackle the challenges of the day.

suggestions for relaxation and other methods of stress reduction are presented in Figure 14-5. If you can accomplish these you are less likely to need tranquilizing medication to keep you calm and in control. Your stress symptoms will ordinarily return, however, if you do not eliminate and modify the stressor. If the stress is an emotional conflict you do not see or understand, assistance from a mental health professional is recommended.

- ✪ Give in to your emotions. If you are angry, disgusted, or confused, admit your feelings. Suppressing your emotions adds to stress.
- ✪ Take a brief break from the stressful situation and do something small and constructive, such as washing your car, emptying a wastebasket, or getting a haircut.
- ✪ Get a massage, because it can loosen tight muscles, improve your blood circulation, and calm you down.
- ✪ Get help with your stressful task from a coworker, supervisor, or friend.
- ✪ Concentrate intensely on reading, surfing the Internet, a sport, or a hobby. Contrary to common sense, concentration is at the heart of stress reduction.
- ✪ Have a quiet place at home and have a brief idle period there every day.
- ✪ Take a leisurely day off from your routine.
- ✪ Finish something you have started, however small. Accomplishing almost anything reduces some stress.
- ✪ Stop to smell the flowers, make friends with a young child or elderly person, or play with a kitten or puppy.
- ✪ Strive to do a good job, but not a perfect job.
- ✪ Work with your hands, doing a pleasant task.
- ✪ Find somebody or something that makes you laugh, and have a good laugh.
- ✪ Minimize drinking caffeinated or alcoholic beverages, and drink fruit juice or water instead. Grab a piece of fruit rather than a can of beer.
- ✪ Help somebody less fortunate than you. The flood of good feelings will act like endorphins.

FIGURE 14-5 Stress Busters

Use the Freeze-Frame Technique

A scientifically based method of stress reduction that emphasizes reappraising a difficult event, along with some symptom management, is the **freeze-frame technique** developed by the HeartMath Institute. The method proceeds as follows:

Step One. *Recognize the stressful feeling and freeze-frame it.* See your problem as a still photo, not a movie. Stop the inner conversation about it.

Step Two. Make a sincere effort to *shift your focus* away from the racing mind or disturbed emotions in the area around your heart. Pretend you are breathing through your heart to help focus energy in this area. Stay focused there for 10 seconds or more.

Step Three. *Recall a positive fun feeling or time* you've had in your life and visualize experiencing it again.

Step Four. Using your intuition, common sense, and sincerity, *ask your heart what would be a more efficient response* to the situation—one that will minimize future stress.

Step Five. *Listen to what your heart says* in answer to your question. Here you are using an in-house source of common sense solutions.

You may hear nothing, but at least you will feel calmer. You may receive confirmation of something you already know. Equally important, you may gain a perspective shift and see the problem in a different way. Although we may not have control over the event, we do have control over how we perceive it.[20]

freeze-frame technique A scientifically based method of stress reduction that emphasizes reappraising a difficult event, along with some symptom management.

IMPROVING PERSONAL PRODUCTIVITY

Achieving personal productivity is more in vogue than ever. Companies strive to operate with smaller staffs than in the past by pushing workers to achieve higher productivity. At the same time, there is a movement toward simplifying personal life by reducing clutter and cutting back on tasks that do not add much to the quality of life. **Personal productivity** refers to the amount of resources, including time, you consume to achieve a certain level of output. We approach productivity improvement from four perspectives: (1) dealing with procrastination, (2) attitudes and values that enhance personal productivity, (3) work habits and skills that enhance personal productivity, and (4) overcoming time wasters.

personal productivity The amount of resources, including time, you consume to achieve a certain level of output.

DEALING WITH PROCRASTINATION

◄ Learning Objective 4

The person who **procrastinates** delays action for no good reason. Procrastination lowers productivity because it wastes time and many important tasks never get done. Even productive people sometimes procrastinate. If these people did not procrastinate, they would be even more productive.

Many people regard procrastination as a laughable weakness, particularly because procrastinators themselves joke about the problem. Yet procrastination has been evaluated as a profound, debilitating problem, with about 20 percent of working adults identifying themselves as chronic procrastinators.[21] Approximately 70 percent of college students report problems with overdue papers and delayed studying.[22] The enormity of the procrastination problem makes it worthwhile to examine methods for bringing it under control. Do Self-Assessment Quiz 14-1 to think through your own tendencies toward procrastination—and don't wait until tomorrow.

Choose from among the following suggestions for controlling procrastination, based on those that appear to best fit your type of procrastination. A combination of techniques is likely to be the most effective.

procrastination Delaying action for no good reason.

SELF-ASSESSMENT QUIZ 14-1

PROCRASTINATION TENDENCIES

Directions: Circle yes or no for each item:

1.	I usually do my best work under the pressure of deadlines.	Yes	No
2.	Before starting a project I go through such rituals as sharpening every pencil, straightening up my desk more than once, and reading and responding to all possible e-mail.	Yes	No
3.	I crave the excitement of the "last-minute rush," such as researching and writing a paper right before the deadline.	Yes	No
4.	I often think that if I delay something, it will go away, or the person who asked for it will forget about it.	Yes	No
5.	I extensively research something before taking action, such as obtaining three different estimates before getting the brakes repaired on my car.	Yes	No
6.	I have a great deal of difficulty getting started on most projects, even those I enjoy.	Yes	No
7.	I keep waiting for the right time to do something, such as getting started on an important report.	Yes	No
8.	I often underestimate the time needed to do a project, and say to myself, "I can do this quickly, so I'll wait until next week."	Yes	No
9.	It is difficult for me to finish most projects or activities.	Yes	No
10.	I have several favorite diversions or distractions that I use to keep me from doing something unpleasant, such as a difficult homework assignment.	Yes	No

Total Yes Responses _____

Scoring and Interpretation: The greater the number of "yes" responses, the more likely it is that you have a serious procrastination problem. A score of 8, 9, or 10 strongly suggests that your procrastination is lowering your productivity.

1. **Calculate the cost of procrastination.** You can reduce procrastination by calculating its cost. You might lose out on obtaining a high-paying job you really want by not having your résumé and cover letter ready on time. Your cost of procrastination would include the difference in compensation between the job you do find and the one you really wanted. Another cost would be the loss of potential job satisfaction.

2. **Follow the WIFO principle, which stands for "worst in, first out."**[23] If you tackle the worst task on your list first, doing the other tasks may function like a small reward. You get to do what you dislike the least by doing first what you dislike the most. WIFO is particularly effective when faced with a number of tasks simultaneously.

3. **Break the task into manageable chunks.** To reduce procrastination, cut down a task that seems overwhelming into smaller projects that seem less formidable. If your job calls for preparing an enormous database, begin by assembling some readily available information. Then take the next step by assembling another small segment of the database—perhaps all customers

whose last names begin with *Z*. Think of your task as pulling together a series of small databases that will fit into a master database.

4. **Make a commitment to other people.** Try to make it imperative that you get something done on time by making it a commitment to one or more other people. You might announce to coworkers that you are going to get something accomplished by a certain date. If you fail to meet this date, you are likely to feel embarrassed.

5. **Remove some clutter from your mind.** Procrastination escalates when people have many unfinished projects in the back of their mind, draining their concentration. Too much to do can freeze us into inaction. Just eliminating a few trivial items from your to-do list can give you enough mental energy to overcome procrastination on a few major tasks. Notice carefully that this approach to overcoming procrastination requires that you apply enough self-discipline to take the first step.

6. **Satisfy your stimulation quota in constructive ways.** If you procrastinate because you enjoy the rush of scrambling to make deadlines, find a more constructive way of using busyness to keep you humming. If you need a high level of stimulation, enrich your life with extra projects and learning new skills. The fullness of your schedule will provide you the stimulation you had been receiving from squeezing yourself to make deadlines and reach appointments on time.[24]

7. **Eliminate tangible rewards you are giving yourself for procrastinating.** If you are procrastinating through socializing with coworkers, taking a walk to obtain a beverage, surfing the Net, or any other pleasant experience—stop rewarding yourself. Just sit alone in your work area doing nothing while procrastinating. If you remove the pleasant activities from your stalling routine, you may be able to reduce procrastination.[25]

ENHANCING PERSONAL PRODUCTIVITY THROUGH ATTITUDES AND VALUES

◄ Learning Objective 5

Developing good work habits and time-management practices is often a matter of developing the right attitudes toward your work and toward time. If, for example, you think that your schoolwork or job is important and that time is a precious resource, you will be on your way toward developing good work habits. In this section, we describe a group of attitudes, values, and beliefs that can help a person become more productive through better use of time and improved work habits.

Begin with a Mission and Goals

A mission, or general purpose, propels you toward being productive. Assume that a person says, "My mission is to be an outstanding professional in my field and a loving, constructive spouse and parent." The mission serves as a compass to direct your activities, such as being well organized in order to accomplish more work and be highly valued by your employer. Goals are more specific than mission statements; they support the mission statement, but the effect is the same. Being committed to a goal also propels you toward good use of time. If you know that you can obtain the position in international business that you really want by mastering a second language, you are likely to work diligently on learning that language. Skill-Building Exercise 14-2 gives you the opportunity to establish a mission statement and supporting goals.

Play the Inner Game of Work

Timothy Gallwey developed the inner game of tennis to help tennis players focus better on their game. Over time the inner game spread to skiing, other sports, life in general, and work. The key concept is that by removing inner obstacles such as self-criticism, you can dramatically improve your ability to focus, learn, and perform.

USING A MISSION STATEMENT AND GOALS TO POWER WORK HABITS

People with a well-defined mission statement and supporting goals tend to have better work habits and time management than those who do not. The following exercise is designed to help you establish a mission statement and goals so you will be energized to be more productive.

A. Mission Statement: To help develop your mission statement, or general purpose in life, ask yourself, "What are my five biggest wishes in life?" These wishes give you a hint to your purpose because they point toward an ideal purpose in life. Feel free to think big, because mission statements tend toward being idealistic.

B. Long-Range Goals to Support Mission Statement: Now write down what long-range goals would support your mission statement. Suppose your mission statement related to "creating a better life for people who are disadvantaged." Your long-range goals might include establishing a foundation that would fund your efforts. You would also need to be successful enough in your career to get the foundation started.

C. Intermediate-Range Goals to Support Long-Range Goals: Write down the intermediate-range goals needed to support the long-range goals. You will probably need to complete your education, obtain broad experience, and identify a lucrative form of self-employment.

D. Weekly Goals to Support Intermediate-Range Goals: Write down what you have to do this week to help you complete your education, such as researching and writing a paper for a particular course, registering for courses for next term, and inquiring about career opportunities in your field.

E. Today's Goals to Support Weekly Goals (My To-Do List): Here's where your lofty purpose in life gets translated into reality. What do you have to do today to get that paper written? Do you need to get your car battery replaced so you can get to the library so you can write your paper, so you can graduate, so you can become rich, so you can ultimately help all those people who are disadvantaged? Get going.

According to Gallwey, two selves exist inside each person. Self 1 is the critical, fearful, self-doubting voice that sends out messages like, "You have almost solved this tough problem for the customer. Don't blow it now." Intimidating comments like these hinder Self 2 from getting the job done. Self 2 encompasses all the inner resources— both actual and potential—of the individual.

Self 1 must be suppressed so Self 2 can accomplish its task and learn effectively without being lectured. The process required to move Self 1 aside is to focus your attention on a critical variable related to performance rather than on the performance you are attempting to achieve. An example would be for a customer service representative to focus on the amount of tension in a caller's voice.[26] Or, you might focus on the facial expressions of your manager as you attempt to sell him or her on an idea for improving productivity.

Work Smarter, Not Harder

People caught up in trying to accomplish a job often wind up working hard, but not in an imaginative way that leads to good results. Much time and energy are therefore wasted. A working-smart approach also requires that you spend a few minutes carefully planning how to implement your task. An example of working smarter, not harder is to invest a few minutes of critical thinking before conducting a telemarketing campaign for home replacement windows. Develop a list of homeowners of houses of at least 15 years old. People with relatively new homes are poor prospects for replacing their windows.

Value Orderliness and Cleanliness

An orderly desk, work area, briefcase, or hard drive does not inevitably indicate an orderly mind. Yet it does help most people become more productive because they can better focus their mind. Also, less time is wasted and less energy is expended if you do not have to hunt for information that you thought you had on hand. According to time-management consultant Barbara Hemphill, the average person spends 150 hours per year searching for misplaced information. Hemphill says, "Your ability to accomplish any task or goal is directly related to your ability to find the right information at the right time."[27] Knowing where information is and what information you have available is a way of being in control of your job. When your job gets out of control, you are probably working at less than peak efficiency. Valuing cleanliness improves productivity in several ways. According to the Japanese system, cleanliness is the bedrock of quality. Also, after you have thoroughly cleaned your work area, you will usually attain a fresh outlook.

Back to the Opening Case

The cleanup helped Dever manage her time better: "I was constantly finding myself saying, 'Where did I put that file?' When you have a clear desk, you can just come in in the morning and pull out the file you're working on and feel like you're more in control."

Value Good Attendance and Punctuality

Good attendance and punctuality are expected of both experienced and inexperienced employees. You cannot be productive unless you are physically present in your work area. The same principle applies whether you work on company premises or at home. One exception is that some people can work through solutions to job problems while engaged in recreation. Keep in mind, too, that being late for or absent from meetings sends the silent message that you do not regard the meeting as being important.

The relationship of lateness to absenteeism and work performance has been researched. Based on 30 studies and over 9,000 workers, it was found that employees who were late also tended to have high absenteeism records. In addition, employees who were late tended to have poorer work performance than workers who were prompt, but the relationship was not strong.[28] Despite this weak association, being late must still be regarded as a productivity drain.

Attain a Balance in Life and Avoid Being a Workaholic

A productive attitude to maintain is that overwork can lead to negative stress and burnout. Proper physical rest and relaxation can contribute to mental alertness and an improved ability to cope with frustration. A strategy for preventing overwork is to strive for a balance in which you derive satisfaction from various spheres of life. Major spheres in addition to work include family life, romance, sports, the arts and music, faith, and intellectual growth.

A strongly recommended technique for attaining balance between work and other spheres of life is to learn how to say no diplomatically to your boss and family members.[29] For example, your boss might ask you to take on a project when you are already overloaded. It would be necessary to *occasionally* explain that you are so

workaholism An addiction to work in which not working is an uncomfortable experience.

Time management is more than making up a to-do list. Not doing the right things to begin with gets you nowhere faster. Time management is the foundation for creating balance in our lives in vital areas, such as health and family.
—Don Wetmore, president of the Productivity Institute, reported in *HR Magazine*, November 2003, p. 103

Learning Objective 6 ▶

overloaded that you could not do a good job with the new assignment. And, you might have to *occasionally* turn down your family's or friend's request to take a weekend vacation when you face heavy work demands.

Neglecting the normal need for rest and relaxation can lead to **workaholism**, an addiction to work in which not working is an uncomfortable experience. Some types of workaholics are perfectionists who are never satisfied with their work and therefore find it difficult to leave work behind. In addition, the perfectionist-type workaholic may become heavily focused on control, leading to rigid behavior and strained interpersonal relationships. However, some people who work long and hard are classified as achievement-oriented workaholics who thrive on hard work and are usually highly productive.[30] For example, a person with strong family values might nevertheless work 65 hours per week for one year while establishing a new business.

ENHANCING PERSONAL PRODUCTIVITY THROUGH WORK HABITS AND SKILLS

Overcoming procrastination and developing the right attitudes contribute to personal productivity. Effective work habits and skills are also essential for high productivity. Six key work habits and skills are described next. They represent a mixture of traditional productivity boosters and those geared toward information technology.

Prepare a To-Do List and Set Priorities

At the heart of every time-management system is list making, whether the list is placed on an index card, in a leather-bound planner, or in a palm-size computer. As already described, the to-do list is the basic tool for achieving your daily goals, which in turn helps you achieve bigger goals and your mission. Almost every successful person in any field composes a list of important and less important tasks that need to be done. Before you compose a useful list, you need to set aside a few minutes of quiet time every day to sort out the tasks at hand. This is the most basic aspect of planning.

As is well known, it is helpful to set priorities for items on the to-do list. A typical system is to use A to signify critical or essential items, B to signify important items, and C for the least important ones. Although an item might be regarded as a C (for example, emptying the wood shavings from the electronic pencil sharpener), it still makes a contribution to your management of time and sense of well-being. Accomplishing anything reduces some stress. Also, many people obtain satisfaction from crossing off an item on their list, however trivial. If you are at all conscientious, small, unaccomplished items will come back to interfere with your concentration.

Time-management consultant Harold Taylor warns that preparing to-do lists should not become an end in itself, with so much time devoted to list making that accomplishing some of the tasks get neglected.[31] Another danger is filling the to-do list with items you would have to accomplish anyway, such as "check e-mail." The to-do list can become so long that it becomes an overwhelming task.

Streamline Your Work and Emphasize Important Tasks

As companies continue to operate with fewer workers than in the past despite prosperity, more unproductive work must be eliminated. Getting rid of unproductive work is part of *business process improvement* in which work processes are radically redesigned and simplified. Every employee is expected to get rid of work that does not contribute to productivity or help customers. In general, to streamline your work, look for duplication of effort and waste. An example of duplication of effort would be to routinely send people e-mail and fax messages covering the same topic. An example of waste would be to call a meeting for disseminating information that could easily be communicated by e-mail.

Emphasizing important tasks means that you make sure to take care of A items on your to-do list. It also implies that you search to accomplish a few work activities that, if done well, would make a big difference in your job performance. Although important tasks may take less time to accomplish than many routine tasks, they can represent the difference between success and failure. Five minutes of telephone conversation with a major customer might do more good for your company than three hours of arranging obsolete inventory in the warehouse.

Concentrate on One Important Task at a Time Instead of Multitasking

While working on important tasks, concentrate on what you are doing. Effective executives and professionals have a well-developed capacity to concentrate on the problem or person facing them, however surrounded they are with other obligations. Intense concentration leads to crisper judgment and analysis and also minimizes major errors. Another useful by-product of concentration is that it helps reduce absentmindedness. If you really concentrate on what you are doing, the chances diminish that you will forget what you intended to do.

While concentrating on an important task, such as performing analytical work or writing a report, avoid multitasking, or performing more than one activity simultaneously. Common forms of multitasking include surfing the Internet or reading e-mail while engaged in a phone conversation with a coworker or customer. Both experimental evidence and opinion has accumulated that multitasking while performing important tasks leads to problems in concentration, along with significant errors—for most people. Multitasking on routine tasks has less negative consequences, and can sometimes be a legitimate time saver. A classic experiment on the topic demonstrated that switching back and forth between tasks actually results in more time required to complete a task.[32]

According to time-management guru Stephanie Winston, the biggest mistake most people make is multitasking. She observes that successful CEOs do not multitask. Instead they concentrate on one thing at a time. "What stops the rest of us from doing likewise, is a reluctance to set boundaries," she says. "People tell me that they feel guilty if they turn off their instant messaging, even if it drives them crazy." Constant distractions interfere with accomplishing good work, so it is better to say, "No, I'm busy right now."[33]

Stay in Control of Paperwork and Electronic Work

Although it is fashionable to complain about paperwork in responsible jobs, the effective career person does not neglect paperwork. (Paperwork includes electronic work such as electronic mail and voice mail.) Paperwork involves taking care of administrative details such as correspondence, invoices, human resource reports, and inventory forms. A considerable amount of electronic work results in paperwork because many e-mail messages and attachments wind up being printed. Unless paperwork and electronic work are attended to, a person's job may get out of control. A small amount of time should be invested in paperwork every day. Nonprime time (when you are at less than your peak of efficiency but not overfatigued) is the best time to take care of paperwork.

An effective technique is to respond quickly to high-priority e-mail messages, and permanently delete those you will most likely not need to refer to again. Print and file only those e-mail messages of high importance to avoid being overwhelmed with piles of old messages.

Work Productively from Your Home Office or Virtual Office

A growing segment of the workforce works either full or part time from home or from a **virtual office**. Such an office is a place of work without a fixed physical location from which the worker or workers communicate their output electronically. A virtual office might be in a car, train, airplane, or hotel room; on a park bench; or wherever the worker happens to be at the time. Many people adapt well to working at home and from virtual offices because they are self-starters and self-disciplined. Many other workers lack the self-discipline and effective work habits necessary to be productive outside of a traditional office. Following is a list of representative suggestions for being productive while working independently.[34]

virtual office A place of work without a fixed physical location, where the output is communicated electronically.

- Act as if you work in a traditional office. Set specific working hours, get dressed, go outside the house for a few minutes, then return and get to work. Also, close your office at home or virtual office at some regular time. Otherwise, you are open for business all the time. If you work at home, establish a clear workspace and let your family and friends know when you cannot be disturbed.

- Stay in touch with teammates to enhance your team player skills and not lose out on important information that could lower your effectiveness (such as missing an appointment at the traditional office).

- Minimize conducting your personal life at the same time as working (for example, working while watching television, talking to neighbors, or shopping over the Internet).

- Schedule regular times for meals and snacks; otherwise, you will lose many minutes and gain many pounds taking food and beverage breaks.

The practice of working at home or from virtual offices is increasing rapidly, so these suggestions merit careful consideration. Several of the productivity ideas also fit the conventional office.

Enhance Your Internet Search Skills

An important job skill is searching the Internet for a variety of information. It follows that if you develop your Internet search skills you will be more productive by obtaining the results you need within a reasonable time. First, it is helpful to rely on several search engines to seek needed information. Several meta-search engines claim to be so comprehensive that no other engine is required. Such claims are exaggerated, because the same search word entered into several different comprehensive engines will reveal a different list of sources.

Second, give careful thought to the search word or phrase you use. The more specific you are, the better. Assume that you wanted to find software to enhance your productivity, and that you enter the word "software" into a search engine. You will probably receive a message indicating that 1.4 billion entries have been located in response to your personal inquiry. You are better advised to use the search phrase "Software for increasing personal productivity."

Third, for many searches, framing the query as a phrase by enclosing it in quotation marks refines the number of hits (or sites) returned. Place quotation marks before and after the search word, such as "software for improving work habits." Fourth, if you don't find what you want in your initial search, reframe your question in another way or change the terms. How about "software for time management" or "computer programs for increasing personal efficiency"? Skill-Building Exercise 14-3 will help you make better use of the Internet to enhance your personal productivity.

SKILL-BUILDING EXERCISE 14-3

PRODUCTIVITY BOOSTING
THROUGH WORK HABITS

The chapter has already given you ideas about using work habits to increase productivity. Here is a chance to make some personal applications of your own. Gather into small teams or work individually to identify 10 ways in which good work habits, as well as using the Internet, can increase personal productivity either on the job or at home. To supplement your own thinking, you might search the Internet for ideas on how the Internet is supposed to boost productivity.

OVERCOMING TIME WASTERS

Another basic thrust to improve personal productivity is to minimize wasting time. Many of the techniques already described in this chapter help save time, such as eliminating nonessential work. Whether or not an activity is a time waster depends on the purpose of the activity. Suppose you play computer solitaire for 10 minutes to reduce stress and then return to work refreshed. In contrast, another worker who spends 10 minutes playing solitaire just for fun is wasting time.

Figure 14-6 presents a list of common time wasters. Being aware of time wasters will help sensitize you to the importance of minimizing them. Even if you saved just 10 minutes per workday, the productivity gain over a year could be enormous.

To analyze whether you might be wasting time, do Skill-Building Exercise 14-4. Self-Assessment Quiz 14-2 gives you an opportunity to think through your tendencies toward a subtle type of time wasting.

1. Use a time log for two weeks to track time wasters. (See Skill-Building Exercise 14-4.)
2. Minimize daydreaming on the job by forcing yourself to concentrate.
3. Avoid the computer as a diversion from work, such as sending jokes back and forth to work members, playing video games, and checking out recreational Web sites during working hours.
4. Cluster together tasks such as returning phone calls or responding to e-mail messages. For example, in most jobs it is possible to be polite and productive by reserving two or three 15-minute periods per day for taking care of e-mail correspondence.
5. Socialize on the job just enough to build your network. Chatting with coworkers is a major productivity drain.
6. Be prepared for meetings by, for example, having a clear agenda and sorting through the documents you will be referring to. Make sure electronic equipment is in working order before attempting to use it during the meeting.
7. Keep track of important names, places, and things to avoid wasting time searching for them.
8. Set a time limit for tasks after you have done them once or twice.
9. Prepare a computer template for letters and computer documents that you send frequently. (The template is essentially a form letter, especially with respect to the salutation and return address.)
10. When you arrive at work, be ready to get started working immediately. Greet people quickly, avoid checking your personal e-mail, and shut off your cell phone.
11. Take care of as much e-mail correspondence as you can after you have finished your other work, unless a key part of your job is dealing with e-mail. It consumes substantial time.
12. Avoid perfectionism, which leads you to keep redoing a project. Let go and move on to another project.
13. Make use of bits of time—for instance, five minutes between appointments. Invest those five minutes in sending a work-related e-mail message or revising your to-do list.
14. Minimize procrastination, the number one time waster for most people.
15. Avoid spreading yourself too thin by doing too many things at once, such as having one project too many to handle. When you are overloaded, time can be wasted because of too many errors.
16. Manage interruptions by letting coworkers know when you are available for consultation, and when you need to work independently—except for emergencies. Respond to instant messages only if your job requires responding immediately. Batch your instant messages just as you would other e-mails.

FIGURE 14–6 Ways to Prevent and Overcome Time Wasting

Sources: Suggestions 4, 5, and 6 are based on Stephen R. Covey with Hyrum Smith, "What If You Could Chop an Hour from Your Day for Things That Matter Most?" *USA Weekend,* January 22–24, 1999, pp. 4–5; suggestion 10 is from Anita Bruzzese, "Tips to Avoid Wasting Time," Gannet News Service, August 9, 2004. Data about the productivity drain of interruptions are analyzed in Quintus R. Jett and Jennifer M. George, "Work Interrupted: A Closer Look at the Role of Interruptions in Organizational Life," *Academy of Management Review,* July 2003, pp. 494–507.

SKILL-BUILDING EXERCISE 14-4

MAINTAINING A TIME LOG

An effective starting point to avoid wasting time is to identify how you spend the 168 hours you have each week (24 hours × 7 days). For two weeks catalog all the time you spend, down to as much detail as you can tolerate. Include the large obvious items, as well as the small items that are easy to forget. Keep track of any activity that requires at least five minutes. Major items would include working, attending class, studying, reading, watching television, sleeping, eating, going places, spending time with loved ones and friends (hanging out). Small items would include visiting the coffee shop or vending machine, purchasing gum, and clipping your nails. If you multitask, such as walking and listening to music, do not double-count the time.

When your time logs have been completed, search for complete wastes of time, or activities that could be shortened. You might find, for example, that you spend about 45 minutes per day in the pursuit and consumption of coffee. If you reduced that time to 30 minutes you would have an additional 15 minutes per day that you could invest in your career. However, if coffee time includes forming alliances with people or maintaining relationships, maybe the 45-minute-per-day investment is worthwhile.

SELF-ASSESSMENT QUIZ 14-2

TENDENCIES TOWARD PERFECTIONISM

Directions: Many perfectionists hold some of the behaviors and attitudes described below. To help understand your tendencies toward perfectionism, rate how strongly you agree with each of the statements below on a scale of 0 to 4 by circling the appropriate number. 0 means disagree, 4 means agree.

1.	Many people have told me that I am a perfectionist.	0	1	2	3	4
2.	I often correct the speech of others.	0	1	2	3	4
3.	It takes me a long time to write an e-mail because I keep checking and rechecking my writing.	0	1	2	3	4
4.	I often criticize the color combinations my friends are wearing.	0	1	2	3	4
5.	When I purchase food at a supermarket, I usually look at the expiration date so I can purchase the freshest.	0	1	2	3	4
6.	I can't stand when people use the term "remote" instead of "remote control."	0	1	2	3	4
7.	If a company representative asked me "What is your *social*," I would reply something like, "Do you mean my *social security number?*"	0	1	2	3	4
8.	I hate to see dust on furniture.	0	1	2	3	4
9.	I like the Martha Stewart idea of having every decoration in the home just right.	0	1	2	3	4
10.	I never put a map back in the glove compartment until it is folded just right.	0	1	2	3	4

11. Once an eraser on a pencil of mine becomes hard and useless, I throw away the pencil.   0 1 2 3 4

12. I adjust all my watches and clocks so they show exactly the same time.   0 1 2 3 4

13. It bothers me that clocks on personal computers are often wrong by a few minutes.   0 1 2 3 4

14. I clean the keyboard on my computer at least once a week.   0 1 2 3 4

15. I organize my e-mail messages and computer documents into many different, clearly labeled files.   0 1 2 3 4

16. You won't find old coffee cups or soft-drink containers on my desk.   0 1 2 3 4

17. I rarely start a new project or assignment until I have completed my present project or assignment.   0 1 2 3 4

18. It is very difficult for me to concentrate when my work area is disorganized.   0 1 2 3 4

19. Cobwebs in chandeliers and other lighting fixtures bother me.   0 1 2 3 4

20. It takes me a long time to make a purchase such as a digital camera because I keep studying the features on various models.   0 1 2 3 4

21. When I balance my checkbook, it usually comes out right within a few dollars.   0 1 2 3 4

22. I carry enough small coins and dollar bills with me so when I shop I can pay the exact amount without requiring change.   0 1 2 3 4

23. I throw out any underwear or tee-shirts that have even the smallest holes or tears.   0 1 2 3 4

24. I become upset with myself if I make a mistake.   0 1 2 3 4

25. When a fingernail of mine is broken or chipped, I fix it as soon as possible.   0 1 2 3 4

26. I am carefully groomed whenever I leave my home.   0 1 2 3 4

27. When I notice packaged goods or cans on the floor in a supermarket, I will often place them back on the shelf.   0 1 2 3 4

28. I think that carrying around antibacterial cleaner for the hands is an excellent idea.   0 1 2 3 4

29. If I am with a friend, and he or she has a loose hair on the shoulder, I will remove it without asking.   0 1 2 3 4

30. I am a perfectionist.   0 1 2 3 4

Total Score _____

Scoring and Interpretation: Add the numbers you circled to obtain your total score.

91 or over: You have strong perfectionist tendencies to the point that it could interfere with your taking quick action when necessary. Also, you may annoy many people with your perfectionism.

61–90: You have a moderate degree of perfectionism that could lead you to produce high-quality work and be a dependable person.

31–60: You have a mild degree of perfectionism. You might be a perfectionist in some situations quite important to you, but not in others.

0–30: You are not a perfectionist. You might be too casual about getting things done right, meeting deadlines, and being aware of details.

SUMMARY

A major challenge facing any worker who wants to stay healthy and have good interpersonal relationships is to manage stress effectively. Individual differences play a big role in determining whether an event will lead to stress. The physiological changes that take place within the body in response to stress are responsible for most of the stress symptoms. The fight-or-flight response is the battle against the stressor. Updated information suggests that women are more likely to cope with a stressor through tend and befriend.

The activation of hormones when the body has to cope with a stressor produces short-term physiological reactions, including an increase in heart rate and blood pressure. When stress levels rarely subside, the physiological changes create damage. However, the right amount of stress prepares us for meeting difficult challenges and improves performance. An optimum level of stress exists for most people and most tasks. In general, performance tends to be best under moderate amounts of stress. Performance decreases are less likely with certain worker characteristics such as high self-esteem.

One of the major problems of prolonged stress is that it may lead to burnout, a condition of emotional, mental, and physical exhaustion in response to long-term stressors. Burnout also creates cynicism and a distancing from tasks and people. Workers who perceive the cause of burnout to be external are more likely to become less committed to the firm and more cynical.

Four personality factors predisposing people toward stress are low perceived control, low self-efficacy, Type A behavior, and negative affectivity. The heart attack triggers associated with Type A behavior are hostility, anger, cynicism, and suspiciousness, with hostility having the biggest impact. Four frequently encountered job stressors are role overload, role conflict and ambiguity, adverse environmental conditions including carpal tunnel syndrome, and job insecurity.

Managing stress refers to controlling stress by making it become a constructive force in your life. Coping with, or managing, stress includes hundreds of activities, with substantial individual differences in which technique is effective. Eight representative stress-management methods are to eliminate or modify the stressor, get appropriate physical exercise, rest sufficiently, maintain a healthy diet, build a support network, practice visualization, practice everyday methods of stress reduction, and use the freeze-frame technique.

Achieving high personal productivity on the job is more in demand than ever. A starting point in improving productivity is to minimize procrastination, an enormous problem for many people that can be approached as follows: Calculate the cost of procrastination; follow the worst in, first out (WIFO) principle; break the task into manageable chunks; make a commitment to other people; remove some clutter from your mind; satisfy your stimulation quota in constructive ways; and eliminate rewards for procrastinating.

Developing good work habits and time-management practices is often a matter of developing the right attitudes toward your work and toward time, as follows: (1) begin with a mission and goals; (2) play the inner game of work, (3) work smarter, not harder; (4) value orderliness and cleanliness; (5) value good attendance and punctuality; and (6) attain a balance in life and avoid being a workaholic.

Effective work habits and skills are essential for high productivity, including the following: (1) Prepare a to-do list and set priorities; (2) streamline your work and emphasize important tasks; (3) concentrate on one important task at a time instead of multitasking; (4) stay in control of paperwork and electronic work; (5) work productively from your home office or virtual office; and (6) enhance your Internet search skills.

Another basic thrust to improved personal productivity is to minimize time wasting. Whether or not an activity is a time waster depends on its purpose. Being aware of time wasters such as those presented in Figure 14-5 will sensitize you to the importance of minimizing them.

QUESTIONS FOR DISCUSSION AND REVIEW

1. Why might it be true that people who love their work live much longer than people who retire early because they dislike working?

2. A student told his instructor, "You have to give me a deadline for my paper. Otherwise, I can't handle it." What does this statement tell you about (a) the stressor he faces and (b) how pressure influences his work performance?

3. Why might having your stress under control improve your interpersonal relationships?

4. A student commented to the class, "It's not worth studying stress because it's all in your head. If you don't think about stress, you won't have to worry about it." What is your reaction to her comment?

5. Interview a person in a high-pressure job in any field. Find out whether the person experiences significant stress and what method he or she uses to cope with it.

6. Provide an example from your own or somebody else's life of how having a major goal in life can help a person be better organized.

7. Describe any way in which you have used information technology to make you more productive.

8. Many people who use a personal digital assistant (such as contained in a handheld computer) find that they are no more organized or productive than before. What could be their problem?

9. Use information in this chapter to explain how a person might be well organized yet still not get very far in his or her career.

10. Ask an experienced high-level worker to identify his or her most effective method of time management.

GO TO THE WEB

http://www.theinnergame.com
(The inner game of work, sports, and teambuilding)

http://www.stress.org
(Institute for Stress Management)

http://stress.about.com
(Considerable information about stress plus several self-quizzes)

http://www.napo.net
(National Association of Professional Organizers)

AN INTERPERSONAL RELATIONS CASE PROBLEM

THE NEW MARKETING ASSISTANT

One year ago Jennie DaSilva returned enthusiastically to the workforce after 12 years of being a full-time homemaker and a part-time direct sales representative for beauty products. Jennie's major motive for finding a full-time professional job was to work toward her career goal as a marketing manager in a medium-size or large company. To help prepare for this career, DaSilva completed a business degree over a five-year period.

Another compelling reason for returning to full-time employment was financial need. DaSilva's husband owned and operated an appliance and electronics store that was becoming less profitable each year. Several large appliance stores had moved into the area, resulting in fewer customers for Northside Appliances (the name of the family business). DaSilva and her husband, Fred, concluded that the family could not cover its bills unless Jennie earned the equivalent of a full-time income.

After three months of searching for full-time employment, Jennie responded to a newspaper ad for a marketing assistant position. The ad described the position as part of a management training program with an excellent future. Ten days after submitting her cover letter and résumé, Jennie was invited for an interview. The company proved to be a national provider of long-distance telephone service. The human resources interviewer and hiring manager both explained that Jennie's initial assignment would be as a telemarketer. Both people advised Jennie that large numbers of people were applying for these telemarketing positions.

Jennie would be required to telephone individual consumers and small-business owners, and make a sales pitch for them to transfer their long-distance telephone service to her company. The company supplied a computerized list with an almost inexhaustible list of names and telephone numbers across the country. In this way Jennie could take advantage of time-zone differences to telephone people during their dinnertime, as well as at other times. Jennie would receive a small commission for each customer who made the switch to her company. Her major responsibility, in addition to telephone soliciting, would be to enter the results of her conversations into a computer, as well as prepare summaries.

One week after the interview, Jennie was extended a job offer. She accepted the offer despite some concern that the position was a little too far removed from the professional marketing position she sought. Jennie was assigned to a small cubicle in a large room with about 25 other telemarketers. She found the training program exciting, particularly with respect to techniques for overcoming customer resistance. Jennie reasoned that this experience, combined with her direct selling of beauty products, would give her excellent insights into how consumers think and behave. For the first two weeks Jennie found the calls to be uplifting. She experienced a surge of excitement when a customer agreed to switch to her company. As was the custom in the office, she shouted "Yes!" after concluding each customer conversion to her company.

As the weeks moved slowly on, Jennie became increasingly restless and concerned about the job. Her success ratio was falling below the company standard of a 3 percent success rate on the cold calls. A thought kept running through Jennie's mind, "Even if I'm doing well at this job, 97 percent of people I call will practically hang up on me. And I can't stand keyboarding all these worthless reports explaining what happened as a result of my calls. It's a horrible waste of time."

Jennie soon found it difficult to sleep peacefully, often pacing the apartment after Fred had fallen asleep. She also noticed that she was arguing much more with Fred and the two children. Jennie's stomach churned so much that she found eating uncomfortable. She often poked at her food, but drank coffee and diet soft drinks much more than previously. After six months of working at the long-distance carrier, her weight plunged from 135 pounds to 123 pounds. Jennie's left thumb and wrists were constantly sore. One night when Fred asked her why she was rubbing the region below her thumb, Jennie said, "I keep pushing the mouse around so much during the day that my thumb feels like it's falling off."

During the next several months, Jennie spoke with her supervisor twice about her future in the company. Both times the supervisor explained that the best telemarketers become eligible for supervisory positions, providing they have proved themselves for at least three years. The supervisor also cautioned Jennie that her performance was adequate, but not exceptional. Jennie thought to herself, "I'm banging my head against the wall, and I'm considered just average."

As Jennie approached a full year in her position, she and Fred reviewed the family finances. He said,

"Sales at the store are getting worse and worse. I predict that this year your salary will be higher than profits from the store. It's great that we can count on at least one stable salary in the family. The kids and I really appreciate it."

Jennie thought to herself, "Now is the worst time to tell Fred how I really feel about my job. I'm falling apart inside, and the family needs my salary. What a mess."

Case Questions

1. What aspects of work stress are revealed in this case?
2. What suggestions can you make to the company for decreasing the stressors in the position of telemarketer?
3. What advice can you offer Jennie to help her improve her productivity on the job?

AN INTERPERSONAL RELATIONS CASE PROBLEM

GEOMANIA NAPS

Geomania is a telecommunications firm based in the information technology section of New York City. Some of the several hundred employees live in Manhattan, but many have commutes of up to two hours from other cities. Having survived the downturn in the telecommunications business during the late 1990s and early 2000s, Geomania is understaffed. Many staff members in professional, technical, support, and managerial jobs are doing work that was once performed by two people.

A case researcher asked human resources manager Stephanie Cohen what impact the heavy workload was having on employees. She replied, "We've got a bunch of great soldiers here, but the overload problem is taking its toll. Some staff members are having many more fights at home. More people are having serious medical problems like chest pains, migraine headaches, and stomach ulcers. I also think the error rate in work is going up. Manuel Gomez, the customer service manager, tells me Geomania is receiving more complaints about our systems not working."

The case researcher pointed out that Cohen's observations were to be expected when so many people are working so hard. She was asked if she noticed any other unusual behavior in the office in recent months. Cohen said that her assistant, Bonnie Boswell, had made some observations about unusual behavior, and that Boswell should be asked to participate in the interview.

Boswell got right to the heart of the matter, explaining that she has observed some behavior that could be helping productivity, hurting productivity, or a combination of both. "What I've noticed," said Boswell" is that our people are finding more and more creative ways to take naps on the job. The motto has become, 'You snooze you win,' instead of 'You snooze you lose.'

"There certainly is a positive side to napping. According to one NASA survey, 71% of corporate aviation pilots, 80% of regional pilots, and 60% of hospital workers said they took naps on the job. Another NASA study found that airline pilots who fell asleep on average for 26 minutes had a 34% improvement in performance and a 54% improvement in alertness. Of course, they were not sleeping while flying!

"But on the negative side, if you are sleeping you are not producing for the company. Besides that it looks so totally unprofessional to be sacked out in your cubicle, especially if you snore or scream because you are having a terrifying dream."

When asked where and how these workers were napping, both Boswell and Cohen had plenty of answers. Cohen said it has always been easy for executives to nap because they have private offices. Several keep their offices equipped with pillows, so they can nap comfortably on a couch, at their desk, or on the floor under the desk. Cohen said that she had walked in on napping executives by mistakes, and an office assistant told her about the pillows.

Boswell said that cubicle dwellers have to be more creative about napping because other workers can readily see them. She explained, "Quite often they catch a nap during meetings. At some meetings half the audience is listing to one side or nap jerking (falling asleep, then quickly jerking the head to awake). One napper closes his eyes on his desk, and holds on to a bottle of eye drops to make it appear he is in the process of self-medication.

Many nappers sleep in their car during lunch break. "Some of the most stressed-out workers catch a few winks in the office supplies room by resting their head on a box."

Cohen said she was even wondering if Geomania should hire as a consultant, psychologist Bill Anthony who founded the Napping Company to promote productive naps in the workplace. He contends that companies do not have to set up special sleeping rooms. Instead, they can institutionalize nap breaks the way they have coffee breaks.

"My concern right now," concluded Cohen, "is what to recommend to top management. I think our CEO is opposed to napping on the job (except for his little 40 winks now and then), and napping does not look professional. Yet, a formal napping program could be a real productivity booster. Maybe we could even cut down on some medical problems."

Source: Some of the facts in this case are from Jared Sandberg, "As Bosses Power Nap, Cubicle Dwellers Doze Under Clever Disguise," *The Wall Street Journal,* July 23, 2003, p. B1.

Case Questions

1. If you worked for Geomania, and were stationed in a cubicle, explain why you would or would not nap on the job.

2. Would it be a good idea for management to just let workers decide for themselves whether to nap on the job? Explain your reasoning.

3. As the human resources director for Geomania, develop a written policy for napping on company time. (A policy is a general guideline to follow.) Include such aspects of napping as to when, where, under what circumstances, and for how long might workers nap. Mention whether or not Geomania should have a separate napping area.

4. How might a program of napping contribute to employee stress management at Geomania?

Appendix 1

Expressing

Source: Messages: The Communications Skills Book, 1995, Second Edition
By Matt McKay, Ph.D., Patrick Flanning, and Martha Davis, Ph.D.
New Harbinger Publications, Oakland, CA 94609
Copyright © 1995 by New Harbinger Publications.

Sam: "Do we have to go down to the P.T.A. meeting tonight?"

Jane: "Why, does it bother you?"

Sam: "It's just the same old thing. I don't know."

Jane: "Did something happen last time?"

Sam: "It's nothing. Sometimes the speakers are interesting, but I don't know . . . and Mrs. Williams is running it now."

Jane: "You don't like how she's handling it?"

Sam: "She's all right. She's so . . . organized. Forget it, let's get a move on if we're going."

Sam is in for another deadly evening. Mrs. Williams will carry on like General Patton. A speaker will drone about "multicultural awareness." If Sam had been able to express himself, he might have persuaded Jane to skip a night, or to help him push for changes in the meeting format. As it is, Jane has no idea what's irking him and can't respond to his needs.

This chapter is about expressing yourself when it counts and to the people who matter to you. It doesn't tell you how to assertively ask your butcher for a good cut of meat. But it does tell you how to make clear and complete statements about your inner experience.

The Four Kinds of Expression

Your communications to other people can be broken down into four categories: expressing your observations, thoughts, feelings, and needs. Each category requires a different style of expression, and often a very different vocabulary.

Observations

This is the language of the scientist, the detective, the TV repairman. It means reporting what your senses tell you. There are no speculations, inferences, or conclusions. Everything is simple fact. Here are some examples of observations:

1. "I read in the *Enquirer* that an ice age is due to start within five hundred years."

2. "My old address was 1996 Fell Street."

3. "She plans to wear a chiffon dress with white ruffled collar."

4. "I broke the toaster this morning."

5. "It was a very hot day when I left Kansas. A slight wind riffled the fields and a thunderhead was beginning to form up north."

All of these statements adhere strictly to what the person has heard, read, or personally experienced. If Sam had been able to talk about his observations at the P.T.A. meeting, he might have pointed out that the meetings invariably went overtime, that the speakers were selected by Mrs. Williams without consulting the group, and that certain parent-teacher problems were never discussed.

Thoughts

Your thoughts are conclusions, inferences drawn from what you have heard, read, and observed. They are attempts to synthesize your observations so you can see what's really going on and understand why and how events occur. They may also incorporate value judgments in which you decide that something is good or bad, wrong or right. Beliefs, opinions, and theories are all varieties of conclusions. Here are some examples:

1. "Unselfishness is essential for a successful marriage." *(belief)*

2. "I think the universe will keep exploding and collapsing, exploding and collapsing, forever." *(theory)*

3. "He must be afraid of his wife; he always seems nervous around her." *(theory)*

4. "Log Cabin is the only syrup worth buying." *(theory)*

5. "You were wrong to just stop seeing her." *(value judgment)*

If Sam had been able to express his thoughts about the P.T.A. meeting, he might have said that Mrs. Williams was dominating and grandiose. He might have suggested that she was deliberately squelching conflicts because she was friendly with the school administration.

Feelings

Probably the most difficult part of communication is expressing your feelings. Some people don't want to hear what you feel. They get bored or upset when feelings come up. Some people are selectively receptive. They can hear about your post-divorce melancholy, but not about your fear of death. Anger is the most discouraged feeling because it's threatening to the listener's self-esteem.

Since people are often threatened or frightened by emotion, you may have decided to keep many feelings to yourself. Yet how you feel is a large part of what makes you unique and special. Shared feelings are the building blocks of intimacy. When others are allowed to know what angers, frightens, and pleases you, two things happen: They have greater empathy and understanding and are better able to modify their behavior to meet your needs.

Examples of some feeling statements are:

1. "I missed Al and felt a real loss when he left for Europe."

2. "I feel like I let you down, and it really gnaws at me."

3. "I sit alone in the house, feel this tingling going up and down my spine, and get this wave of anxiety."

4. "I light up with joy when I see you. I feel this incredible rush of affection."

5. "I'm checking my reactions, and I feel stunned and a little angry."

Note that feeling statements are not observations, value judgments or opinions. For example, "Sometimes I feel that you are very rigid," has nothing to do with feelings. It's just a slightly buffered judgment.

If Sam had expressed his feelings to Jane, he might have told her that he felt bored at the meetings and that he was angry at Mrs. Williams. He also might have discussed his worries that the school has serious curriculum inadequacies and his frustration that nothing was

Needs

No one knows what you want, except you. You are the expert, the highest authority on yourself. However, you may have a heavy injunction against expressing needs. You hope friends and family will be sensitive or clairvoyant enough to know what you want. "If you loved me, you'd know what's wrong" is a common assumption. Since you feel it's bad to ask for anything, your needs are often expressed with a head of anger or resentment. The anger says "I'm wrong to ask, and you're wrong to make me have to."

Trying to have a close relationship in which you don't express your needs is like driving a car without a steering wheel. You can go fast, but you can't change directions or steer around chuckholes. Relationships change, accommodate, and grow when both people can clearly and supportively express what they need. Some typical need statements are:

1. "Can you be home before seven? I'd love to go to a movie."

2. "I'm exhausted. Will you do the dishes and see that the kids are in bed?"

3. "I need a day to myself this weekend. Can we get together Sunday night?"

4. "I need to reserve time with you so we can sit down and work this out."

5. "Could you just hug me for a while?"

Needs are not pejorative or judgmental. They don't blame or assign fault. They are simple statements about what would help or please you.

Returning to the Sam and Jane story, Sam might have told Jane that he really needs rest and wants to spend time with her alone. "Let's light the fire and snuggle up tonight."

Whole Messages

Whole messages include all four kinds of expressions: what you see, think, feel, and need. Intimate relationships thrive on whole messages. Your closest friends, your mate, and your family can't know the real you unless you share all of your experiences. That means not leaving things out, not covering up your anger, not squelching your wants. It means giving accurate feedback about what you observe, clearly stating your inferences and conclusions, saying how it all makes you feel, and if you need something or see possibilities for change, making straight-forward requests or suggestions.

When you leave something out, it's called a *partial message*. Partial messages create confusion and distrust. People sense something is missing, but they don't know what. They're turned off when they hear judgments untempered by your feelings and hopes. They resist hearing anger that doesn't include the story of your frustration or hurt. They are suspicious of conclusions without supporting observations. They are uncomfortable with demands growing from unexpressed feelings and assumptions.

Not every relationship or situation requires whole messages. Effective communication with your garage mechanic probably won't involve a lot of deep feeling or discussion of your emotional needs. Even with intimates, the majority of messages are just informational. But partial messages, with something important left out or obscured, are always dangerous. They become relational boobytraps when used to express the complex issues that are an inevitable part of closeness.

You can test whether you are giving whole or partial messages by asking the following questions:

1. Have I expressed what I actually know to be fact? Is it based on what I've observed, read, or heard?

2. Have I expressed and clearly labeled my inferences and conclusions?

3. Have I expressed my feelings without blame or judgment?

4. Have I shared my needs without blame or judgment?

Contaminated Messages

Contamination takes place when your messages are mixed or mislabeled. For example, you might be contaminating feelings, thoughts, and observations if you said to your daughter, "I see you're wearing that old dress again." What you really needed to say were three very distinct things:

1. "That dress is a little frayed and still has the ink spot we were never able to get out." (*observation*)

2. "I don't think it's nice enough for a Sunday visit to Grandpa's." (*thought*)

3. "I feel anxious that your grandfather will think I'm not a very good parent if I let you wear a dress like that." (*feeling*)

Contaminated messages are at best confusing and at worst deeply alienating. The message "I see your wife gave you two juicy oranges for lunch" is confusing because the observation is contaminated by need. The need is only hinted at, and the listener has to decide if what he heard was really a covert appeal. The message "While you were feeding your dog, my dinner got cold" is alienating because what appears to be a simple observation contains undercurrents of anger and judgment ("You care more about your dog than me").

Contaminated messages differ from partial messages in that the problem is not merely one of omission. You haven't left the anger, the conclusion, or the need out of it. It's there all right, but in a disguised and covert form. The following are some examples of contaminated messages:

1. "Why don't you act a little human for a change?" In this message need is contaminated with a value judgment (*thought*). A whole message might have been, "You say very little, and when you do it's in a soft, flat voice (*observation*). It makes me think that you don't care, that you have no emotions (*thought*). I feel hurt (*emotion*), but what I really want is for you to talk to me (*need*)."

2. "Every year you come home to visit with a different man. I don't know how you move from one to another like that." Said in an acid tone, this would be an observation contaminated with a value judgment (*thought*). The whole message might be "Each year you come home with someone else (*observation*). I wonder if it creates a sort of callousness, a shallow affection (*thought*). I worry, and also feel disappointed when I start liking your friend and never see him again (*feeling*). I hope you'll make a commitment to a life partner (*need*)."

3. "I know what your problem is, you like to get paid but you don't like to work." This is an example of feeling contaminated with a value judgment (*thought*). The whole statement might be "You've been late six times in the last two weeks (*observation*). It makes me think that you're trying to work as little as possible (*thought*). The lateness irritates me (*feeling*) and I want you to be late no more than once a month (*need*)."

4. "I need to go home . . . another one of those headaches." Said in an angry voice at a party, this is an example of feelings contaminated with need. The person really wants to say "I've been standing by myself (*observation*). You don't seem to care or draw me into conversation (*thought*). I get to feeling hurt and angry (*feeling*). I want you to involve me in things or I don't

5. "You eat your breakfast without a word, you get your hat, you leave, you get home, you mix a drink, you read the paper, you talk about golf and your secretary's legs at dinner, you fall asleep in front of the TV, and that's the way it is." In this case, observation is contaminated with feelings. It seems like a straightforward recital of events, but the speaker really wants to say "I'm lonely and angry, please pay attention to me."

The easiest way to contaminate your messages is to make the content simple and straightforward, but say it in a tone of voice that betrays your feelings. "I want to stop interviewing people, we have enough already" can be said in a matter-of-fact or very annoyed voice. In one case it's a clear statement of need. In the other, need is contaminated with unacknowledged anger. The secret of avoiding contaminated messages is to separate out and express each part of the communication.

Preparing Your Message

Self-Awareness

The only way you can be sure to give whole messages, and to avoid partial and contaminated ones, is to examine your own inner experience. What you are observing, thinking, feeling, and wanting? What is the purpose of this communication? Is the stated purpose the same as your real purpose? What are you afraid of saying? What do you need to communicate?

Awareness may include a bit of a rehearsal, particularly while getting used to whole messages. You run things over in your mind until each part of the message is clear and distinct. You separate what you observe and know from what you surmise and believe. You contact your feelings and find a way to say them. You arrive at a nonthreatening way to express your need.

Other Awareness

A certain amount of audience analysis should precede any important message. If your friend just lost a job, he may not be receptive to a diatribe about your low rate of pay. What kind of shape is the other person in? Is he or she rushed, in pain, angry, or able to listen?

Other awareness also means keeping track of the listener's response while you're talking: facial expressions, eye contact, and body language. Is he or she asking questions, giving feedback, or sitting like a lump in the chair?

Place Awareness

Important messages are usually delivered when two people are alone, in a nondistracting environment. Talking where you can be overheard discourages whole messages. Partial and contaminated messages increase as you feel the need to compress and sanitize your comments for public consumption. Here are some general rules for finding the right environment to talk:

1. Find some privacy.

2. Find a place where you won't be interrupted.

3. Find a place that's congenial and physically comfortable.

4. Find a place that's quiet, with few distractions.

Practicing Whole Messages

In the following exercise, try making a whole message out of each statement. Write it using first person sentences ("I noticed that you've been very quiet. . . .").

1. "I see you're getting uptight again." (This is in an annoyed voice, which covers a certain amount of anxiety and hurt. His wife has been silent for thirty minutes following his late arrival home.)

OBSERVATIONS:

THOUGHTS:

FEELINGS:

NEEDS:

2. "Should we be talking like this?" (Between new lovers who've suddenly launched into fantasies of kids and marriage. The speaker is anxious that her partner may feel pressured, and may withdraw.)

OBSERVATIONS:

THOUGHTS:

FEELINGS:

NEEDS:

3. "A person runs out of time, something just changes in them." (A man trying to explain why he quit his job. Passed over for promotion, he was depressed and fearful of getting older without finding satisfying work. He's trying to get his fourteen-year-old daughter to understand.)

OBSERVATIONS:

THOUGHTS:

FEELINGS:

NEEDS:

4. "I'm here, aren't I?" (Said to the boss, after being asked how he felt having to work overtime. He's missing his ten-year-old's play, and wants to be home in time to help with the cast party.)

OBSERVATIONS:

THOUGHTS:

FEELINGS:

NEEDS:

5. "I know, I know, you don't have to tell me," (After being reminded of upcoming finals for the fourth time. A sixteen-year-old is feeling over-controlled by her parents.)

OBSERVATIONS:

THOUGHTS:

FEELINGS:

NEEDS:

Here are examples of whole messages for the above statements. See how yours compare.

1. "You haven't said anything since I got home, and I assume you're angry. When you withdraw like that I get angry too. I'd rather talk about it than do this."

2. "We're fantasizing about a lifetime together after two weeks. I'm worried that one of us may get scared and withdraw. Does it feel okay to you to do this?"

3. "I'd been passed over for a long time and didn't really like what I was doing anyway. I don't think it's healthy to grow old someplace doing work you don't like. I was getting depressed and wanted to take a chance on finding something that really felt good. It's hard and I need your support."

4. "I'm missing my ten-year-old's play. I should be there. It's frustrating. But I do want to be home by nine to help with the cast party."

5. "You've reminded me four times, and I get the impression you think I'm stupid or irresponsible. I feel watched and it makes me angry. Let me handle this myself and we can talk about it if I mess up."

The ability to make whole rather than partial or contaminated messages is a skill. It is acquired with practice. This this exercise:

1. Select a friend or family member whom you trust.

2. Explain the concept of whole messages.

3. Arrange a time to practice.

4. Select something you want to talk about, something that was important enough to affect you emotionally. It can be something in the past, or something going on right now; something involving others; or something directly related to the person you practice with.

5. Talk about your chosen subject, using the four components of a whole message: Talk about what happened and what you observed; describe what you thought and concluded; say

something about how it all made you feel; and describe your needs in the situation.

6. When you finish, your partner should repeat back in his or her own words each part of the message.

7. You should correct anything that he or she didn't get quite right.

8. Reverse the whole process, and let your partner describe an experience using whole messages.

Now make an agreement with your partner that every significant communication between you will involve whole messages. Commit yourself to practicing whole messages for two weeks. Always be sure to give each other feedback about what was heard and what was left out of the message. At the end of two weeks, evaluate your experience. The goal is for whole messages to become automatic. Eventually you can expand your exercise program to include other significant people. The exercises will sharpen your awareness so you can rapidly look inside yourself for the information necessary to make whole messages.

Rules for Effective Expression

Messages Should Be Direct

The first requirement for effective self-expression is knowing when something needs to be said. This means that you don't assume people know what you think or want.

Indirectness can be emotionally costly. Here are a few examples. One man whose wife divorced him after fifteen years complained that she had no right to call him undemonstrative. "She knew I loved her. I didn't have to say it in so many words. A thing like that is obvious." But it wasn't obvious. His wife withered emotionally without direct expression of his affection. A woman who had been distressed by her child's performance in school stopped nagging when his grades went up. She was surprised to learn that her son felt unappreciated and wanted some direct approval. A man who had developed a chronic back problem was afraid to ask for help with gardening and household maintenance. He suffered through these tasks in pain and experienced a growing irritation and resentment toward his family. A fifteen-year-old retreated to her room when her divorced mother became interested in a new man. She complained of headaches and excused herself whenever the boyfriend arrived. Her mother, who once told the children they would always come first, assumed that her daughter was just embarrassed and would soon get over it.

These are all examples of people who have something important to communicate. But they don't know it. They assume others realize how they feel. Communicating directly means you don't make any assumptions. In fact, you should assume that people are poor mind readers and haven't the faintest idea what goes on inside you.

Some people are aware of the times when they need to communicate, but are afraid to do so. Instead they try hinting, or telling third parties in hope that the target person will eventually hear. This indirectness is risky. Hints are often misinterpreted or ignored. One woman kept turning the sound down on the TV during commercials. She hoped her husband would take the hint and converse a little at the breaks. Instead he read the sports page until she finally blew up at him. Third party communications are extremely dangerous because of the likelihood that your message will be distorted. Even if the message is accurately delivered, no one wants to hear about your anger, disappointment, or even your love secondhand.

Messages Should Be Immediate

If you're hurt or angry, or needing to change something, delaying communication will often exacerbate your feelings. Your anger may smoulder, your frustrated need become a chronic irritant. What you couldn't express at the moment will be communicated later in subtle or passive-aggressive ways. One woman was quite hurt at the thought of not being invited to Thanksgiving at her sister's house. She said nothing, but broke a date they had to go to the planetarium and "forgot" to send a Christmas card.

Sometimes unexpressed feeling is gunnysacked to the point where a small transgression triggers a major dumping of the accumulated rage and hurt. These dumping episodes alienate family and friends. A hospital ward secretary had a reputation with peers for being dangerous and volatile. For months she would be sweet, considerate, and accommodating. But sooner or later the explosion came. A slight criticism would be answered with megatons of gripes and resentments.

There are two main advantages to immediate communication: (1) Immediate feedback increases the likelihood that people will learn what you need and adjust their behavior accordingly. This is because a clear relationship is established between what they do (for example, driving too fast) and the consequences (your expressed anxiety). (2) Immediate communication increases intimacy because you share your responses now. You don't wait three weeks for things to get stale. Here-and-now communications are more exciting and serve to intensify your relationships.

Messages Should Be Clear

A clear message is a complete and accurate reflection of your thoughts, feelings, needs, and observations. You don't leave things out. You don't fudge by being vague or abstract. Some people are afraid to say what they really mean. They talk in muddy, theoretical jargon. Everything is explained by "vibes" or by psychological interpretations. One woman who was afraid to tell her boyfriend she was turned off by public petting said that she felt "a little strange" that day and thought that her parents' upcoming visit was "repressing her sexuality." This ambiguous message allowed her boyfriend to interpret her discomfort as a temporary condition. He never learned her true needs.

Keeping your messages clear depends on awareness. You have to know what you've observed, and then how you reacted to it. What you see and hear in the outside world is so easily confused with what you think and feel inside. Separating these elements will go a long way toward helping you express yourself clearly.

Here are some tips for staying clear:

1. Don't ask questions when you need to make a statement. Husband to wife: "Why do you have to go back to school? You have plenty of things to keep you busy." The statement hidden in the question is "I'm afraid if you go back to school I won't see you enough, I'll feel lonely. As you grow in independence I'll feel less control over the direction of our lives."

Wife to husband: "Do you think we need to make an appearance at your boss's barbeque today?" Imbedded in the question is the unexpressed need to relax and putter in the garden. By failing to plead her case clearly, her husband can either miss or safely ignore her needs.

Daughter to father: "Are we going to have a little three-foot tree this year?" What she thinks but doesn't say is that she likes the big trees seen at friends' houses—the ones full of lights and tinsel around which the family gathers. She wishes that her family did more things together, and thinks Christmas decorating would be a good place to start.

Father to son: "How much did that paint job cost?" He really wants to talk about the fact that his son lives above his means, and then borrows from Mom without any intention of paying back. He's worried about his son's relationship to money and angry because he feels circumvented.

2. Keep your messages congruent. The content, your tone of voice, and your body language should all fit together. If you congratulate someone on getting a fellowship, his response is congruent if the voice, facial gestures, and spoken messages all reflect pleasure. Incongruence is apparent if he thanks you with a frown, suggesting that he doesn't really want the compliment

Incongruence confuses communication. Congruence promotes clarity and understanding. A man who spent the day in his delivery truck arrived home to a request that he make a run to the supermarket. His response was, "Sure, whatever you want." But his tone was sarcastic and his body slumped. His wife got the message and went herself. But she was irritated by the sarcastic tone and later started a fight about the dishes. A model asked soothingly to hear about her roommate's "boyfriend in trouble." But while the story unfolded, her eyes flitted always to the mirror and she sat on the edge of her chair. Her voice said, "I care," but her body said, "I'm bored, hurry up."

3. Avoid double messages. Double messages are like kicking a dog and petting it at the same time. They occur when you say two contradictory things at once. Husband to wife: "I want to take you, I do. I'll be lonely without you. But I don't think the convention will be much fun. Really, you'd be bored to death." This is a double message, because on the surface the husband seems to want his wife's company. But when you read between the lines, it's evident that he's trying to discourage her from coming.

Father to son: "Go ahead, have a good time. By the way, I noticed your report card has some real goof-off grades. What are you doing about them?" This is a rather obvious double message, but the effect is confusing. One message undercuts the other, and the son is left unclear about his father's real position. The most malignant double messages are the "come close, go away" and "I love you, I hate you" messages. These communications are found in parent-child and lover relationships, and inflict heavy psychological damage.

4. Be clear about your wants and feelings. Hinting around about your feelings and needs may seem safer than stating them clearly. But you end up confusing the listener. Friend to friend: "Why don't you quit volunteering at that crazy free clinic?" The clear message would be: "I'm afraid for you struggling in that conflict-ridden place. I think you are exhausting yourself, and I miss the days when we have time to spend an afternoon together. I want you to protect your health and have more time for me."

Husband to wife: "I see the professors and their wives at the faculty party, and I shudder at some of the grotesque relationships." The real message that couldn't be said was "When I see that terrible unhappiness, I realize what a fine life we have and how much I love you."

Mother to daughter: "I hope you visit Grandma this week." On the surface this seems straightforward, but underneath lurks the guilt and anxiety she feels about Grandma's loneliness. She worries about the old woman's health and, without explaining any of this, badgers her daughter to make frequent visits.

Two lovers: "I waited while you were on the phone and now our dinners are cold." The underlying statement is "I wonder how much you care about me when you take a phone call in the middle of dinner. I'm feeling hurt and angry."

5. Distinguish between observations and thoughts. You have to separate what you see and hear from your judgments, theories, beliefs, and opinions. "I see you've been fishing with Joe again" could be a straightforward observation. But in the context of a longstanding conflict about Joe, it becomes a barbed conclusion. Review the section on contaminated messages for more discussion of this issue.

6. Focus on one thing at a time. This means that you don't start complaining about your daughter's Spanish grades in the middle of a discussion about her boyfriend's marijuana habits. Stick with the topic at hand until both parties have made clear, whole messages. If you get unfocused, try using one of the following statements to clarify the message: "I'm feeling lost . . . what are we really talking about?" or "What do you hear me saying? I sense we've gotten off the track."

Messages Should Be Straight

A straight message is one in which the stated purpose is identical with the real purpose of the communication. Disguised intentions and hidden agendas destroy intimacy because they put you in a position of manipulating rather than relating to people. You can check if your messages are straight by asking these two questions: (1) Why am I saying this to this person? (2) Do I want him or her to hear it, or something else?

Hidden agendas are dealt with at length in another chapter. They are usually necessitated by feelings of inadequacy and poor self-worth. You have to protect yourself, and that means creating a certain image. Some people take the *I'm good* position. Most of their communications are subtle opportunities to boast. Others pay the *I'm good but you aren't* game. They are very busy putting everyone down and presenting themselves, by implication, as smarter, stronger, more successful. Agendas such as *I'm helpless, I'm fragile, I'm tough,* and *I know it all* are good defensive maneuvers to keep you from getting hurt. But the stated purpose of your communication is always different from your real purpose. While you are ostensibly discoursing on intricate Middle East politics, the real purpose is to show how knowledgeable you are. We all succumb to little vanities, but when your communications are dominated by one such agenda, you aren't being straight.

Being straight also means that you tell the truth. You state your real needs and feelings. You don't say you're tired and want to go home if you're really angry and want more attention. You don't angle for compliments or reassurance by putting yourself down. You don't say you're anxious about going to a couples therapist when actually you feel angry about being pushed to go. You don't describe your feelings as depression because your mate prefers that to irritation. You don't say you enjoy visiting your girlfriend's brother when the experience is one step below fingernails scraping on the chalkboard. Lies cut you off from others. Lies keep them from knowing what you need or feel. You lie to be nice, you lie to protect yourself, but you end up feeling alone with your closest friends.

Messages Should Be Supportive

Being supportive means you want the other person to be able to hear you without getting blown away. Ask yourself, "Do I want my message to be heard defensively or accurately? Is my purpose to hurt someone, to aggrandize myself, or to communicate?"

The Fair Fighting chapter explores step-by-step methods of working through anger. However, if you prefer to hurt your listener with your messages, use these six tactics:

1. Global labels. Stupid, ugly, selfish, evil, assinine, mean, disgusting, worthless, and lazy are a few of the huge list of hurtful words. The labels are most damaging when used in a "You're a fool, a coward, a drunk," and so on format. Making your point that way creates a total indictment of the person, instead of just a commentary on some specific behavior.

2. Sarcasm. This form of humor very clearly tells the listener that you have contempt for him. It's often a cover for feelings of anger and hurt. The effect on the listener is to push him away or make him angry.

3. Dragging up the past. This destroys any chance of clarifying how each of you feels about a present situation. You rake over old wounds and betrayals instead of examining your current dilemma.

4. Negative comparisons. "Why aren't you generous like your brother?" "Why don't you come home at six like other men?" "Sarah's getting A's and you can't even get a B in music appreciation." Comparisons are deadly because they not only contain "you're bad" messages, but they make people feel inferior to friends and family.

5. Judgmental "you messages." These are attacks that use an accusing form. "You don't love me anymore." "You're never here when I need you." "You never help around the house." "You turn me on about as much as a 1964 Plymouth."

6. Threats. If you want to bring meaningful communication to a halt, get out the big guns. Threaten to move out, threaten to quit, threaten violence. Threats are good topic changers, because instead of talking about uncomfortable issues, you can talk about the hostile things you plan to do.

Communicating supportively means that you avoid "win/lose" and "right/wrong" games. These are interactions in which the intention of one or both players is "winning" or proving the other person "wrong" rather than sharing and understanding. Your intention in communication will guide you toward a predictable result. Real communication produces understanding and closeness, while "win/lose" games produce warfare and distance. Ask yourself, "Do I want to win or do I want to communicate? Do I want to be right or do I want mutual understanding?" If you find yourself feeling defensive and wanting to criticize the other person, that's a clue that you're playing "win/lose."

Win/lose interactions can be avoided by sticking rigidly to the whole-message structure. You can also get around the win/lose pattern by making clear observations on your process. "I'm feeling pretty defensive and angry right now, and it looks like I've fallen into the old win/lose syndrome."

Appendix 2

Managing Job Stress
by Tim Blood

When you experience work related stress (work overload, time urgency, job complexity, decision making stress for example), your body usually senses that there's a source of danger. Then, as it's been doing for millions of years, it mobilizes various systems in the body to help you escape from or combat this perceived danger. A queasy stomach, shallow breathing, tense muscles, and alarming thoughts are all part of the "stress response"--the body's way of preparing you for "fight or flight."

For most of our human history the challenges our ancestors faced required them to respond to threatening situations in a physical way. Tense muscles, for example, were necessary to run away from or fight physical danger. But in the modern world, tense muscles and other aspects of the stress response are seldom necessary to respond to the challenges we face. In fact, when we mobilize for action over and over, we can get worn out and suffer from stress related illness.

To illustrate this, imagine that the human body is a car and you're driving along behind a slow moving truck. When it's finally clear to pass, you press the accelerator to the floor and speed by the truck. Then you ease off the accelerator and continue at a moderate speed. Most cars can handle these short bursts of full speed operation without damage. But if you drove for mile after mile at full speed, your engine would probably break down before long. Likewise our bodies can handle brief periods of full speed operation but tend to break down without a rest.

For example, if you suddenly smelled smoke and heard a fire alarm, your body would mobilize it's energy to help you quickly leave the building. This would be an appropriate response to this situation. It would not be desirable to sit around saying to yourself "no need to get stressed out here, I'm going to just stay cool and see what happens. . ." The point is that the stress response is desirable when it prepares us for a situation that requires fight or flight, but it's usually an "obsolete" response to the stress of our modern world.

Much of the advice regarding stress in the popular media fails to account for the complexity of modern life and the uniqueness of each of us as individuals. To be effective, stress management needs to be comprehensive.

A comprehensive stress management program consists of three elements or levels:

1. **Life-Situation Interventions:** Avoid, manage, and modify stressors (causes of stress) in your immediate environment.

2. **Perception Interventions:** Modify the way you think about stressors.

3. **Emotional and Physiological Arousal Interventions:** Manage the way your body responds to stress.

The first step in each of these levels of managing stress involves increasing your self-awareness. On the first level, you're becoming more aware of the causes of stress and of options for modifying or avoiding those stressors. On the second level, you're paying attention to your thoughts and noticing which ones are helpful and which ones increase your stress level. On the third level, you're tuning in to your body and noticing, for example, where you hold tension and when your breathing becomes shallow.

1. **Life-Situation Interventions**: Avoid, manage, and modify stressors (causes of stress) in your immediate environment.

By applying what you are learning in **Human Relations at Work** you will be helping to avoid, manage, and modify many of the causes of stress in your work environment. For example, by using effective communication skills you will help avoid misunderstandings with coworkers and customers that can lead to stressful situations. Behaving assertively can help you stand up for your rights while respecting the rights of others. Working as part of a team and negotiating for win-win solutions to conflicts will help minimize the stress that often results when there are unresolved differences of opinion. Developing an appreciation for diversity
will help you welcome differences among people rather than feeling threatened when you encounter someone with a different work style or world view. Learning about change in the workplace will help you understand what you and your coworkers are likely to be experiencing during times of transition.

2. **Perception Interventions**: Modify the way you <u>think</u> about stressors.

If you slow down a bit and pay close attention to your thought process, you may make some interesting discoveries. Many people find that their <u>way</u> of thinking about things actually increases their stress level in many situations. Developing awareness of your thought process is the first step in modifying the way you think about stressors.

Here's an exercise you can try now that will help you become more aware of your thought process:

If you're not in a quiet location right now, try to find one where you will be undisturbed for about five minutes. Sit in a comfortable position (but not so comfortable that you'll fall asleep). Take a couple of slow, deep breathes. Notice the feelings in your body as you inhale. . . exhale. . . Take note of any thoughts that are occurring to you as you continue breathing fully. After you've noted the thought, return your attention to your breathing.

What did you notice? Most people find they have an ongoing dialog occurring in their head. Thoughts like, "What if someone comes to the door now. This seems like a dumb exercise. What am I having for dinner. I'm worried about _____. Am I doing this right? Is five minutes up yet? I wonder what's on TV." Some people find they have more than one "voice," or source of thought. I'm not referring to actually "hearing voices" in your head, but to the possibility of more than one source for your thoughts. For example, a person might notice they're hearing the voice of a parent or boss who is saying something like "you should be doing better" and also the voice of a close friend who is saying something like "nice going."

When noticing how your thought process effects your stress level, there is a key question that is important to ask yourself. The question addresses whether the <u>way</u> you're thinking about the situation is unnecessarily <u>adding</u> to your stress level. You could phrase the question something like, "Is it possible that the way I'm thinking about this is needlessly increasing my stress level?" Another way of asking would be, "As I notice the voice I'm paying attention to, is it part of the solution or is it part of the problem?"

When the answer to your question suggests that your thoughts are adding to your stress, try to modify your way of thinking about what's going on. This, of course, is easier said than done. You have spent years developing your way of thinking and even if you notice that it's sometimes not real helpful, it's going to take some effort to make changes. Fortunately, this is not an "all or nothing" proposition. Each time you catch yourself listening to an unhelpful or irrational voice, try to replace it with a helpful, rational voice.

Listed below are four common types of irrational thinking that tend to increase stress. Next to each type are some ways to challenge and replace these thinking styles:

Distorted or Irrational Thinking Style	Tools to Challenge Distorted or Irrational Thoughts
Filtering: selectively looking at only one part of a situation (usually the bad) while disregarding the positive.	Consider the "big picture." Ask yourself what other interpretations might be possible.
Over generalizing: reaching a broad conclusion based on one small bit of evidence.	Question the logic of the assumption you're making, ask for evidence, look for exceptions.
Polarized thinking: perceiving everything at the extremes with nothing in between--things are perfect or terrible, with no middle ground.	Challenge simplistic thinking, consider that you can handle a more complex explanation for this situation, look for creative approaches.
Catastrophizing: expect the worst, exaggerate the bad.	Reassure the voice that's warning you of danger that you can respond effectively without considering this situation a major emergency.

This process of "Rational Emotive Thinking" is described by Gerald Kranzler in You Can Change How You Feel. "Cognitive Restructuring" is described by Aaron Beck in Cognitive Therapy and Emotional Disorders.

Try the exercise again now and see if you notice more than one "voice" or source for your thoughts.

What did you notice this time? Could you identify some of the voices in your internal dialog? It can be helpful to develop an analogy or representational system for your thought process. Here are two possibilities:

The courtroom. In this analogy, you have a prosecuting attorney and a defense attorney arguing about you. The prosecutor is saying things like, "When you forgot that appointment, you really messed up. How could you be so stupid? You're always screwing things up. What an idiot." The defensive attorney is saying things like, "OK, so you forgot the appoint-ment, everybody makes an occasional mistake. It wasn't intentional. Now what can we do to improve the situation?" The courtroom judge runs the trial and decides who gets to speak.

The VCR remote control. In this analogy, there is a remote control device that can switch from one channel or movie to another in your head. One channel might have lots of drama with the characters angrily criticizing each other. Another channel might have a sarcastic comedy where the criticism is disguised as humor. Another channel shows a peaceful beach with a person walking along, enjoying him or herself.

Take a moment now to try out these analogies and see if either one feels right for you. If not, try designing an analogy for your thinking process that would work. Additional ideas could include a cast of cartoon characters, a group of musicians, a committee of people sitting around a table, talking animals, a collection of cassette tapes that you could play in a tape player, or something else.

Now, experiment with altering the thoughts you're having by modifying the "voices." If you're using the courtroom analogy, you be the judge who gets to choose which attorney gets to speak. Let the prosecutor speak for five or ten seconds. OK, that's enough! Now, listen to the defense attorney who is calm and rational and supportive of you. When the prosecutor jumps up and starts yelling, have the judge tell him/her to be quiet and wait until they have permission to speak. Let the defense attorney continue to speak and listen to this supportive, helpful voice.

With the VCR remote control analogy, imagine pressing the buttons to change the channel when there's a movie playing that is not enjoyable or helpful to you. Choose a movie that's constructive and nurturing and useful to watch.

3. **Emotional and Physiological Arousal Interventions**: Manage the way your body responds to stress.
    A. BREATHE DEEPLY.
    B. Use Relaxation Training to reduce Physical/Emotional Arousal.
    C. Use Exercise to utilize the energy created by the stress response.

©Tim Blood, Lane Community College

Appendix 3

Anger management   Source: <u>Make Anger Your Ally</u> by Neil Clark Warren

A. General principles
1. Anger is usually a secondary emotion as a response to hurt, frustration, or fear.
2. Anger is physiological arousal - basically a stress response.
3. Anger and aggression are significantly different.
4. How we use anger is learned.
5. The expression of anger can come under your control.
6. Anger is a useful emotion when it motivates you to: right a wrong, resolve a conflict, or change a negative situation. "Express anger appropriately in defense of yourself".

B. Common strategies for mismanaging anger
1. Exploding
2. Self-punishing
3. Under handing, passive aggressive

C. Anger "values"
1. Do you want to be in control when you're angry?
2. If so are you willing to spend the energy to stay "ahead of the action"?
3. When you get angry with people, how do you want to end up with them?
4. Overall, what do you most want the outcome of your anger to be?

E. Recognize the "invitation" to get angry
1. Stay in close touch with your feelings
        a. Once a day, write about how you're feeling right now - write for 10-20 minutes.
        b. Keep an "anger diary" where you write about times when you get angry.
2. Remember that you can refuse the invitation to get angry

F. Develop an "early warning system"
1. Learn to recognize the physiological arousal (muscle tension, rapid heartbeat, shallow breathing, churning stomach etc.) that can signal the beginning of anger.

G. Clarifying the feeling
1. Notice if your primary emotion might be hurt, frustration, or fear.
2. Use an "I" statement to describe your feelings.

H. Take a "time-out", get grounded and centered
1. Short: take a deep breathe
2. Longer: several minutes or hours where you remove yourself from the situation to slow down and stop the anger process. Lay "groundwork" for longer time-outs.
3. Possibilities: take a brisk walk, dissipate the energy from the stress response in a non-destructive way, notice and challenge irrational thinking, put the situation in perspective, recite positive affirmations...learn what works best for you.

I. Resolution
1. Use communication skills, assertive behavior, negotiation skills etc. to resolve the situation.
2. Ask WHAT do I want from this encounter that will contribute most to the kind of long-term relationship   I want with this person and HOW can I best get what I really want? Be creative.

214

Appendix 4

Nonviolent Communication, A Language of Compassion
by Marshall Rosenberg
ISBN 1-892005-02-6
PuddleDancer Press

Chapter summaries copied from web site: http://www.puddledancer.com/

Chapter Summary:

1. Giving From The Heart

NVC helps us connect with ourselves and each other in a way that allows our natural compassion to flourish. It guides us to reframe the way we express ourselves and listen to others by focusing our consciousness on four areas: what we are observing, feeling, and needing and what we are requesting to enrich our lives. NVC fosters deep listening, respect, and empathy and engenders a mutual desire to give from the heart. Some people use NVC to respond compassionately to themselves, some to create greater depth in their personal relationships, and still others to build effective relationships at work or in the political arena. Worldwide, NVC is used to mediate disputes and conflicts at all levels.

2. Communication That Blocks Compassion

It is our nature to enjoy giving and receiving compassionately. We have, however, learned many forms of "life-alienating communication" which lead us to speak and behave in ways that injure ourselves and others. One form of life-alienating communication is the use of moralistic judgments that imply wrongness or badness on the part of those who don't act in harmony with our values. Another form of such communication is the use of comparisons, which can block compassion both for ourselves and others. Life-alienating communication also obscures our awareness that we are each responsible for our own thoughts, feelings, and actions. Communicating our desires in the form of demands is yet another characteristic of language that blocks compassion.

3. Observing Without Evaluating

The first component of NVC entails the separation of observation from evaluation. When we combine observation with evaluation, others are apt to hear criticism and resist what we are saying. NVC is a process language that discourages static generalizations. Instead, observations are to be made specific to time and context, e.g. "Hank Smith has not scored a goal in 20 games" rather than "Hank Smith is a poor soccer player."

4. Identifying and Expressing Feelings

The second component necessary for expressing ourselves is feelings. By developing a vocabulary of feelings that allows us to clearly and specifically name or identify our emotions, we can connect more easily with one another. Allowing ourselves to be vulnerable by expressing our feelings can help resolve conflicts. NVC distinguishes the expression of actual feelings from words and statements that describe thoughts, assessments, and interpretations.

5. Taking Responsibility for Our Feelings

The third component of NVC is the acknowledgment of the needs behind our feelings. What others say and do may be the stimulus, but never the cause, of our feelings. When someone communicates negatively, we have four options as to how to receive the message: (1) blame ourselves, (2) blame others, (3) sense our own feelings and needs, (4) sense the feelings and needs hidden in the other person's negative message. Judgments, criticisms, diagnoses, and interpretations of others are all alienated expressions of our own needs and values. When others hear criticism, they tend to invest their energy in selfdefense or counterattack. The more directly we can connect our feelings to our needs, the easier it is for others to respond compassionately. In a world where we are often harshly judged for identifying and revealing our needs, doing so can be very frightening, especially for women who are socialized to ignore their own needs while caring for others. In the course of developing emotional responsibility, most of us experience three stages: (1) "emotional slavery"-believing ourselves responsible for the feelings of others, (2) "the obnoxious stage"-in which we refuse to admit to caring what anyone else feels or needs, and (3) "emotional liberation"-in which we accept full responsibility for our own feelings but not the feelings of others, while being aware that we can never meet our own needs at the expense of others.

6. Requesting That Which Would Enrich Life

The fourth component of NVC addresses the question of what we would like to request of each other to enrich each of our lives. We try to avoid vague, abstract, or ambiguous phrasing, and remember to use positive action language by stating what we are requesting rather than what we are not. When we speak, the clearer we are about what we want back, the more likely we are to get it. Since the message we send is not always the message that's received, we need to learn how to find out if our message has been accurately heard. Especially when we are expressing ourselves in a group, we need to be clear about the nature of the response we are wanting back. Otherwise we may be initiating unproductive conversations that waste considerable group time. Requests are received as demands when listeners believe that they will be blamed or punished if they do not comply. We can help others trust that we are requesting, not demanding, by indicating our desire for them to comply only if they can do so willingly. The objective of NVC is not to change people and their behavior in order to get our way; it is to establish relationships based on honesty and empathy which will eventually fulfill everyone's needs

7. Receiving Empathically

Empathy is a respectful understanding of what others are experiencing. Instead of offering empathy, we often have a strong urge to give advice or reassurance and to explain our own position or feeling. Empathy, however, calls upon us to empty our mind and listen to others with our whole being. In NVC, no matter what words others may use to express themselves, we simply listen for their observations, feelings, needs, and requests. Then we may wish to reflect back, paraphrasing what we have understood. We stay with empathy, allowing others the opportunity to fully express themselves before we turn our attention to solutions or requests for relief. We need empathy to give empathy. When we sense ourselves being defensive or unable to empathize, we need to (a) stop, breathe, give ourselves empathy, (b) scream nonviolently, or (c) take time out.

8. The Power of Empathy

Our ability to offer empathy can allow us to stay vulnerable, defuse potential violence, help us hear the word "no" without taking it as a rejection, revive a lifeless conversation, and even hear the feelings and needs expressed through silence. Time and again people transcend the paralyzing effects of psychological pain when they have sufficient contact with someone who can hear them empathically

9. Expressing Anger Fully

Blaming and punishing others are superficial expressions of anger. If we wish to fully express anger, the first step is to divorce the other person from any responsibility for our anger. Instead we shine the light of consciousness on our own feelings and needs. By expressing our needs, we are far more likely to get them met than by our judging, blaming, or punishing others. The four steps to expressing anger are (1) stop and breathe, (2) identify our judgmental thoughts, (3) connect with our needs, and (4) express our feelings and unmet needs. Sometimes in between steps 3 and 4 we may choose to empathize with the other person so that he or she will be better able to hear us when we express ourselves in Step 4. We need to take our time in both learning and applying the process of NVC

10. The Protective Use of Force

In situations where there is no opportunity for communication, such as in instances of imminent danger, we may need to resort to the protective use of force. The intention behind the protective use of force is to prevent injury or injustice, never to punish or to cause individuals to suffer, repent, or change. The punitive use of force tends to generate hostility and to reinforce resistance to the very behavior we are seeking. Punishment damages goodwill and selfesteem, and shifts our attention from the intrinsic value of an action to external consequences. Blaming and punishing fail to contribute to the motivations we would like to inspire in others.

11. Liberating Ourselves and Counseling Others

NVC enhances inner communication by helping us translate negative internal messages into feelings and needs. Our ability to distinguish our own feelings and needs and to empathize with them can free us from depression. We can replace "dream-killing language" with NVC and recognize the existence of choice in all our actions. By showing us how to focus on what we are truly wanting rather than on what is wrong with ourselves or others, NVC gives us the tools and understanding to create a more peaceful state of mind. Professionals in counseling and psychotherapy to engender relationships with clients that are mutual and authentic may also use NVC.

12. Expressing Appreciation in Nonviolent Communication

Conventional compliments often take the form of judgments, however positive, and are sometimes offered to manipulate the behavior of others. NVC encourages the expression of appreciation solely for celebration. We state (1) the action that has contributed to our wellbeing, (2) the particular need of ours that has been fulfilled, and (3) the feeling of pleasure engendered as a result. When we receive appreciation expressed in this way, we can do so without any feeling of superiority or false humility by celebrating along with the person who is offering the appreciation.

GLOSSARY

action plan   A series of steps to achieve a goal.

active listener   A person who listens intensely, with the goal of empathizing with the speaker.

aggressive personality   A person who verbally, and sometimes physically, attacks others frequently.

assertiveness   Being forthright in expressing demands, opinions, feelings, and attitudes.

behavioral feedback   Information given to another person that pinpoints behavior rather than personal characteristics or attitudes.

behavior modification   An attempt to change behavior by manipulating rewards and punishments.

brainstorming   A group problem-solving technique that promotes creativity by encouraging idea generation through noncritical discussion.

brainwriting   Brainstorming by individuals working alone.

burnout   A condition of emotional, mental, and physical exhaustion in response to long-term stressors.

business etiquette   A special code of behavior required in work situations.

career path   A sequence of positions necessary to achieve a goal.

carpal tunnel syndrome   A condition that occurs when repetitive flexing and extension of the wrist causes the tendons to swell, thus trapping and pinching the median nerve.

casual time orientation   A cultural characteristic in which people view time as an unlimited and unending resource and therefore tend to be patient.

character trait   An enduring characteristic of a person that is related to moral and ethical behavior.

charisma   A special quality of leaders whose purposes, powers, and extraordinary determination differentiate them from others. (However, people besides leaders can be charismatic.)

coaching   A method of helping workers grow and develop and improve their job competence by providing suggestions and encouragement.

cognitive factors   The collective term for problem-solving and intellectual skills.

cognitive restructuring   Mentally converting negative aspects into positive ones by looking for the positive elements in a situation.

cognitive style   Mental processes used to perceive and make judgments from situations.

collectivism   A feeling that the group and society should receive top priority, rather than the individual.

communication   The sending, receiving, and understanding of messages.

compromise   Settlement of differences by mutual concessions.

concern for others   An emphasis on personal relationships and a concern for the welfare of others.

conflict   A situation in which two or more goals, values, or events are incompatible or mutually exclusive.

conflict of interest   A situation that occurs when a person's judgment or objectivity is compromised.

consensus   General acceptance by the group of a decision.

cross-functional team   A work group composed of workers from different specialties, and about the same organizational level, who come together to accomplish a task.

cultural fluency   The ability to conduct business in a diverse, international environment.

cultural intelligence (CQ)   An outsider's ability to interpret someone's unfamiliar and ambiguous behavior the same way that person's compatriots would.

cultural sensitivity   An awareness of and willingness to investigate the reasons why people of another culture act as they do.

cultural training   A set of learning experiences designed to help employees understand the customs, traditions, and beliefs of another culture.

cycle-of-service chart   A method of tracking the moments of truth with respect to customer service.

crew   A group of specialists each of whom have specific roles, perform brief events that are closely synchronized with each other, and repeat these events under different environmental conditions.

defensive communication   The tendency to receive messages in such a way that our self-esteem is protected.

defining moment   Choosing between two or more ideals in which one deeply believes.

denial   The suppression of information we find uncomfortable.

developmental need A specific area in which a person needs to change or improve.

difficult person An individual who creates problems for others, even though he or she has the skill and mental ability to do otherwise.

diversity training Training that attempts to bring about workplace harmony by teaching people how to get along better with diverse work associates.

effort-to-performance expectancy The probability assigned by the individual that effort will lead to performing the task correctly.

electronic brainstorming Method of generating ideas with the aid of a computer. Group members simultaneously and anonymously enter their suggestions into a computer, and the ideas are distributed to monitors of other group members.

emotional intelligence Qualities such as understanding one's own feelings, empathy for others, and the regulation of emotion to enhance living.

empathy In communication, imagining oneself in the receiver's role, and assuming the viewpoints and emotions of that individual.

empowerment The process of managers transferring, or sharing, power with lower ranking employees.

ethical screening Running a contemplated decision or action through an ethics test.

ethics The moral choices a person makes. Also, what is good and bad, right and wrong, just and unjust, and what people should do.

expectancy theory A motivation theory based on the premise that the effort people expend depends on the reward they expect to receive in return.

feedback In communication, messages sent back from the receiver to the sender.

fight-or-flight response The body's physiological and chemical battle against a stressor in which the person tries to cope with the adversity head-on or tries to flee from the scene.

formality A cultural characteristic of attaching considerable importance to tradition, ceremony, social rules, and rank.

frame of reference The fact that people perceive words and concepts differently because their vantage points and perspectives differ.

freeze-frame technique A scientifically based method of stress reduction that emphasizes reappraising a difficult event, along with some symptom management.

g (general) factor A factor in intelligence that contributes to the ability to perform well in many tasks.

group decision making The process of reaching a judgment based on feedback from more than one individual.

group norms The unwritten set of expectations for group members.

groupthink A deterioration of mental efficiency, reality testing, and moral judgment in the interest of group solidarity.

high-context culture A culture that makes extensive use of body language.

impression management A set of behaviors directed at enhancing one's image by drawing attention to oneself.

incivility In human relations, employees' lack of regard for each other.

individual differences Variations in how people respond to the same situation based on personal characteristics.

individualism A mental set in which people see themselves first as individuals and believe that their own interests take priority.

informal learning The acquisition of knowledge and skills that take place naturally outside a structured learning environment.

informality A cultural characteristic of a casual attitude toward tradition, ceremony, social rules, and rank.

intelligence The capacity to acquire and apply knowledge, including solving problems.

intermittent reward A reward that is given for good performance occasionally, but not always.

interpersonal skill training The teaching of skills in dealing with others so they can be put into practice.

intuition An experience-based way of knowing or reasoning in which the weighing and balancing of evidence are done automatically.

law of effect Behavior that leads to a positive consequence for the individual tends to be repeated, whereas behavior that leads to a negative consequence tends not to be repeated.

leader-exchange model A theory explaining that group leaders establish unique working relationships with group members, thereby creating in-groups and out-groups.

leadership The ability to inspire support and confidence among the people who are needed to achieve common goals.

learning style The way in which a person best learns new information.

materialism An emphasis on assertiveness and the acquisition of money and material objects.

mentor An individual with advanced experience and knowledge who is committed to giving support and career advice to a less experienced person.

message A purpose or idea to be conveyed.

metacommunication To communicate about your communication to help overcome barriers or resolve a problem.

microinequity A small, semiconscious message we send with a powerful impact on the receiver.

micromanager One who closely monitors most aspects of group members' activities, sometimes to the point of being a control freak.

mirroring Subtly imitating someone.

moments of truth Situations in which a customer comes in contact with a company and forms an impression of its service.

moral intensity In ethical decision making, how deeply others might be affected by the decision.

motivation An internal state that leads to effort expended toward objectives; an activity performed by one person to get another to accomplish work.

motivational state   Any active needs and interests operating at a given time.

multiple intelligences   A theory of intelligence contending that people know and understand the world in distinctly different ways and learn in different ways.

negative affectivity   A tendency to experience aversive emotional states.

negative reinforcement (avoidance motivation)   Rewarding people by taking away an uncomfortable consequence of their behavior.

negotiating   Conferring with another person to resolve a problem.

networking   Developing contacts with influential people, including gaining their trust and confidence. Also, contacting friends and acquaintances and building systematically on these relationships to create a still wider set of contacts that might lead to employment.

noise   Anything that disrupts communication, including the attitudes and emotions of the receiver.

nominal group technique (NGT)   A group problem-solving technique that calls people together in a structured meeting with limited interaction.

nonverbal communication   The transmission of messages through means other than words.

nurturing person   One who promotes the growth of others.

organization culture   A system of shared values and beliefs that influence worker behavior.

organizational citizenship behavior   The willingness to go beyond one's job description.

organizational politics   Gaining power through any means other than merit or luck.

participative leadership   Sharing authority with the group.

perceived control   The belief that an individual has at his or her disposal a response that can control the negative aspects of an event.

performance-to-outcome expectancy   The probability assigned by the individual that performance will lead to outcomes or rewards.

personality   Persistent and enduring behavior patterns that tend to be expressed in a wide variety of situations.

personality clash   An antagonistic relationship between two people based on differences in personal attributes, preferences, interests, values, and styles.

personal productivity   The amount of resources, including time, you consume to achieve a certain level of output.

person–organization fit   The compatibility of the individual and the organization.

person–role conflict   The situation that occurs when the demands made by the organization clash with the basic values of the individual.

political decision-making model   The assumption about decision making that people bring preconceived notions and biases into the decision-making situation.

positive gossip   Unofficial information that supports others, is based on truth, and respects not leak confidential information.

positive reinforcement   Increasing the probability that behavior will be repeated by rewarding people for making the desired response.

power   The ability or potential to control anything of value and to influence decisions.

proactive personality   A person who is relatively unconstrained by situational forces and who brings about environmental change.

procrastination   Delaying action for no good reason.

protégé   The less experienced person in a mentoring relationship who is helped by the mentor.

Pygmalion effect   The phenomenon that people will rise (or fall) to the expectations that another person has of them.

rational decision-making model   The traditional, logical approach to decision making based on the scientific method.

role ambiguity   A condition in which the job holder receives confusing or poorly defined expectations.

role conflict   The situation that occurs when a person has to choose between two competing demands or expectations.

role overload   Having too much work to do.

s (special) factors   Specific components of intelligence that contribute to problem-solving ability.

self-efficacy   The confidence in your ability to carry out a specific task.

self-managing work team   A small group of employees responsible for managing and performing technical tasks to deliver a product or service to an external or internal customer.

sexual harassment   Unwanted sexually oriented behavior in the workplace that results in discomfort and/or interference with the job.

social loafing   The psychological term for shirking individual responsibility in a group setting.

stress   An adaptive response that is the consequence of any action, situation, or event that places special demands on a person.

stressor   The external or internal force that brings about stress.

summarization   The process of summarizing, pulling together, condensing, and thereby clarifying the main points communicated by another person.

support network   A group of people who can listen to your problems and provide emotional support.

synergy   A situation in which the group's total output exceeds the sum of each individual's contribution.

team   A small number of people with complementary skills who are committed to a common purpose, set of performance goals, and approach for which they hold themselves mutually accountable.

toxic person   One who negatively affects others.

training   The process of helping others acquire a job-related skill.

triarchic theory of intelligence   An explanation of mental ability holding that intelligence is composed of three different subtypes: analytical, creative, and practical.

Type A behavior   A behavior pattern in which the individual is demanding, impatient, and overstriving, and therefore prone to negative stress.

universal training need   An area for improvement common to most people.

urgent time orientation   A cultural characteristic of perceiving time as a scarce resource and tending to be impatient.

valence   The value, worth, or attractiveness of an outcome.

value   The importance a person attaches to something.

virtual office   A place of work without a fixed physical location, where the output is communicated electronically.

virtual team   A small group of people who conduct almost all of their collaborative work by electronic communication rather than face-to-face meetings.

win–win   The belief that after conflict has been resolved both sides should gain something of value.

workaholism   An addiction to work in which not working is an uncomfortable experience.

work–family conflict   A state that occurs when an individual's roles of worker and active participant in social and family life compete with each other.

REFERENCES

CHAPTER 1

1. *Dale Carnegie Training* brochure, Spring–Summer 2005, p. 12.

2. Joanne Lozar Glenn, "Lessons in Human Relations," *Business Education Forum,* October 2003, p. 10.

3. Research cited in Bob Wall, *Working Relationships: The Simple Truth About Getting Along with Friends and Foes at Work* (Palo Alto, CA: Davies-Black, 1999).

4. George B. Yancey, Chante P, Clarkson, Julie D. Baxa, and Rachel N. Clarkson, "Example of Good and Bad Interpersonal Skills at Work," *http://www.psichi.org/pubs/articles/article_368.asp,* p. 2, accessed February 2, 2004.

5. The model presented here is an extension of the one presented in Thomas V. Bonoma and Gerald Zaltman, *Psychology for Management* (Boston: Kent, 1981), pp. 88–92.

6. Gary P. Latham, "The Motivational Benefits of Goal-Setting," *Academy of Management Executive,* November 2004, pp. 126–127.

7. Roger B. Hill, "On-Line Instructional ResourcesLesson 3, Interpersonal Skills," *http://www.coe.uga.edu/~rhill/workethic/less3.htm,* p. 1, accessed March 17, 2005.

8. Nancy Day, "Informal Learning Gets Results," *Workforce,* June 1998, pp. 30–36; Marcia L. Conner, "Informal Learning," *Ageless Learner,* 1997–2005, *http://agelesslearner.com/intros/informal.html,* p. 2.

9. Morgan W. McCall, Jr., *High Flyers: Developing the Next Generation of Leaders* (Boston: Harvard Business School Press, 1998).

CHAPTER 2

1. Marvin Zuckerman, "Are You a Risk Taker?" *Psychology Today,* November/December 2000, p. 53.

2. Remus Ilies and Timothy A. Judge, "On the Heritability of Job Satisfaction: The Mediating Role of Personality," *Journal of Applied Psychology,* August 2003, pp. 750–759.

3. Robert R. McRae and Juri Allik, eds, *The Five-Factor Model of Personality Across Cultures* (New York: Kluwer, 2002).

4. Roger R. McRae and Paul T. Costa, Jr., "Personality Trait Structure as Human Universal," *American Psychologist,* May 1997, pp. 509–516.

5. Lawrence R. James and Michelle D. Mazerolle, *Personality in Work Organizations* (Thousand Oaks, CA: Sage, 2002).

6. "Which Traits Predict Job Performance?" *APA Help Center, http://www.apahelpcenter.org/articles/article.php?id=33,* accessed March 22, 2005.

7. Gregory M. Hurtz and John J. Donovan, "Personality and Job Performance: The Big Five Revisited," *Journal of Applied Psychology,* December 2000, pp. 869–879.

8. David V. Day, Deidra J. Scheleicher, Amy L. Unckless, and Nathan J. Hiller, "Self-Monitoring Personality at Work: A Meta-Analytic Investigation of Construct Validity," *Journal of Applied Psychology,* April 2002, pp. 390–401.

9. Gerald L. Blakely, Martha C. Andrews, and Jack Fuller, "Are Chameleons Good Citizens? A Longitudinal Study of the Relationship Between Self-Monitoring and Organizational Citizenship Behavior," *Journal of Business and Psychology,* Winter 2003, pp. 131–144.

10. L. A. Witt, Lisa A. Burke, Murray R. Barrick, and Michael K. Mount, "The Interactive Effects of Conscientiousness and Agreeableness on Job Performance," *Journal of Applied Psychology,* February 2002, pp. 164–169.

11. Carl J. Thoresen, Jill C. Bradley, Paul D. Bliese, and Joseph D. Thoresen, "The Big Five Personality Traits and Individual Job Performance Growth Trajectories in Maintenance and Transitional Job Stages," *Journal of Applied Psychology,* October 2004, pp. 835–853.

12. L. A. Burke and L. A. Witt, "Personality and High-Maintenance Employee Behavior," *Journal of Business and Psychology,* Spring 2004, pp. 349–363.

13. Cited in David Stipp, "A Little Worry Is Good for Business," *Fortune,* November 24, 2003, p. 68.

14. The Myers-Briggs Type Indicator (MBTI) is published by Consulting Psychological Press Inc., Palo Alto, CA 94306. Much of the discussion here is based on Robert P. Vecchio, *Organizational Behavior: Core Concepts,* 4th ed. (Fort Worth, TX: Dryden Press, 2000), pp. 44–45; Douglas P. Shuit, "Happy Birthday, Myers-Briggs," *Workforce Management,* December 2003, pp. 72–74.

15. An example of this research is John W. Slocum and Donald Hellreigel, "A Look at How Managers' Minds Work," *Business Horizons,* vol. 26, 1983, pp. 58–68.

16. Brian S. Young, Winfred Arthur, Jr., and John Finch, "Predictors of Managerial Performance: More than Cognitive Ability," *Journal of Business and Psychology,* Fall 2000, pp. 53–72.

17. Robert J. Sternberg, *Beyond IQ: A Triarchic Theory of Human Intelligence* (New York: Cambridge University Press, 1985); Bridget Murray, "Sparking Interest in Psychology Class," *APA Monitor,* October 1995, p. 51.

18. Howard Gardner, *Intelligence Reframed: Multiple Intelligence in the 21st Century* (New York: Basic Books, 1999).

19. Daniel Goleman, Richard Boyatzis, and Annie McKee, "Primal Leadership: The Hidden Driver of Great Performance," *Harvard Business Review,* December 2001, pp. 42–51.

20. David A. Morand, "The Emotional Intelligence of Managers: Assessing the Construct Validity of a Nonverbal Measure of People Skills'," *Journal of Business and Psychology,* Fall 2001, pp. 21–33.

21. David C. McClelland, "How Motives, Skills, and Values Determine What People Do," *American Psychologist,* July 1985, p. 815.

CHAPTER 3

1. Joann S. Lublin, "To Win Advancement, You Need to Clean Up Any Bad Speech Habits," *The Wall Street Journal,* October 5, 2004, p. B1.

2. Ritch Sorenson, Grace DeBord, and Ida Ramirez, *Business and Management Communication: A Guide Book,* 4th ed. (Upper Saddle River, NJ: Prentice Hall, 2001), pp. 6–10.

3. Sue Morem, "Nonverbal Communication Help for Salespeople," *http://www.careerknowhow/com/ask_sue/nonverbal.htm.*

4. Frederick Golden, "Lying Faces Unmasked," *Time,* April 5, 1999, pp. 52–53.

5. Jeffrey Jacobi, *The Vocal Advantage* (Upper Saddle River, NJ: Prentice Hall, 1996).

6. Roberta H. Krapels and Vanessa D. Arnold, "Speaker's Credibility in Persuasive Work Situations," *Business Education Forum,* December 1997, p. 25.

7. Mark Henricks, "Can We Talk? Speaking Up About the Value of Dialogue," *Entrepreneur,* January 1998, p. 82.

8. Sharon Lund O'Neil, "An Empowered Attitude Can Enhance Communication Skills," *Business Education Forum,* April 1998, pp. 28–30.

9. Jimmy Calano and Jeff Salzman, "Persuasiveness: Make It Your Power Booster," *Working Woman,* October 1988, pp. 124–125; Krapels and Arnold, "Speaker's Credibility," pp. 24–26; Gayle Theiss, "Say It Smart," *Aspire,* November–December 1998, pp. 3–4.

10. Jean Mausehund and R. Neil Dortch, "Communications Presentation Skills in the Digital Age," *Business Education Forum,* April 1999, pp. 30–32.

11. For more details, see Brian Fugere, Chelsea Hardaway, and Jon Warshawsky, *Why Business People Speak Like Idiots* (New York: Free Press, 2005).

12. Joann Baney, *Guide to Interpersonal Communication* (Upper Saddle River, NJ: Pearson/Prentice Hall, 2004), p. 7.

13. The information in this section is from Holly Weeks, "Taking the Stress Out of Stressful Conversations," *Harvard Business Review,* July–August 2001, pp. 112–119. The quote is from page 117.

14. Deborah Tannen, *Talking from 9 to 5* (New York: William Morrow, 1994); Tannen, "The Power of Talk: Who Gets Heard and Why," *Harvard Business Review,* September–October 1995, pp. 138–148; Daniel J. Canary and Kathryn Dindia, *Sex Differences and Similarities in Communication* (Mahwah, NJ: Erlbaum, 1998), p. 318; John Gray, *Men Are from Mars, Women Are from Venus* (New York: HarperCollins, 1992).

15. Cited in Kris Maher, "The Jungle: Focus on Recruitment, Pay and Getting Ahead," *The Wall Street Journal,* October 19, 2004, p. B10.

CHAPTER 4

1. Reprinted with permission from Chris Penttila, "Heart of Gold: Nonprofits are Reaping the Rewards of Starting For-Profit Ventures," *Entrepreneur,* September 2004, p. 19.

2. Conference Board report cited in "CEO Leadership Skips Teamwork, Article Says," Rochester, New York, *Democrat and Chronicle,* February 17, 2002, p. 1E.

3. Jon R. Katzenbach and Douglas K. Smith, "The Discipline of Teams," *Harvard Business Review,* March–April 1993, p. 112.

4. Deal E. Yeatts and Coyd Hyten, *High Performing Self-Managed Work Teams: A Comparison of Theory and Practice* (Thousands Oaks, CA: Sage, 1998), p. xiii.

5. Rudy M. Yandrick, "A Team Effort," *HR Magazine,* June 2001, p. 138.

6. Claus W. Langfred, "Too Much Trust a Good Thing? Negative Effects of High Trust and Individual Autonomy in Self-Managing Teams," *Academy of Management Journal,* June 2004, pp. 385–399.

7. "Shepherding Communications When the Flock Is Scattered," *Flexible Workplace Management,* sample issue, 2001.

8. Shelia Simsarian Webber and Richard J. Klimoski, "Crews: A Distinct Type of Work Team," *Journal of Business and Psychology,* Spring 2004, pp. 261–279.

9. "When Committees Spell Trouble: Don't Let Individuals Hide Within a Group," *WorkingSMART,* August 1998, p. 1.

10. Irving L. Janus, *Victims of Groupthink: A Psychological Study of Foreign Policy Decisions and Fiascos* (Boston: Houghton Mifflin, 1972); Glen Whyte, "Groupthink Reconsidered," *Academy of Management Review,* January 1989, pp. 40–56.

11. Martha A. Peak, "Treating Trauma in Teamland," *Management Review,* September 1997, p. 1.

12. "R. Meredith Belbin," in *Business: The Ultimate Resource* (Cambridge, MA: Perseus, 2002), pp. 966–967; Belbin, *Management Teams* (London: Elsevier Butterworth-Heinemann, 2003); Belbin® Team-Roles, *http://www.belbin.com/belbin-teamroles.htm.*

13. From a review of Meredith Belbin, *Management Teams,* by Colin Thomson appearing in *http://www.accountingweb. co.uk.,* accessed April 14, 2004.

14. "Fly in Formation: Easy Ways to Build Team Spirit," *WorkingSMART,* March 2000, p. 6.

15. Pamela Lovell, "Healthy Teams Display Strong Vital Signs," *Teamwork,* sample issue, the Dartnell Corporation, 1997.

16. Glenn M. Parker, *Cross-Functional Teams: Working with Allies, Enemies, & Other Strangers* (San Francisco: Jossey-Bass, 1994), p. 170.

17. Mary J. Waller et al., "The Effect of Individual Perceptions of Deadlines on Team Performance," *Academy of Management Review,* October 2001, p. 597.

18. Mark G. Ehrhant and Stefanie E. Naumann, "Organizational Citizenship Behavior in Work Groups: A Group Norms Approach," *Journal of Applied Psychology,* December 2004, pp. 960–974.

CHAPTER 5

1. "Spacecraft Will Examine Mars in Greater Detail than Ever Before," *http://mars.jpl.nasa.gov/mro/spotlight/2004706.html,* accessed July 6, 2004.

2. Andrew E. Schwartz and Joy Levin, "Better Group Decision Making," *Supervisory Management,* June 1990, p. 4.

3. Michael Mercer, *Absolutely Fabulous Organizational Change* (Castlegate, 2000); Duncan Maxwell Anderson, "Hidden Forces," *Success,* April 1995, p. 1.

4. Kay Lovelace, Debra L. Shapiro, and Laurie R. Weingart, "Minimizing Cross-Functional New Product Teams' Innovativeness and Constraint Adherence: A Conflict Communications Perspective," *Academy of Management Journal,* August 2001, pp. 779–793.

5. David A. Garvin and Michael A. Roberto, "What You Don't Know about Making Decisions," *Harvard Business Review,* September 2001, pp. 110–111.

6. Leigh Thompson, "Improving the Creativity of Work Groups," *Academy of Management Executive,* February 2003, p. 99.

7. "Future Edisons of America: Turn Your Employees into Inventors," *WorkingSMART,* June 2000, p. 2.

8. R. Brent Gallupe, William H. Cooper, Mary-Liz Grise, and Lana M. Bastianutti, "Blocking Electronic Brainstorms," *Journal of Applied Psychology,* February 1994, pp. 77–78.

9. Keng L. Siau, "Electronic Brainstorming," *Innovative Leader,* April 1997, p. 3.

10. Allen C. Bluedorn, Daniel B. Turban, and Mary Sue Love, "The Effects of Stand-Up and Sit-Down Meeting Formats on Meeting Outcomes," *Journal of Applied Psychology,* April 1999, pp. 277–285.

11. Cathy Olofson, "The Ritz Puts on Stand-Up Meetings," *Fast Company,* September 1998, *http://www.fastcompany.com/magzine/17/minm.html.*

12. Howard Baker, "Promoting Interaction and Teamwork with Electronic Mail," *Business Education Forum,* October 1994, pp. 30–31.

13. "Introduction to Groupware," *http://www.usabilityfirst.com/groupware/intro.html.*

CHAPTER 6

1. Margaret M. Clark, "Religion vs. Sexual Orientation," *HR Magazine,* August 2004, pp. 54–59.

2. Arvind V. Phatak, *International Dimensions of Management* (Boston: Kent, 1983), p. 167.

3. P. Christopher Earley and Elaine Mosakowski, "Cultural Intelligence," *Harvard Business Review,* October 2004, p. 140. The example is from the same source, same page.

4. Earley and Mosakowski, "Toward Culture Intelligence: Turning Cultural Differences into a Workplace Advantage," *Academy of Management Executive,* August 2004, pp. 154–155.

5. Scott B. Button, "Organizational Efforts to Affirm Sexual Diversity: A Cross-Level Examination," *Journal of Applied Psychology,* February 2001, pp. 17–28.

6. Charlene Marmer Solomon, "Global Operations Demand That HR Rethink Diversity," *Personnel Journal,* July 1994, p. 50.

7. Geert Hofstede, *Culture's Consequences: International Differences in Work Related Values* (Beverly Hills, CA: Sage, 1980); updated and expanded in "A Conversation with Geert Hofstede," *Organizational Dynamics,* Spring 1993, pp. 53–61; Jim Kennedy and Anna Everest, "Put Diversity in Context," *Personnel Journal,* September 1991, pp. 50–54.

8. Lee Gardenswartz and Anita Rowe, "Cross-Cultural Awareness," *HR Magazine,* March 2001, p. 139.

9. Rick Borelli, "A Worldwide Language Trap," *Management Review,* October 1997, pp. 52–54.

10. Daren Fonda, "Selling in Tongues," *Time,* November 26, 2001, pp. B12–B13.

11. Carolena Lyons Lawrence, "Teaching Students How Gestures Communicate Across Cultures," *Business Education Forum,* February 2003, p. 39.

12. Roger E. Axtell, *Gestures: The Do's and Taboos of Body Language Around the World* (New York: Wiley, 1990).

13. Siri Carpenter, "Why Do They All Look Alike'?" *Monitor on Psychology,* December 2000, p. 44.

14. "Diversity: A New' Tool for Retention," *HRfocus,* June 2000, pp. 1, 14–15.

15. Pamela Babcock, "Diversity Down to the Letter," *HR Magazine,* June 2004, pp. 91, 94.

16. Mei Fong, "Chinese Charm School," *The Wall Street Journal,* January 13, 2004, p. B1.

17. P. Christopher Earley and Randall S. Peterson, "The Elusive Cultural Chameleon: Cultural Intelligence as a New Approach to Intercultural Training for the Global Manager," *Academy of Management Learning and Education,* March 2004, p. 106.

18. Kathryn Tyle, "I Say Potato, You Say *Patata,*" *HR Magazine,* January 2004, p. 85.

19. Joanne M. Glenn, "Wendy's International, Inc.—Managing Cross-Generational Diversity," *Business Education Forum,* February 2000, p. 16.

20. Gillian Flynn, "The Harsh Reality of Diversity Programs," *Workforce,* December 1998, p. 29.

CHAPTER 7

1. Based on facts in David Brown, "IT Culture Creates Discord," *Canadian HR Reporter,* May 3, 2004.

2. Michael R. Frone, "Work-Family Conflict and Employee Psychiatric Disorders: The National Comorbidity Survey", *Journal of Applied Psychology,* December 2000, pp. 888–895.

3. Kathryn Tyler, "Beat the Clock," *HR Magazine,* November 2003, p. 103.

4. Dominic A. Infante, *Arguing Constructively* (Prospect Heights, IL: Waveland Press, 1992).

5. Anne Fisher, "How to Prevent Violence at Work," *Fortune,* February 21, 2005, p. 42.

6. Deborah Smith, "I/O Conference Examines Army Special Forces, Workplace Incivility," *Monitor on Psychology,* June 2003, p. 11.

7. Christine M. Pearson and Christine L. Porath, "On the Nature, Consequences and Remedies of Workplace Incivility: No Time for Nice'? Think Again." *Academy of Management Executive,* February 2005, pp. 7–30. The definition of *incivility* is from the same source, p. 7.

8. Kenneth Thomas, "Conflict and Conflict Management," in Marvin D. Dunnette ed., *Handbook of Industrial and Organizational Psychology* (Chicago: Rand McNally College Publishing, 1976), pp. 900–902. Sone of the information about when to use each style is from Dean Tjosvold, *The Conflict Positive Organization* (Reading, MA: Addison-Wesley, 1991).

9. Simon, cited in Mark Liu, "You Can Learn to Be Less Accommodating If You Want To," Rochester, New York, *Democrat and Chronicle,* April 25, 1999, p. 1C.

10. Robert R. Blake and Jane S. Mouton, *The Managerial Grid III* (Houston, TX: Gulf, 1985), p. 101.

11. The first three suggestions are from Connirae Andreas and Steve Andreas, *Heart of the Mind* (Moab, UT: Real People Press, 1991). Suggestion four is from Deb Koen, "How to Handle Criticism at Work," Rochester, New York, *Democrat and Chronicle,* June 20, 2004.

12. Mark Diener, "Mad Skills," *Entrepreneur,* April 2003, p. 79.

13. Steve Alper, Dean Tjosvold, and Kenneth S. Law, "Conflict Management, Efficacy, and Performance in Organizational Teams," *Personnel Psychology,* Autumn 2000, pp. 625–642.

14. Maria Rotundo, Dung-Hanh Nguyen, and Paul R. Sackett, "A Meta-Analytic Review of Gender Differences in Perceptions of Sexual Harassment," *Journal of Applied Psychology,* October 2001, pp. 914–922.

15. Anne M. O'Leary-Kelly, Ramona L. Paetzold, and Ricky W. Griffin, "Sexual Harassment as Aggressive Behavior: An Actor-Based Perspective," *Academy of Management Review,* April 2000, pp. 372–388.

16. Remus Ilies, Nancy Hauserman, Susan Schwochau, and John Stibal, "Reported Incidence Rates of Work-Related Sexual Harassment in the United States: Using Meta-Analysis to Explain Rate Disparities," *Personnel Psychology,* Autumn 2003, pp. 607–631.

17. Ibid.

18. Joanne Cole, "Sexual Harassment: New Rules, New Behavior," *HRfocus,* March 1999, p. 1.

19. Kimberly T. Schneider, Suzanne Swan, and Louis F. Fitzgerald, "Job-Related and Psychological Effects of Sexual Harassment in the Workplace: Empirical Evidence from Two Organizations," *Journal of Applied Psychology,* June 1997, pp. 412–413.

20. Theresa M. Glomb, Liberty J. Munson, and Charles L. Hulin, "Structural Equation Models of Sexual Harassment: Longitudinal Explorations and Cross-Sectional Generalizations," *Journal of Applied Psychology,* February 1999, pp. 14–28.

21. Kathleen Neville, *Corporate Attractions: An Inside Account of Sexual Harassment with the New Sexual Roles for Men and Women on the Job* (Reston, VA: Acropolis Books, 1992; Joanne Cole, "Sexual Harassment: New Rules, New Behavior," *HRfocus,* March 1999, pp. 1, 14–15.

22. Jathan W. Janove, "Sexual Harassment and the Three Big Surprises," *HR Magazine,* November 2001, p. 123.

23. Robert McGarvey, "Hands Off! How Do the Latest Supreme Court Decisions on Sexual Harassment Affect You?" *Entrepreneur,* September 1998, p. 86; Cole, "Sexual Harassment: New Rules," p. 14.

CHAPTER 8

1. Bill Bradley, "Whatever the Score—Bounce Back," *Parade Magazine,* October 18, 1998, p. 6.

2. Joseph A. Raelin, *Creating Leaderful Organizations: How to Bring Out Leadership in Everyone* (San Francisco: Berrett-Koehler, 2003).

3. George P. Hollenbeck and Douglas T. Hall, "Self-Confidence and Leader Performance," *Organizational Dynamics,* no. 3, 2004, pp. 254–269.

4. Shelley A. Kirkpatrick and Edwin A. Locke, "Leadership: Do Traits Matter?" *Academy of Management Executive,* May 1991, pp. 26–27.

5. Dale E. Zand, *The Leadership Triad: Knowledge, Trust, and Power* (New York: Oxford University Press, 1997).

6. Reported in "Developing Trust Pays Off," *Manager's Edge,* April 1999, p. 9.

7. Douglas R. May, Adrian Y. L. Chan, Timothy D. Hodges, and Bruce J. Avolio, "Developing the Moral Component of Authentic Leadership," *Organizational Dynamics,* no. 3, 2003, pp. 247–260.

8. Anthony Bianco, "The Rise of a Star," *BusinessWeek,* December 21, 1998, p. 63; "AmEx's Ken Chenault Talks about Leadership, Integrity, and the Credit Card Business," *http://www.knowledge@wharton,* April 2005.

9. Bruce J. Avolio, Jane M. Howell, and John J. Sosik, "A Funny Thing Happened on the Way to the Bottom Line: Humor as a Moderator of Leadership Style Effects," *Academy of Management Journal,* April 1999, pp. 219–227.

10. Zand, *The Leadership Triad,* p. 8.

11. Studies on this topic are reviewed in Timothy A. Judge, Amy Colbert, and Remus Ilies, "Intelligence and Leadership: A Quantitative Review and Test of Theoretical Propositions," *Journal of Applied Psychology,* June 2004, p. 548.

12. Bill Breen, "The Clear Leader," *Fast Company,* March 2005, pp. 65–67.

13. Daniel Goleman, "What Makes a Leader?" *Harvard Business Review,* November–December 1998, p. 92; Goleman, "Never Stop Learning," *Harvard Business Review,* January 2004, pp. 28–28.

14. Robert A. Eckert, "Where Leadership Starts," *Harvard Business Review,* November 2001, pp. 53–61. The quote is from page 54.

15. Jay A. Conger, *The Charismatic Leader: Behind the Mystique of Exceptional Leadership* (San Francisco: Jossey-Bass, 1989).

16. Suggestions 7, 9, and 10 are from Roger Dawson, *Secrets of Power Persuasion* (Upper Saddle River, NJ: Prentice Hall, 1992), pp. 181–183.

17. "Bring Out the Leader in Everyone," *Managing People at Work,* sample issue, 2000, p. 4.

18. Jon R. Katzenbach and Douglas K. Smith, "The Discipline of Teams," *Harvard Business Review,* March–April 1993, p. 118.

19. "Bring Out the Leader in Everyone," p. 4.

20. "What It Takes to Be an Effective Team Leader," *Manager's Edge,* March 2000, p. 6.

21. Terri A. Scandura and Chester A. Schrieisheim, "Leader-Member Exchange and Supervisor Career Mentoring as Complementary Constructs in Leadership Research," *Academy of Management Journal,* December 1994, pp. 1588–1602; George Graen and J. F. Cashman, "A Role Making Model of Leadership in Formal Organizations: A Developmental Approach," in J. G. Hunt and L. L. Larson, eds., *Leadership Frontiers* (Kent, OH: Kent State University Press, 1975), pp. 143–165.

22. Francis J. Yammarino, Alan J. Dubinsky, Lucette B. Comer, and Marvin A. Jolson, "Women and Transformational and Contingent Reward Leadership: A Multiple-Levels-of-Analysis Perspective," *Academy of Management Journal,* February 1997, pp. 205–222.

23. Jon R. Katzenbach and Jason A. Santamaria, "Firing Up the Front Line," *Harvard Business Review,* May–June 1999, pp. 116–117.

24. William D. Hitt, *The Model Leader: A Fully Functioning Person* (Columbus, OH: Battelle Press, 1993).

25. Manuel London, *Leadership Development: Paths to Self-Insight and Professional Growth* (Mahwah, NJ: Erlbaum, 2002).

26. Cheryl Dahle, "Natural Leader," *Fast Company,* December 2000, p. 270.

27. Michael E. McGill and John W. Slocum, Jr., "A *Little* Leadership Please?" *Organizational Dynamics,* Winter 1998, p. 48.

28. Bill Breen, "Trickle-Up Leadership," *Fast Company,* November 2001, pp. 70–72.

CHAPTER 9

1. Gerald Kushel, *Reaching the Peak Performance Zone: How to Motivate Yourself and Others to Excel* (New York: AMACOM, 1994), p. 66.

2. Research summarized in "One of These Seven Things Will Motivate Any Employee in the Company," *Motivational Manager,* sample issue, 1998 (Lawrence Ragan Communications, Inc.).

3. Fred Luthans and Alexander D. Stajkovic, "Reinforce for Performance: The Need to Go Beyond Pay and Even Rewards," *Academy of Management Executive,* May 1999, p. 52.

4. Steven Kerr, *Ultimate Rewards: What Really Motivates People to Achieve* (Boston: Harvard Business School Publishing, 1997).

5. "Simple Rewards Are Powerful Motivators," *HRfocus,* August 2001, p. 10.

6. Martin Booe, "Sales Force at Mary Kay China Embraces the American Way," *Workforce Management,* April 2005, pp. 24–25.

7. Jennifer Laabs, "Satisfy Them with More Than Money," *Workforce,* November 1998, p. 43; Charlotte Garvey, "Meaningful Tokens of Appreciation," *HR Magazine,* August 2004, pp. 101–106.

8. "Time Your Praise to Make It Last," *WorkingSMART,* June 2000, p. 2.

9. Andrew J. DuBrin, "Self-Perceived Technical Orientation and Attitudes Toward Being Flattered," *Psychological Reports,* vol. 96, 2005, pp. 852–854.

10. The original version of expectancy theory applied to work motivation is Victor Vroom, *Work and Motivation* (New York: Wiley, 1964).

11. Alexander D. Stajkovic and Fred Luthans, "Social Cognitive Theory and Self-Efficacy: Going Beyond

Traditional Motivational and Behavioral Approaches," *Organizational Dynamics,* Spring 1998, p. 66.

12. Steve McShane, "Getting Emotional about Employee Motivation," *Currents* (published by McGraw-Hill), September 2004, p. 1; Amir Erez and Alice M. Isen, "The Influence of Positive Affect on the Components of Expectancy Motivation," *Journal of Applied Psychology,* December 2002, pp. 1055–1067.

CHAPTER 10

1. Elwood F. Holton III, "New Employee Development Tactics: Perceived Availability, Helpfulness, and Relationship with Job Attitudes," *Journal of Business and Psychology,* Fall 2001, pp. 73–85.

2. Jeffrey Keller, "Associate with Positive People," a supplement to the *Pryor Report,* 1994.

3. Ibid.

4. Monica C. Higgins and Kathy E. Kram, "Reconceptualizing Mentoring at Work: A Developmental Network Perspective," *Academy of Management Review,* April 2001, pp. 264–288.

5. Anne Field, "No Time to Mentor? Do It Online," *BusinessWeek,* March 3, 2003, p. 126; Stephenie Overman, "Mentors without Borders," *HR Magazine,* March 2004, pp. 3–85.

6. Based mostly on Kathy E. Kram, *Mentoring at Work: Developmental Relationships in Organizational Life* (Glenview, IL: Scott Foresman, 1985), pp. 22–39; Erik J. Van Slyke and Bud Van Slyke, "Mentoring: A Results-Oriented Approach," *HRfocus,* February 1998, p. 14.

7. Stephanie C. Payne and Ann H. Huffman, "A Longitudinal Examination of the Influence of Mentoring on Organizational Commitment and Turnover," *Academy of Management Journal,* February 2005, pp. 158–168.

8. Hal Rosenbluth and Diane McFerrin Peters, *Good Company: Caring as Fiercely as You Compete* (Reading, MA: Addison-Wesley, 1998).

9. Editors of *Managers Edge, The Successful Manager's Guide to Giving and Receiving Feedback* (Alexander, VA: Briefings Publishing Group, 2004), p. 14.

10. Anne Fisher, "Turn Star Employees into Superstars," *Fortune,* December 13, 2004, p. 70.

11. "Coach Your Employees to Success with This Plan," *Manager's Edge,* May 2000, p. 1.

12. "Coach with Could,' Not Should,'" *Executive Strategies,* April 1998, p. 1.

13. Bruce Tulgan, "The Under-Management Epidemic," *HR Magazine,* October 2004, p. 119.

14. Kent W. Seibert, "Reflection in Action: Tools for Cultivating On-the-Job Learning Conditions," *Organizational Dynamics,* Winter 1999, p. 55.

15. Career Track seminar, *How to Deal with Difficult People,* 1995; Kenneth Kaye, *Workplace Wars and How to End*

Them: Turning Personal Conflicts into Productive Teamwork* (New York: AMACOM, 1994); Joann S. Lublin, "Feeling Unappreciated? You May Find Griping Makes Things Worse," *The Wall Street Journal,* June 5, 2003, p. B1; Jared Sandberg, "Staff Handfuls' and the Bosses Who Coddle Them," *The Wall Street Journal,* October 8, 2003, p. B1.

16. "How to Deal with Problem' Workers," *Positive Leadership,* sample issue, distributed 2001; Martien Eerhart, "Top 7 Ideas for Dealing with Difficult Employees," *http://top7business.com/archives/personnel/050499.html.*

17. Quoted in Jessica Guynn, "Bullying Behavior Affects Morale as Well as the Bottom Line," Knight Rider syndicated story, November 2, 1998.

18. John C. Maxwell, *Winning with People: Discover the People Principles That Work for You Every Time* (Nashville, TN: Nelson Books, 2004), pp. 1428–1429.

CHAPTER 11

1. William L. Gardner III, "Lessons in Organizational Dramaturgy: The Art of Impression Management," *Organizational Dynamics,* Summer 1992, p. 45.

2. Jim Rucker and Jean Anna Sellers, "Changes in Business Etiquette," *Business Education Forum,* February 1998, p. 43.

3. Rucker and Sellers, "Changes in Business Etiquette," p. 45.

4. This section of the chapter is based on Annette Vincent and Melanie Meche, "It's Time to Teach Business Etiquette," *Business Education Forum,* October 1993, pp. 39–41; "Business Etiquette: Teaching Students the Unwritten Rules," *Keying In,* January 1996, pp. 1–8; Rucker and Sellers, "Changes in Business Etiquette," pp. 43–45; Letitia Baldrige, *The Executive Advantage* (Washington, DC: Georgetown Publishing House, 1999); "Changes in Business Etiquette," pp. 43–45; "Culture Shock?" *Entrepreneur,* May 1998, p. 46; Ann Perry, "Finer Points of the Meet and Eat," *Toronto Star,* http://www.thestar.com, January 2, 2004; Blanca Torres, "Good Dining Manners Can Help Bet a Bigger Slice of the Job Pie," *Baltimore Sun* story, April 5, 2005; Erin White, "The Jungle: Focus on Recruitment, Pay and Getting Ahead," *The Wall Street Journal,* November 2, 2004, p. B8. The quotes are from the same sources.

5. "Disability Etiquette," *Human Resources Forum* (a supplement to *Management Review*), June 1997, p. 3; "Helping Today's Blind Children Become the Winners of Tomorrow," American Blind Children's Council (flyer), 2002.

6. Deb Koen, "Jittery About Networking? Know the Etiquette," Rochester, New York, *Democrat and Chronicle,* April 14, 2002, p. 4E.

7. Brian Hilliard and James Palmer, *Networking Like a Pro* (Atlanta, GA: Agito Consulting, 2003, p. 52).

8. *Monster Career Centre, Monster.com.* "Managing Your Boss—How to Play Your Cards Right, vol. 4, 2002, p. 2.

9. Research reported in Jennifer Reingold, "Suck Up and Move Up," *Fast Company,* January 2005, p. 34.

10. Marshall Goldsmith, "All of Use Are Stuck on Suck-Ups," *Fast Company,* December 2003, p. 117.

11. Cited in Joy Davia, "Make No Mistake: Come Clean When You Make One," Rochester, New York, *Democrat and Chronicle,* February 20, 2005, p. 1E.

12. Shelia Murray Bethel, *Making a Difference* (New York: Putnam's Sons, 1989).

13. Gary M. Stern, "Small Slights Bring Big Problems," *Workforce,* August 2002, p. 17; Joann S. Lublin, "How to Stop the Snubs That Demoralize You and Your Colleagues," *The Wall Street Journal,* December 7, 2004, p. B1.

CHAPTER 12

1. Paul R. Timm, *Customer Service: Career Success Through Customer Satisfaction,* 2nd ed. (Prentice Hall, 2001), p. 8.

2. Anthony J. Rucci, Steven P. Kirn, and Richard T. Quinn, "The Employee-Customer-Profit Chain at Sears," *Harvard Business Review,* January–February 1998, pp. 82–97.

3. Barry M. Stow and Jerry Ross, "Stability in the Midst of Change: A Dispositional Approach to Job Attitudes," *Journal of Applied Psychology,* August 1985, p. 471.

4. Sue Shellenbarger, "Domino Effect: The Unintended Results of Telling Off Customer-Service Staff," *The Wall Street Journal,* February 5, 2004, p. D1.

5. Lance A. Bettencourt, Kevin P. Gwinner, and Matthew L. Meuter, "A Comparison of Attitude, Personality, and Knowledge Predictors of Service-Oriented Organizational Citizenship Behavior," *Journal of Applied Psychology,* February 2001, pp. 29–41.

6. Alex M. Susskind, K. Michele Kacmar, and Carl P. Borchgrevink, "Customer Service Providers' Attitudes Relating to Customer Service and Customer Satisfaction in the Customer-Server Exchange," *Journal of Applied Psychology,* February 2003, pp. 179–187.

7. Adrian J. Slywotzky and David J. Morrison, "Forget the Product: Focus on the Customer," *Leadership* (newsletter of the American Management Association International), February 1999, p. 2.

8. "The Chairman of the Board Looks Back," *Fortune,* May 28, 2001, p. 70.

9. Richard B. Chase and Sriram Dasu, "Want to Perfect Your Company's Service? Use Behavioral Science," *Harvard Business Review,* June 2001, pp. 78–84.

10. Karl Abrecht, *The Only Thing That Matters* (New York: HarperCollins, 1992).

11. Susan Okula, "Customer Service: New Tools for a Timeless Idea," *Business Education Forum,* December 1998, p. 7; Robert F. Gault, "Managing Customer Satisfaction for Profit," *Management Review,* April 1993, p. 23.

12. Amanda C. Kooser, "Crowd Control," *Entrepreneur,* August 2003, pp. 33–34.

13. Adapted from "For Extraordinary Service," *The Customer Service Professional,* October 1997, p. 3.

14. Adapted from *Nation's Restaurant News,* as reported in *Manager's Edge,* April 2000, p. 8.

15. Lorna Ducet, "Service Provider Hostility and Service Quality," *Academy of Management Journal,* October 2004, pp. 761–771.

16. D. J. Cran, "Towards the Validation of the Service Orientation Construct," *The Service Industries Journal,* vol. 14, 1994, p. 36.

17. Dot Yandle, "Helping Your Employees Give Customers What They Want," *Success Workshop* (a supplement to *Manager's Edge*), November 1998, p. 1.

18. Steven Gray, "Flipping Burger King," *The Wall Street Journal,* April 26, 2005, B1.

19. Michelle Conlin and Andrew Park, "Blogging with the Boss's Blessing," *BusinessWeek,* June 28, 2004, p. 100–102.

20. Daniel Akst, book review of *Hug Your Customers* by Jack Mitchell (Hyperion, 2003), appearing in *The Wall Street Journal,* November 14, 2003, p. W9.

21. Research cited in "Service Facts," *Customer Service Professional,* October 1997, p. 1.

22. Hwee Hoon Tan, Maw Der Foo, and Min Hui Kwek, "The Effects of Customer Personality Traits on the Display of Positive Emotions," *Academy of Management Journal,* April 2004, pp. 287-296.

23. Donna Deeprose, "Helping Employees Handle Difficult Customers," *Supervisory Management,* September 1991, p. 6; Chip R. Bell and Ron Zemke, "Service Breakdown—The Road to Recovery," in *Service Wisdom: Creating and Maintaining the Customer Service Edge* (Minneapolis, MN: Lakewood Books, 1992).

24. Patrick J. Kiger, "The Art of the Apology," *Workforce Management,* October 2004, p. 62.

25. Jan Norman, "Caring about Clients Helps Companies Handle Crises," *Knight Ridder* story, December 3, 2000.

26. Hal Hardy, "Five Steps to Pleasing difficult, Demanding Customers," *First-Rate Customer Service,* No. 1, 2005, p. 1.

27. "Customer Problem Clinics," in Making . . . Serving . . . Keeping Customers, published by Dartnell, 4660 Ravenswood Avenue, Chicago, IL 60640.

28. Timm, *Customer Service,* p. 43.

29. Excerpted and paraphrased from Scott Hays, "Exceptional Customer Service Takes the Ritz' Touch," *Workforce,* January 1999, pp. 99–102; Updated slightly from "How to Turn Your Customer Service

Department into a Team of Superheroes," *Executive Focus,* January 2004, p. 12.

CHAPTER 13

1. Gwendolyn Bounds, "Handyman Etiquette: Stay Calm, Avert Eyes," *The Wall Street Journal,* May 10, 2005, pp. B1, B4.

2. Linda K. Treviño and Katherine A. Nelson, *Managing Business Ethics: Straight Talk About How to Do It Right* (New York: Wiley, 1995), pp. 24–35; O. C. Ferrell, John Fraedrich, and Linda Ferrell, *Business Ethics: Ethical Decision Making and Cases,* 4th ed. (Boston: Houghton Mifflin, 2000) pp. 13–16; Anita Bruzzese, "Tools Take Ethics to the Real World," Gannett News Service, May 16, 2005.

3. Thomas M. Jones, "Ethical Decision Making by Individuals in Organizations: An Issue Contingent Model," *Academy of Management Review,* April 1991, p. 391.

4. Linda Kelbe Treviño, "Managing to Be Ethical: Debunking Five Business Ethics Myths," *Academy of Management Executive,* May 2004, pp. 69-72.

5. Data from Ethics Resource Center and Kronos Inc., reported in Sue Shellenbarger, "How and Why We Lie at the Office: From Pilfered Pens to Padded Accounts," *The Wall Street Journal,* March 24, 2005, p. D1.

6. Treviño and Nelson, *Managing Business Ethics,* pp. 47–64.

7. Data reported in "McAfee Anti-Piracy Information," *http://www.networkassociates.com/us/antipircacy_policy. htm,* accessed May 25, 2005.

8. Bruce Nussbaum, "Can You Trust Anybody Anymore?" *BusinessWeek,* January 28, 2002, p. 32.

9. "O'Leary Admits Lying, Quits," Associated Press, December 15, 2001.

10. The concept of the game is from Karen Ireland, "The Ethics Game," *Personnel Journal,* March 1991, p. 74. The scenarios are original.

11. Joseph L. Badaracco, Jr., "The Discipline of Building Character," *Harvard Business Review,* March–April 1998, pp. 114–124.

12. Michael S. Josephson, "Does Character Still Count?" *USA Weekend,* September 23–25, 1994, p. 20.

13. Treviño and Nelson, *Managing Business Ethics,* pp. 71–75.

14. Daniel J. Brass, Kenneth D. Butterfield, and Bruce C. Skaggs, "Relationships and Unethical Behavior: A Social Network Perspective," *Academy of Management Review,* January 1998, pp. 14–31.

15. "Extolling the Virtues of Hot Lines," *Workforce,* June 1998, pp. 125–126; Daryl Koehn, "An Interview with William Griffin," *http://www.stthom.edu/cbes/griffin. html* (Accessed May 27, 2005).

16. "The Optima Awards: They've Got Game," *Workforce Management,* March 2005, p. 44.

CHAPTER 14

1. Erin White, "The Jungle: Focus on Recruitment, Pay and Getting Ahead," *The Wall Street Journal,* December 21, 2004, p. B6.

2. Shelley Taylor, "Biohavioral Responses to Stress in Females: Tend-and-Befriend not Fight-or-Flight," *Psychological Review,* 107, 2000, pp. 411–429; Sadie F. Dingfelder, "What Lies Behind the Female Habit of Tending and Befriending' During Stress," *Monitor on Psychology,* January 2004, p. 15.

3. Jeffrey R. Edwards, "A Cybernetic Theory of Stress, Coping, and Well-Being in Organizations," *Academy of Management Review,* April 1992, p. 248.

4. *British Medical Journal* study reported in "Trop de Stress au Travail Double le Risque de Mourir d'une Crise de Coeur," *Journal de Montréal,* 18 octobre, 2002, p. 7.

5. Gillian E. Hardy, David Woods, and Toby D. Wall, "The Impact of Psychological Distress on Absence from Work," *Journal of Applied Psychology,* April 2003, pp. 306–314.

6. Steve M. Jex, *Stress and Job Performance: Theory, Research, and Implications for Managerial Practice* (Thousands Oaks, CA: Sage, 1998).

7. Quoted in "An Ounce of Prevention Beats Burnout," *HRfocus,* June 1999, p. 1.

8. Christina Maslach, *The Truth About Burnout* (San Francisco: Jossey-Bass, 1997). See also Dirk van Dierendonck, Wilmar B. Schaufeli, and Bram P. Buunk, "The Evaluation of an Individual Burnout Intervention Program: The Role of Equity and Social Support," *Journal of Applied Psychology,* June 1998, pp. 392–407.

9. M. Afalur Rahim, "Relationships of Stress, Locus of Control, and Social Support to Psychiatric Symptoms and Propensity to Leave a Job: A Field Study with Managers," *Journal of Business and Psychology,* Winter 1997, p. 159.

10. Steve M. Jex and Paul D. Bliese, "Efficacy Beliefs as a Moderator of the Impact of Work-Related Stressors: A Multilevel Study," *Journal of Applied Psychology,* June 1999, pp. 349–361; Steve M. Jex, Paul O. Bliese, Sheri Buzell, and Jessica Primeau, "The Impact of Self-Efficacy on Stressor-Strain Relations: Coping Style as an Explanatory Mechanism," *Journal of Applied Psychology,* June 2001, pp. 401–409.

11. John Schaubroeck and Deryl E. Merrit, "Divergent Effects of Job Control on Coping with Work Stressors: The Key Role of Self-Efficacy," *Academy of Management Journal,* June 1997, p. 750.

12. Jeffrey R. Edwards and A. J. Baglioni, Jr., "Relationships between Type A Behavior Pattern and Mental and Physical Symptoms: A Comparison of Global and Component Measures," *Journal of Applied Psychology,* April 1991, p. 276; related research reported in Etienne Benson, "Hostility Is among Best Predictors of

Heart Disease in Men," *Monitor on Psychology,* January 2003, p. 15.

13. Peter Y. Chen and Paul E. Spector, "Negative Affectivity as the Underlying Cause of Correlations between Stressors and Strains," *Journal of Applied Psychology,* June 1991, p. 398.

14. Families and Work Institute survey reported in Adam Geller, "Survey: Third of Americans Overworked," Associated Press, March 16, 2005.

15. William Atkinson, "Causes of Workplace Stress," *HR Magazine,* December 2000, p. 107; Michele Conlin, "Is Your Office Killing You?" Business Week, June 5, 2000, pp. 114–128.

16. The data on vision and carpal tunnel syndrome are from the Computer Vision Syndrome Center reported in Anita Bruzzese, "Computer Users often Strain Eyes," Gannett News Service, September 13, 2004.

17. Richard S. DeFrank and John M. Ivancevich, "Stress on the Job: An Executive Update," *Academy of Management Executive,* August 1998, pp. 56–57.

18. Richard Corliss, "The Power of Yoga," *Time,* April 23, 2001, pp. 54–62; Stacy Forster, "Companies Say Yoga Isn't a Stretch," *The Wall Street Journal* October 14, 2003, p. D4.

19. Lea Winerman, "Sleep Deprivation Threatens Public Health, Says Research Award Winner," July/August 2004, p. 61.

20. Bruce Cyer, Rolin McCraty, and Doc Childre, "Pulling the Plug On Stress," *Harvard Business Review,* July 2003, pp. 102–107; *http://www.HeartMath.com,* 2003.

21. Robert Boice, *Procrastination and Blocking: A Novel, Practical Approach* (Westport, CT: Greenwood Publishing Group, 1996); Data reported in Jared Sandberg, "Fans of Procrastination Say It Boosts Control, Self-Esteem," *The Wall Street Journal,* February 9, 2005, p. B1.

22. Maia Szalavitz, "Stand & Deliver," *Psychology Today,* July/August 2003, p. 50.

23. The term WIFO has been contributed by Shale Paul, as cited in "Tips to Keep Procrastination Under Control," Gannett News Service syndicated story, November 9, 1998.

24. Dru Scott, *How to Put More Time in Your Life* (New York: New American Library, 1980), p. 1.

25. "Don't Procrastinate," *Practical Supervision,* undated sample issue, p. 7.

26. Cited in "The Voices in Your Head," *Entrepreneur,* July 2000, pp. 105–107.

27. Curtis Sittenfeld, "She's a Paper Tiger," *Fast Company,* August 2002, p. 34.

28. Meni Koslowky and Abraham Sagie, "Correlates of Employee Lateness: Some Theoretical Considerations," *Journal of Applied Psychology,* February 1997, pp. 79–88.

29. Anne Fisher, "The Rebalancing Act," *Fortune,* October 6, 2003, p. 110; Andrea Kay, "Avoid Traps' to Gain the Free Time You Need," *Gannet News Service,* January 10, 2005.

30. Kathryn Tyler, "Stress Management for Workaholics," *HR Magazine,* September 1999, pp. 34–40; Mildred L. Culp, "Working Productively with Workaholics While Minimizing Legal Risks," Passage Media syndicated story, 1997.

31. Cited in Jared Sandberg, "To-Do Lists Can Take More Time than Doing, But That Isn't the Point," *The Wall Street Journal,* September 8, 2004, p. B1.

32. Joshua S. Rubinstein, David E Meyer, and Jeffrey E. Evans, "Executive Control of Cognitive Processes in Task Switching," *Journal of Experimental Psychology—Human Perception and Performance,* Vol. 26, January 2000, No. 4, pp. 763–769.

33. Anne Fisher, "Get Organized at Work Painlessly," *Fortune,* January 10, 2005, p. 30.

34. Amy Dunkin, "Saying 'Adios' to the Office," *BusinessWeek,* October 12, 1998, p. 153; Heather Page, "Remote Control," *Entrepreneur,* October 1998, p. 148; Jenny C. McCune, "Telecommuting Revisited," *Management Review,* February 1998, p. 14; E. Jeffrey Hill, Brent C. Miller, Sara P. Weiner, and Joe Colihan, "Influences of the Virtual Office on Aspects of Work/Life Balance," *Personnel Psychology,* Autumn 1998, pp. 667–683.

CHAPTER 15

1. Joann S. Lublin, "Job-Hunt Workshops Can Boost Confidence of Grads Seeking Work," *The Wall Street Journal,* February 1, 2005. p. B1.

2. "Kat & Dale Talk Jobs," King Features Syndicate, April 14, 2002.

3. Chris Pentila, "Risky Business," *Entrepreneur,* September 2003, pp. 78–79.

4. Edward A. Robinson, "Beware Job Seekers Have No Secrets," *Fortune,* December 29, 1997, p. 285.

5. Peg Thomas et al., "Resume Characteristics as Predictors as an Invitation to Interview," *Journal of Business and Psychology,* Spring 1999, pp. 339–356.

6. Updated June 2005, from Carol Kleiman, "Key Words Bosses Seek When Scanning Résumés," *Chicago Tribune* syndicated story, October 27, 1997.

7. Jim Pawlak, "Keep Job Application Cover Letter Short," *detnews.com,* April 15, 2005.

8. Louis Lavelle, "Résumés: Beware of Getting Creative'," *BusinessWeek,* October 22, 2001, p. 134E6.

9. Anne Field, "Coach, Help Me Out With This Interview," *BusinessWeek,* October 22, 2001, p. 134E2.

10. Richard Boyatzis, Annie McKee, and Daniel Goleman, "Reawakening Your Passion for Work," *Harvard Business Review,* April 2002, pp. 86–94.

11. Jeff Bailey, "Devoted Work Wins Customers Willing to Pay," *The Wall Street Journal,* October 14, 2003.

12. Scott E. Seibert, Maria L. Kraimer, and J. Michael Crant, "What Do Proactive People Do? A Longitudinal Model Linking Proactive Personality and Career Success," *Personnel Psychology,* Winter 2001, pp. 845–874; Scott E. Seibert, J. Michael Crant, and Maria L. Kraimer, "Proactive Personality and Career Success," *Journal of Applied Psychology,* June 1999, pp. 416–427.

13. Cited in Cheryl Dahle, "Showing Your Worth Without Showing Off," *nytimes.com,* September 19, 2004; *http://www.bragbetter.com.*

14. Philip L. Hunsaker, "Projecting the Appropriate Image," *Supervisory Management,* May 1989, p. 26.

15. Quoted in Anne Field, "What Is Business Casual?" *BusinessWeek,* October 20, 2000, pp. 180–190.

16. Quoted in "Taking Charge in a Temp World," *Fortune,* October 21, 1998, pp. 247–248.

17. Jim Loehr and Tony Schwartz, "The Making of the Corporate Athlete," *Harvard Business Review,* January 2001, pp. 120–128.

18. Anne Fisher, "How to Networkand Enjoy It," *Fortune,* April 4, 2005, p. 38.

19. Quoted in "Network Your Way Up," *WorkingSMART,* February 1997, p. 4.

20. Daniel L. Cable and Timothy A. Judge, "Interviewers' Perceptions of Person–Organization Fit and Organizational Selection Decisions," *Journal of Applied Psychology,* August 1997, pp. 546–561.

21. Amy L. Kristof-Brown, Ryan D. Zimmerman, and Erin C. Johnson, "Consequences of Individuals' Fit at Work: A Meta-Analysis of Person-Job, Person-Organization, Person-Group, and Person-Supervisor Fit," *Personnel Psychology,* Summer 2005, pp. 281–342.

22. From *Industry Week's* CEO of the year profile, as quoted in *Executive Leadership,* March 2001, p. 1.

23. David Wessel, "The Future of Jobs: New Ones Arise, Wage Gap Widens, "*The Wall Street Journal,*" April 2, 2004; Peter Svensson, "Hands-On Jobs May Be the Safest," Associated Press, July 9, 2004.

INDEX

234